French Historical Studies

Volume 47 · Number 2 · May 2024

War Makes Monsters: Crime and Criminality in Times of Conflict

CLAIRE ELDRIDGE and JULIE M. POWELL, Special Issue Editors

T0335209

War/Crime

CLAIRE ELDRIDGE and JULIE M. POWELL

Choosing a single image to represent a collection of articles is always a challenge. Selecting the cover for this special issue was no exception. Ultimately, a desire to encapsulate the complex intersection of war and crime
brought us back to the iconic figure of Henri Désiré Landru, a serial murderer
whose story belongs at once to the history of the First World War and to broader
histories of crime. Landru cloaked himself in the chaos of the war to move
beyond the litany of frauds he had committed in the prewar era. While the police
were distracted and many of the men away at war, Landru escalated his crimes,
producing a list of casualties that rivaled many soldiers at the front. Arrested in
1919, he was charged with and convicted of the murders of twelve women and
one man. Landru, though, was no singular aberration. The "Bluebeard of Gambais," as he was dubbed in the press, was one among a handful of serial murderers active during the First World War, including Fritz Haarmann, "Butcher of
Hanover"; Carl Großmann, "Butcher of Berlin"; George Joseph Smith, "Brides in
the Bath Killer"; and Helmuth Schmidt, "American Bluebeard."[1] If the First
World War "made" these monsters, it did so conditionally. That is, it provided
conditions favorable to the exercise of monstrosities.[2] Moving beyond the First
World War, the conditional making of monsters might just as well apply to the
actions of the "ordinary men" who perpetrated the Holocaust in Poland or the
French paratroopers who committed torture during the Algerian War of Independence (1954–62).[3]

If war makes "monsters" conditionally, it also makes them imaginatively
and contextually. The dehumanization of the enemy has historically been central

---

1. See, e.g., Watson, *Trial of George Joseph Smith*; Buhk, *Shocking Story of Helmuth Schmidt*; Béraud,
Bourcier, and Salmon, *L'affaire Landru*; Elder, *Murder Scenes*; and Aubenas, *Les vampires*.
2. This ideas is most famously encapsulated in George Mosse's "brutalization thesis" and attendant
debates. See Mosse, *Fallen Soldiers*. The most pertinent critique of this position for the French context is
Prost, "Les limites de la brutalisation."
3. Browning, *Ordinary Men*; Branche, *La torture et l'armée*.

French Historical Studies • Vol. 47, No. 2 (May 2024) • DOI 10.1215/00161071-11025095
Copyright 2024 by Society for French Historical Studies   171

to warfare and pivotal in modern genocides.[4] Ideological opponents are imagined as "monstrous," but "monsters" are also imagined. Famously, the memory of civilian guerrillas in the Franco-Prussian War led to collective delusion among German soldiers in 1914. The belief that they were surrounded by *francs-tireurs*, monsters brought to life by the clash of past and present, led to the deaths of some sixty-five hundred Belgian and French civilians—retribution for imagined crimes.[5] From imagined monsters we move to contextual "monsters," those whose deeds are ordinary and perfectly lawful outside of the context of war. Conflict renders those same actions criminal and thereby criminalizes the actor. Regime change often turns the tables of legality and illegality overnight.

It is this last category of monster making that comprises most of the articles here. Importantly, though, such categories are not discrete. State terror in the French Revolution, for example, resulted from the collision of the conditional, imaginative, and contextual making of "monsters." The *représentants en mission*, ostensibly well-intentioned men, unleashed horrors on enemies both real and imagined. Failures by otherwise law-abiding citizens to appear sufficiently loyal to the new republic marked them as counterrevolutionaries, and they were punished accordingly.[6] It is this tangle of lawful and unlawful, of villain and hero, of monster and man, that emerges when we consider the nature of crime and the criminal in the context of war and conflict. In the "fog of war," right and wrong become blurred and confusion leads to all manner of violations. What this special issue seeks to investigate, primarily, though not exclusively, is the relative nature of crime in wartime. Notions of crime and criminality are not fixed but are constantly under negotiation, particularly in times of crisis and great societal change.

Yet while it is not hard to find evidence to support the adage "war makes monsters," which frames this collection, this aphorism tells only part of the story. Evidence suggests that war makes criminals of some while exonerating others. It creates a context for the renegotiation of what constitutes "crime" and provides cover for certain varieties of misdeed while training a spotlight on others. During the First World War, for example, French senator Louis Martin proposed the suspension of legal penalties for abortion in the invaded territories where the rape of French women by advancing German forces was endemic.[7] The London Blitz of 1940–41 created diversions that allowed nefarious activity to

---

4. See, e.g., Harrison, *Dark Trophies*; and Hatzfeld, *Machete Season*.

5. Horne and Kramer, *German Atrocities*.

6. See, e.g., Tackett, *Coming of the Terror*; Palmer, *Twelve Who Ruled*; Lucas, *Structure of the Terror*; and Martin, *Violence et Révolution*.

7. For fuller discussion of this issue, see Audoin-Rouzeau, *L'enfant de l'ennemi* ; and Harris, "'Child of the Barbarian.'"

flourish, from the smashing of shop windows and looting of stores to murder.[8] The history of the European empires is replete with examples of legal exceptionalism, particularly during moments of violent confrontation, within which the systematic use of torture by the French state during the Algerian War of Independence stands as a particularly notorious example.[9] During the Cold War leftist thought became tantamount to subversion in the United States, and Senator Joseph McCarthy brought hundreds of Americans before the House Un-American Activities Committee to investigate treason.[10] Though such examples both are highly selective and pertain to quite different, even incomparable contexts, it is precisely the variable, unstable, and often contradictory nature of the relationship between war and crime that the authors of this special issue aim to elucidate further.

A desire to explore in more detail this multifaceted and often fraught relationship between war and crime/criminality provided the impetus for a gathering of interdisciplinary scholars from the United States and Europe in June 2022 at the Humanities Institute of University College Dublin. The workshop, "War Makes Monsters: Crime and Criminality in Times of Conflict," took a global approach to understanding crime in wartime from a wide-ranging set of perspectives. Yet within that diversity, a cohesive set of French-focused contributions emerged that we decided collectively to develop further. Spanning the fifteenth to the twentieth centuries, encompassing both metropole and the empire, the case studies presented in this issue include constructions of military criminality in the wake of the Hundred Years' War and during the First World War, the drawing of distinctions between legitimate violence and murder in the French Revolution, the mid-twentieth-century criminalization of Algerian black marketeers, and the criminalization of war itself through association with a famed serial murderer. They are united in that they all recognize crime in wartime as both a cultural construction and a product of circumstances. As Joseph Clarke noted in his original workshop paper, "Conflict complicates things. Acts that normally appear intolerable, aberrant, an affront to every known norm—the act of killing, for example—suddenly become acceptable, instrumentalized, even admirable in wartime." This collection of articles digs into this complexity, into the instability of definitions and understandings of crime and criminality in specific historical moments, and into the worlds of a range of historical actors whose lives were far richer and more interesting than externally affixed labels such as *criminal* or *monster* might suggest.

8. See Staveley-Wadham, "Investigating Blackout Crime"; and Francis, *Flyer*, 147–51.
9. The classic text here is Branche, *La torture et l'armée*. For legal exceptionalism, see, for example, discussions of the *indigénat* in Mann, "What Was the *Indigénat*?"; Saada, "La loi, le droit et l'indigène"; and Thénault, "L'indigénat dans l'empire français."
10. See, e.g., Fried, *Nightmare in Red*.

Since the fifteenth century French history has not lacked for major conflicts: the Hundred Years' War, the Wars of Religion, the French Revolution, the Napoleonic Wars, the world wars, and the wars of conquest and liberation that marked the rise and fall of the First and Second French Empires. Each of these episodes has been extensively studied, not only from legal and intellectual perspectives but also in terms of "war as practice," from qualitative and quantitative angles, from the top down and the bottom up, as well as in comparative frames. Within this body of scholarship, questions of crime and criminality appear in multiple guises. As the footnotes to our respective articles attest, the contributors are very conscious of how our work engages with and is indebted to this extensive hinterland. Although a summary of this vast historiography is simply not possible in the space of this introduction, there are certain key themes and debates that have particularly informed the framing of this collection. Much of the discussion within this special issue relates to the challenges war posed to existing legal systems and processes, whether their authority was royal, republican, or military in nature. This is particularly well-trodden ground for the late medieval and early modern periods.[11] The contributors to this special issue share with these scholars an interest in the gap between perception and practice. Writing about the French Wars of Religion, for example, Tom Hamilton has pushed back, both qualitatively and quantitatively, against the assumption that criminal justice was already so weak that it effectively ceased to function during this turbulent period.[12] In a similar vein, the supposed "laxity" of fifteenth-century monarchs and the widely touted "harshness" of military justice during the First World War are critically interrogated here to reveal more complex realities about the roles judicial systems actually play in maintaining or undermining different forms of authority and social cohesion during times of conflict.

In a collection about war, the military unsurprisingly looms large. Until the second part of the twentieth century, military criminality was mostly approached through questions relating to the practice of military justice, and primarily investigated by legal scholars, former military judges, and critics of military justice.[13] Even as military justice remains a point of reference, we seek

11. Useful surveys of this literature include Parker, "Early Modern Europe"; Gunn, Grummitt, and Cools, "War and the State in Early Modern Europe"; Wilson, "Warfare in Europe"; and Bowd, *Renaissance Mass Murder*. For the French context specifically, see Verreycken, *Crimes et gens de guerre au Moyen Age*; Skoda, *Medieval Violence*; Cohen, "Hundred Years' War and Crime in Paris"; Carroll, "Violence, Civil Society, and Civilization"; Carroll, "Political Justice and the Outbreak of the Wars of Religion"; Hamilton, "Adjudicating the Troubles"; Margolf, *Religion and Royal Justice*; Nassiet, *La violence*; Paresys, *Aux marges du royaume*; Prétou, *Crime et justice en Gascogne*; Potter, "'Rigueur de Justice'"; and Roberts, "Royal Authority and Justice."
12. Hamilton, *Widow's Vengeance*; Hamilton, "Crisis and Recovery of Criminal Justice."
13. For an overview of this historiography, see Campion et al., introduction.

to build on the work of scholars who have done so much to broaden the field in terms of method and approach in recent decades.[14] This is evident, we hope, in our focus on the experiences of the soldiers and civilians caught up in these conflicts. In particular, we see these articles as complementing the distinct yet interconnected literatures that, on the one hand, tackle the links among conscription, draft evasion, and criminality—a particularly vibrant subfield for the revolutionary period—and, on the other hand, deal with banditry and brigandage.[15] Like this special issue, both sets of scholarship speak to the social tensions produced by war, particularly during periods of mass conscription; to the agency of those who sought to challenge or subvert the systems and controls imposed upon them; and to the marginal spaces and blurred boundaries where these individuals often found themselves.[16]

In addition to crossing chronological boundaries, "War Makes Monsters" also straddles the metropole/colony divide. Reflecting the French state's preoccupations with maintaining control across its colonial territories, substantive scholarship addresses law, order, and policing in these spaces. Most of this work focuses either on the empire—be it a single territory or a broader panorama[17]— or on communities of colonized peoples who found themselves living and working in metropolitan France.[18] Placing metropole and colony in the same analytic frame, pieces like the ones here on the multiethnic Armée d'Afrique in First World War France and on black marketeers in Algiers and Marseille thus join a

14. With respect to military justice, for the earlier time period covered by this special issue, see, e.g., Staiano-Daniels, "Masters in the Things of War"; Cazaux, *Les capitaines dans le royaume de France*; Kaeuper, *War, Justice, and Public Order*; Maffi, *Tra Marte e Astrea*; Meumann, "Civilians, the French Army, and Military Justice"; Musson and Ramsay, *Courts of Chivalry and Admiralty*; and Schnerr, *"L'honneur de la Maréchaussée."* For the later periods, see Germani, "Military Justice under the Directory"; Bach, *Justice militaire*; Bock, "Les parlementaires et la justice militaire"; and Saint-Fuscien, "Entre guerre et paix."

15. In addition to Eric Hobsbawn's classic work *Bandits*, see Wright, "'Pillagers' and 'Brigands,'"; Toureille, *Vol et brigandage au Moyen Age*; Furon, *Les écorcheurs*; Broers, *Napoleon's Other War*; Sottocasa, *Les brigands*; Sottocasa, *Les brigands et la Révolution*; Kwass, *Louis Mandrin*; Plarier, "Le banditisme rural en Algérie"; Kalman, "Criminalizing Dissent"; Dejeux, "Un bandit d'honneur dans l'Aurès"; and Colonna, *Le meunier, les moines, et le bandit*. On the interconnections among conscription, draft evasion, and criminality, see Forrest, *Conscripts and Deserters*; Brown, *Ending the Revolution*; Cobb, *Police and the People*; Bell, *First Total War*; Auvray, *Objecteurs, insoumis, déserteurs*; Perry, *Mutinous Memories*; and Ruquet, *Déserteurs et insoumis*.

16. For a non-French example of this approach, see Emsley, *Soldier, Sailor, Beggarman, Thief*.

17. Algeria has emerged as a focal point for such work: Crane, "Housing as Battleground"; House, "Intervening on 'Problem' Areas and Their Inhabitants"; Thénault, *Violence ordinaire dans l'Algérie coloniale*; Surkis, *Sex, Law, and Sovereignty in French Algeria*; Bouzaher, *La justice répressive dans l'Algérie coloniale*; and Cole, *Lethal Provocation*. See also Blanchard and Glasman, "Le maintien de l'ordre dans l'empire français"; Blanchard, Blombergen, and Lauro, *Policing in Colonial Empires*; Thomas, *Empires of Intelligence*; Thomas, *Violence and Colonial Order*; Kalman, "Policing the French Empire"; Keller, *Colonial Suspects*; and Boittin, *Undesirable*.

18. Blanchard, *La police parisienne et les Algériens*; Frank, *Hostages of Empire*; Prakash, *Empire on the Seine*.

growing body of work that seeks to expand these discussions, underscoring the porousness of these spaces without ignoring the distinctions between them.[19]

Historians often turn to crime, and to the institutions charged with preventing and prosecuting such acts, because of the richness of associated sources and the diversity of historical actors and voices that can be found within them. The authors in this collection are no different. Carolyn Steedman's observation that the law "mattered to eighteenth-century people out of necessity, because it was there—in their face—shaping and dictating the lives they led, the love they felt, the labor they exchanged for livelihood," applies more broadly across the centuries under consideration.[20] It mattered just as much, and perhaps even more so, in moments when the law and its associated categories were fickle and in flux, liable to change from one moment to the next, with significant real-world consequences—all hallmarks of the periods of conflict under discussion here. Indeed, wars often transform the nature of the state itself and the claims it makes upon its citizens/subjects, reconfiguring the relationship between the ruler and the ruled, thereby engendering new categories of crime and criminal, which in turn require new agents of law enforcement, all processes that leave a paper trail. By maintaining, modifying, but also creating new points and types of contact between the state and people at all layers of society, as well as introducing new actors and institutions claiming authority over the populace, wars can thus be particularly generative when it comes to historical records.

In seeking to take advantage of this situation, the "War Makes Monsters" contributors share a concern to locate the experiences of "ordinary" people caught up in these turbulent times. In this way, we follow historians such as Elwin Hofman, Rebekka Habermas, Katie Barclay, and Laura Kounine who, as Hofman puts it, "have adopted the perspective of 'doing justice,' giving more attention to the role of the actors in criminal justice, their different degrees of power and their negotiations, spaces, bodies and emotions," although we extend this approach to the remit of military as well as civilian justice.[21] Such work entails drawing on a wide array of source materials, such as royal pardon letters, revolutionary engravings, census data, military interrogation transcripts, films, novels and *bandes dessinées*. These last sources in particular remind us that crime and criminality are defined not only in the courtroom but also in the cultural sphere. Accounts of the trials of Landru, as well as those of Henriette Caillaux, Marguerite (Meg) Steinheil, Violette Nozière, and Captain Alfred Dreyfus, are illustrative in this

---

19. For other examples, see Thénault, "L'état d'urgence."
20. Steedman, *History and the Law*, 223.
21. Hofman, *Trials of the Self*, 8; Habermas, *Thieves in Court*; Kounine, *Imagining the Witch*; Barclay, *Men on Trial*. For discussion of these issues in the medieval period, see Goodich, *Voices from the Bench*.

regard.[22] But just as criminals are tried in the court of public opinion, so too are victims. Hallie Rubenhold's *The Five* acknowledges, and indeed refutes, the historical criminalization of the victims of Jack the Ripper.[23]

But we need look no further than present-day press coverage of sexual assaults and police violence to see the role culture plays in turning crime narratives on their head, often inverting victim and perpetrator and excusing all manner of wrongdoing.[24] In considering such sources, we acknowledge a debt to cultural histories of crime, a field indelibly associated with Dominique Kalifa.[25] Unintentionally evoking images of war graves that dot the French countryside and the myriad memorials that anchor its urban landscapes, Kalifa suggested in 1995 that violent crimes create their own maps of "fatal footprints, puddles of blood, and corpses," geographic identities that constitute "another History of France, hierarchical and orderly, possessing its own saints, martyrs, and monsters."[26] Yet, as the special issue demonstrates, Kalifa's history of crime is not "another" history but an integral part of history more broadly, wherein the histories of war and crime regularly intersect and notions of criminality and war are made and remade not separately but together.

Taking a particular theme, in this case the relationship between war and crime/criminality, and exploring it across different historical moments is, of course, not a unique approach, especially for a special issue. Nonetheless, by adopting a comparative and chronologically expansive view, we hope to draw some of the different historiographies outlined above further into conversation with each other. When it comes to large-scale conflicts with global ramifications like the ones covered in this issue—the Hundred Years' War, the revolutionary era, the two world wars—their multidimensional and multiscalar significance create powerful gravitational forces that tend to produce constellations of scholarship bound to and bounded by those events. This collection represents a small effort to redirect some of that scholarly energy by looking out and across seemingly disparate time periods for threads of continuity when it comes to the war/crime nexus and the historical actors drawn into its orbit. In so doing, it becomes clear just how unstable and malleable the boundaries between legal and illegal

22. Harris, *Man on Devil's Island*; Horowitz, *Red Widow*; Maza, *Violette Nozière*; Berensen, *Trial of Madame Caillaux*.

23. Rubenhold, *Five*.

24. An example is the question of rape during wartime, which went unstudied for a long time. Susan Brownmiller was one of the first to broach the topic in *Against Our Will*. Subsequently, the sociologist J. Robert Lilly struggled to publish his book on rapes committed by American GIs in France. The text was finally published in French in 2003 and a few years later in English: Lilly, *La face cachée des GI's*; and Lilly, *Taken by Force*.

25. Among his extensive oeuvre, see in particular Kalifa, *L'encre et le sang*; and Kalifa, *Crime et culture au XIXe siècle*.

26. Kalifa, *L'encre et le sang*, 274–75.

have been in wartime throughout French history, not least because of the wider questions being posed about loyalty, authority, and belonging in those same moments.

Central to many of these histories of warfare are the histories of those (usually men) engaged to fight in them. The articles presented here are no exception. Starting in the fifteenth century, Quentin Verreycken's "Mercy at War: Military Violence and the Politics of Royal Pardon in Fifteenth-Century France" opens up the recurring question of how the exceptional circumstances of conflict impacted which behaviors were considered legal and/or legitimate for those in the military. Analyzing when and how royal pardons were granted to soldiers who perpetrated offenses against civilian populations in fifteenth-century France, Verreycken exposes the complex mix of (often competing) factors weighed in these decisions as the king sought to balance an imperative to exercise justice and protect his subjects against the very practical need to ensure he could retain loyal soldiers, maintain an army, and continue to wage war. In drawing our attention to the constructed, subjective, and situational definition of "crimes" and enactment of punishments, this piece exemplifies a set of themes that underpin all the contributions to this special issue.

Moving the chronology forward to the revolutionary period, the second article in this collection, "The Burning of Bédoin: Crime, Complicity, and Civil War in Revolutionary France," broaches the question of "how a society can come to terms with crime when the very notion of crime is itself constantly changing." Focusing less on the rank and file and more on those giving the orders, Joseph Clarke uses "the burning of Bédoin"—a horrifying example of collective punishment inflicted on a small town following the uprooting of its liberty tree by persons unknown—to draw our attention to "the immense difficulties involved in defining what crime and criminality meant in a civil war context." Committed at the height of the revolutionary terror of the year II, the burning of Bédoin and associated summary mass executions in May 1794 were initially approved by the Committee of Public Safety and even applauded when reported to the National Convention. Yet, only a few months later, in January 1795 the principal instigator of these events, Etienne Maignet, was under investigation by the same Convention for perpetrating such "disgusting horrors." That he ultimately escaped punishment on the grounds that to indict him would require acknowledging the complicity of the Convention, and thus the edifice of revolutionary government, offers another example in the collection where "justice" was redefined and subordinated to other priorities, in this case preserving the fledgling republic.

Where and how the boundary between acceptable and unacceptable violence was drawn is also a theme tackled by Claire Eldridge in "'Brutal by Temperament and Taste': Violence between Comrades in France's Armée d'Afrique,

1914–1918," which explores the prosecution by military justice tribunals of instances of serious interpersonal violence between comrades in France's multiethnic Armée d'Afrique during the First World War. In the same way that fifteenth-century pardon letters allow us to see how ordinary soldiers constructed particular images of themselves while revealing invaluable incidental details about their personal histories, the multivocal military justice sources on which this case study rests give us access to the voices, perspectives, and wider lives of a group of racially and socioeconomically marginalized historical actors. Testimonies provided by accused soldiers, as well as victims and witnesses, are used to illustrate the different ways individuals reacted to the pressures they were placed under between 1914 and 1918, how they related to the men around them within this highly fraught context, how they chose to frame and justify their choices when called upon to explain themselves and their behaviors, and the role that race and racial stereotypes played in all of the above.

Extending the focus beyond the military but remaining attentive to the entanglement of metropole and empire, Danielle Beaujon's contribution to this special issue, "The Algerian Enemy Within: Policing the Black Market in Marseille and Algiers, 1939–1950," offers a multisited investigation into the policing of the black market in Marseille and Algiers during and immediately following the Second World War. It too demonstrates the centrality of colonial knowledge and racial stereotypes to the construction of notions of criminality, embedding these within a discussion of the spatiality and materiality of crime. In both cities, preexisting ideas about North Africans as "suspicious" and even as "internal enemies" led to the demonization and disproportionate targeting of areas associated with this community, while illegal economic activity by Europeans went largely unremarked and unchecked. This selective policing of black market activity speaks to how old discourses were superimposed onto new preoccupations and priorities, usefully reminding us that for all war is often conceived of as a moment of rupture or a set of exceptional circumstances, some things—such as racialized practices of policing and control—remain constant.

The last article in the collection, Julie M. Powell's "Dead but Not Buried: Serial Murderer Henri Désiré Landru and a Century of War Critique," opens the discussion of the relationship between war and crime further into the realm of cultural representation and considers it in the *longue durée*. As Powell notes, from 1919 into the twenty-first century, Landru and the wartime murders for which he was convicted generated a remarkable volume of cultural material—fiction and nonfiction narratives, films, spectacles, and television and radio broadcasts. An examination of this oeuvre reveals how Landru, described by one contemporary as an "allegory of large and obvious content," has been used, time and again, to critique modern war.[27] The slaughter of the Western Front provides the context for Landru's crimes, and as works from 1926, 1947, 1963, and 2006 demonstrate, comparison is inevitable. By shedding light on the incongruity of celebrating one form of mass murder while condemning another, such critiques remind the public that war is monstrous. Just as notions of criminality are historically contingent, however, so too are ideas about the righteousness of warfare. The article makes clear that a society's contemporary relationship to war plays a significant role in whether war itself can be considered a crime.

Events in recent years have underlined the contemporary salience of the themes that this issue explores. The sociologists Sveinung Sandberg and Gustavo Fondevila argue that volatile periods "give rise to new types of criminal, reignite old ones, and repurpose justifications for crime."[28] Amid a time of intense social disorder—including the COVID-19 pandemic; the rise of social justice movements, particularly in response to racialized instances of police brutality; and a resurgence of grassroots organizing—many have begun questioning the legal systems and cultural milieus that criminalize and target the marginalized while whitewashing certain varieties of crimes and shielding the perpetrators. At the heart of movements for social and economic justice that now span the globe are efforts to understand and, ultimately, rewrite the legal codes and cultural scripts that define what crime is and who the criminals are. At the heart of each contribution to this special issue lies the same concern to unpack the negotiations, contestations, and power dynamics underpinning determinations of what is and is not a crime, who is and is not a criminal, and how and why these designations change. By investigating the contingent nature of crime and criminality and exposing how they have historically been made and unmade, our hope is that this issue contributes to this important effort.

CLAIRE ELDRIDGE is professor of the history of the Francophone world at the University of Leeds. She is author of "Conflict and Community in the Trenches: Military Justice Archives and Interactions between Soldiers in France's Armée d'Afrique, 1914–1918" in *History Workshop Journal* (2022) and "Migrations of Decolonization, Welfare, and the Unevenness of Citizenship in the UK, France, and Portugal," with Christoph Kalter and Becky Taylor, in *Past and Present* (2023).

JULIE M. POWELL is adjunct research fellow at University College Dublin. She is the author of *Bodies of Work: The First World War and the Transnational Making of Rehabilitation* (2023) and "Doctoring the Script: Crime Writing, Order, and Medical Authority in the Oeuvre of Dr Augustin Cabanès, 1894–1928" (2022).

27. Bolitho, *Murder for Profit*.
28. Sandberg and Fondevila, "Corona Crimes," 224.

Acknowledgments

In addition to the contributors featured here, we would like to thank Angélique Ibáñez Aristondo, Andrew McKeown, Jessica Meyer, Ariel Mond, Chloë Peters, and Katja Pyötsiä for their thoughtful contributions to the "War Makes Monsters" workshop. We are also grateful to the Humanities Institute and the College of Arts and Humanities at University College Dublin, the Irish Research Council, and the National University of Ireland whose generous financial support made this event possible. Finally, we would like to thank the members of the online Histories of Crime and Criminal Justice reading group started in autumn 2020 by Briony Neilson. Not only did this forum bring Claire and Julie together in the first place, but the stimulating and supportive conversations the group has hosted over the years have also immeasurably enriched our thinking on the issues addressed in this collection.

References

Aubenas, Maurice. *Les vampires*. Paris, 1930.

Audoin-Rouzeau, Stéphane. *L'enfant de l'ennemi: Viol, avortement, infanticide pendant la Grande Guerre*. Paris, 1995.

Auvray, Michel. *Objecteurs, insoumis, déserteurs: Histoire des réfractaires en France*. Paris, 1983.

Bach, André. *Justice militaire, 1915–1916*. Paris, 2013.

Barclay, Katie. *Men on Trial: Performing Emotion, Embodiment, and Identity in Ireland, 1800–1845*. Manchester, 2019.

Bell, David. *The First Total War: Napoleon's Europe and the Birth of Warfare as We Know It*. London, 2007.

Béraud, Henri, Emmanuel Bourcier, and André Salmon. *L'affaire Landru*. Paris, 1924.

Berensen, Edward. *The Trial of Madame Caillaux*. Berkeley, CA, 1993.

Blanchard, Emmanuel. *La police parisienne et les Algériens (1944–1962)*. Paris, 2011.

Blanchard, Emmanuel, Marieke Blombergen, and Amandine Lauro, eds. *Policing in Colonial Empires: Cases, Connection, Boundaries (ca. 1850–1970)*. Brussels, 2017.

Blanchard, Emmanuel, and Joël Glasman. "Le maintien de l'ordre dans l'empire français: Une historiographie émergente." In *Maintenir l'ordre colonial: Afrique et Madagascar, XIXe–XXe siècles*, edited by Jean-Pierre Bat and Nicolas Courtin, 11–41. Rennes, 2012.

Bock, Fabienne. "Les parlementaires et la justice militaire pendant la Grande Guerre." In *Justice, politique et république: De l'affaire Dreyfus à la guerre d'Algérie*, edited by Marc Olivier Baruch and Vincent Duclert, 197–208. Paris, 2002.

Boittin, Jennifer Anne. *Undesirable: Passionate Mobility and Women's Defiance of French Colonial Policing, 1919–1952*. Chicago, 2022.

Bolitho, William. *Murder for Profit*. London, 1962.

Bouzaher, Hocine. *La justice répressive dans l'Algérie coloniale, 1830–1962*. Algiers, 2004.

Bowd, Stephen D. *Renaissance Mass Murder: Civilians and Soldiers during the Italian Wars*. Oxford, 2018.

Branche, Raphaëlle. *La torture et l'armée pendant la guerre d'Algérie*. Paris, 2001.

Broers, Michael. *Napoleon's Other War: Bandits, Rebels, and Their Pursuers in the Age of Revolutions*. Oxford, 2010.

Brown, Howard G. *Ending the Revolution: Violence, Justice, and Repression from the Terror to Napoleon*. Charlottesville, VA, 2006.

Browning, Christopher. *Ordinary Men: Reserve Police Battalion 101 and the Final Solution in Poland*. New York, 1992.

Brownmiller, Susan. *Against Our Will: Men, Women, and Rape.* New York, 1975.

Buhk, Tobin T. *The Shocking Story of Helmuth Schmidt: Michigan's Original Lonely Hearts Killer.* Charleston, SC, 2013.

Campion, Jonas, Xavier Rousseaux, Jean-Marc Berlière, and Luigi Lacchè. Introduction to *Justices militaires et guerres mondiales (Europe, 1914–1950) / Military Justices and World Wars (Europe, 1914–1950)*, edited by Jean-Marc Berlière, Jonas Campion, Luigi Lacchè, and Xavier Rousseaux, 9–38. Louvain-la-Neuve, 2013.

Carroll, Stuart. "Political Justice and the Outbreak of the Wars of Religion." *French History* 33, no. 2 (2019): 177–98.

Carroll, Stuart. "Violence, Civil Society, and Civilization." In vol. 3 of *The Cambridge World History of Violence*, edited by Robert Antony, Stuart Carroll, and Caroline Dodds Pennock, 660–78. Cambridge, 2020.

Cazaux, Loïc. *Les capitaines dans le royaume de France: Guerre, pouvoir et justice au bas Moyen Age.* Paris, 2022.

Cobb, Richard. *The Police and the People: French Popular Protest, 1789–1820.* Oxford, 1970.

Cohen, Ester. "The Hundred Years' War and Crime in Paris, 1332–1488." In *The Civilization of Crime: Violence in Town and Country since the Middle Ages*, edited by Eric A. Johnson and Eric H. Monkkonen, 109–24. Urbana, IL, 1996.

Cole, Joshua. *Lethal Provocation: The Constantine Murders and the Politics of French Algeria.* Ithaca, NY, 2020.

Colonna, Fanny. *Le meunier, les moines, et le bandit: Des vies quotidiennes dans l'Aurès (Algérie) du XXe siècle.* Arles, 2010.

Crane, Sheila. "Housing as Battleground: Targeting the City in the Battles of Algiers." *City and Society* 29, no. 1 (2017): 187–212.

Dejeux, Jean. "Un bandit d'honneur dans l'Aurès, de 1917 à 1921." *Revue de l'Occident musulman et de la Méditerranée*, no. 26 (1978): 35–54.

Elder, Sace. *Murder Scenes: Normality, Deviance, and Criminal Violence in Weimar Berlin.* Ann Arbor, MI, 2010.

Emsley, Clive. *Soldier, Sailor, Beggarman, Thief: Crime and the British Armed Services since 1914.* Oxford, 2013.

Forrest, Alan. *Conscripts and Deserters: The Army and French Society during the Revolution and Empire.* Oxford, 1990.

Francis, Martin. *The Flyer: British Culture and the Royal Air Force, 1939–1945.* Oxford, 2011.

Frank, Sarah Ann. *Hostages of Empire: Colonial Prisoners of War in Vichy France.* Lincoln, NE, 2021.

Fried, Richard M. *Nightmare in Red: The McCarthy Era in Perspective.* New York, 1991.

Furon, Christophe. *Les écorcheurs: Guerre et pillage à la fin du Moyen Age.* Paris, 2023.

Germani, Ian. "Military Justice under the Directory: The Armies of Italy and of the Sambre and Meuse." *French History* 23, no. 1 (2009): 47–68.

Goodich, Michael, ed. *Voices from the Bench: The Narratives of Lesser Folk in Medieval Trials.* New York, 2006.

Gunn, Steven, David Grummitt, and Hans Cools. "War and the State in Early Modern Europe: Widening the Debate." *War in History* 15, no. 4 (2008): 371–88.

Habermas, Rebekka. *Thieves in Court: The Making of the German Legal System in the Nineteenth Century.* New York, 2016.

Hamilton, Tom. "Adjudicating the Troubles: Violence, Memory, and Criminal Justice at the End of the Wars of Religion." *French History* 34, no. 4 (2020): 417–34.

Hamilton, Tom. "The Crisis and Recovery of Criminal Justice in Late Sixteenth-Century France." *Sixteenth Century Journal* (forthcoming).

Hamilton, Tom. *A Widow's Vengeance: Violence and Justice in Late Renaissance France*. Oxford, 2024.

Harris, Ruth. "'Child of the Barbarian': Rape, Race, and Nationalism in France during the First World War." *Past and Present*, no. 141 (1993): 170–206.

Harris, Ruth. *The Man on Devil's Island: Alfred Dreyfus and the Affair That Divided France*. London, 2010.

Harrison, Simon. *Dark Trophies: Hunting and the Enemy Body in Modern War*. New York, 2012.

Hatzfeld, Jean. *Machete Season: The Killers in Rwanda Speak*. New York, 2005.

Hobsbawn, Eric. *Bandits*. London, 1969.

Hofman, Elwin. *Trials of the Self: Murder, Mayhem, and the Remaking of the Mind, 1750–1830*. Manchester, 2021.

Horne, John, and Alan Kramer. *German Atrocities, 1914: A History of Denial*. New Haven, CT, 2001.

Horowitz, Sarah. *The Red Widow: The Scandal That Shook Paris and the Woman Behind It All*. Naperville, IL, 2022.

House, Jim. "Intervening on 'Problem' Areas and Their Inhabitants: The Sociopolitical and Security Logics behind Censuses in the Algiers Shantytowns, 1941–1962." *Histoire et mesure* 34, no. 1 (2019): 121–50.

Kaeuper, Richard W. *War, Justice, and Public Order: England and France in the Later Middle Ages*. Oxford, 1988.

Kalifa, Dominique. *Crime et culture au XIXe siècle*. Paris, 2005.

Kalifa, Dominique. *L'encre et le sang: Récits de crimes et société à la Belle Epoque*. Paris, 1995.

Kalman, Samuel. "Criminalizing Dissent: Policing Banditry in the Constantinois, 1914–1918." In *Algeria Revisited: Contested Identities in the Colonial and Postcolonial Periods*, edited by Rabah Aissoui and Claire Eldridge, 19–38. New York, 2016.

Kalman, Samuel, ed. "Policing the French Empire." Special issue, *Historical Reflections* 46, no. 2 (2020).

Keller, Kathleen. *Colonial Suspects: Suspicion, Imperial Rule, and Colonial Society in French West Africa*. Lincoln, NE, 2018.

Kounine, Laura. *Imagining the Witch: Emotions, Gender, and Selfhood in Early Modern Germany*. Oxford, 2018.

Kwass, Michael. *Louis Mandrin and the Making of a Global Underground*. Boston, 2014.

Lilly, J. Robert. *La face cachée des GI's: Les viols commis par des soldats américains en France, en Angleterre et en Allemagne pendant la Seconde Guerre mondiale*. Paris, 2003.

Lilly, J. Robert. *Taken by Force: Rape and American GIs in Europe in World War II*. New York, 2007.

Lucas, Colin. *The Structure of the Terror: The Example of Javogues and the Loire*. Oxford, 1973.

Maffi, Davide, ed. *Tra Marte e Astrea: Giustizia e giurisdizione militare nell'Europa della prima età moderna (secc. XVI–XVIII)*. Milan, 2012.

Mann, Gregory. "What Was the *Indigénat*? The 'Empire of Law' in French West Africa." *Journal of African History* 50, no. 3 (2009): 331–53.

Margolf, Diane C. *Religion and Royal Justice in Early Modern France: The Paris Chambre de l'Edit, 1598–1665*. Kirksville, MO, 2003.

Martin, Jean-Clément. *Violence et Révolution: Essai sur la naissance d'un mythe national*. Paris, 2006.

Maza, Sarah C. *Violette Nozière: A Story of Murder in 1930s Paris*. Berkeley, CA, 2011.

Meumann, Markus. "Civilians, the French Army, and Military Justice during the Reign of Louis XIV." In *Civilians and War in Europe, 1618–1815*, edited by Erica Charters, Eve Rosenhaft, and Hannah Smith, 100–117. Liverpool, 2012.

Mosse, George. *Fallen Soldiers: Reshaping the Memory of the World Wars*. Oxford, 1990.

Musson, Anthony, and Nigel Ramsay, eds. *Courts of Chivalry and Admiralty in Late Medieval Europe*. Woodbridge, 2018.

Nassiet, Michel. *La violence, une histoire sociale: France, XVIe–XVIIIe siècles*. Seyssel, 2011.

Palmer, R. R. *Twelve Who Ruled: The Year of Terror in the French Revolution*. Princeton, NJ, 2017.

Paresys, Isabelle. *Aux marges du royaume: Violence, justice et société en Picardie sous François Ier*. Paris, 1998.

Parker, Geoffrey. "Early Modern Europe." In *The Laws of War: Constraints on Warfare in the Western World*, edited by Michael Howard, George J. Andreopoulos, and Mark R. Shulman, 40–58. New Haven, CT, 1994.

Perry, Matt, *Mutinous Memories: A Subjective History of French Military Protest in 1919*. Manchester, 2019.

Plarier, Antonin. "Le banditisme rural en Algérie à la période colonial (1871–années 1920)." PhD diss., Université Paris 1 (Panthéon-Sorbonne), 2019.

Potter, David. "'Rigueur de Justice': Crime, Murder, and the Law in Picardy, Fifteenth to Sixteenth Century." *French History* 11, no. 3 (1997): 265–309.

Prakash, Amit. *Empire on the Seine: The Policing of North Africans in Paris, 1925–1975*. Oxford, 2022.

Prétou, Pierre. *Crime et justice en Gascogne à la fin du Moyen Age*. Rennes, 2010.

Prost, Antoine. "Les limites de la brutalisation: Tuer sur le front occidental, 1914–1918." *Vingtième siècle*, no. 81 (2004): 5–20.

Roberts, Penny. "Royal Authority and Justice during the French Religious Wars." *Past and Present*, no. 184 (2004): 3–32.

Rubenhold, Hallie. *The Five: The Untold Lives of the Women Killed by Jack the Ripper*. London, 2019.

Ruquet, Miquèl. *Déserteurs et insoumis de la Grande Guerre (1914–1918) sur la frontière des Pyrénées-Orientales*. Canet, 2009.

Saada, Emmanuelle. "La loi, le droit et l'indigène." *Droits: Revue française de théorie juridique, de philosophie et de culture juridiques*, no. 43 (2006): 165–90.

Saint-Fuscien, Emmanuel. "Entre guerre et paix: La décennie décisive de la justice militaire française." *Mil neuf cent: Revue d'histoire intellectuel (Cahiers Georges Sorel)*, no. 33 (2015): 15–31.

Sandberg, Sveinung, and Gustavo Fondevila. "Corona Crimes: How Pandemic Narratives Change Criminal Landscapes." *Theoretical Criminology* 26, no. 2 (2022): 224–44.

Schnerb, Bertrand. *"L'honneur de la Maréchaussée": Maréchalat et maréchaux en Bourgogne des origines à la fin du XVe siècle*. Turnhout, 2000.

Skoda, Hannah. *Medieval Violence: Physical Brutality in Northern France, 1270–1330*. Oxford, 2013.

Sottocasa, Valérie. *Les brigands: Criminalité et protestation politique (1750–1850)*. Rennes, 2013.

Sottocasa, Valérie. *Les brigands et la Révolution: Violence politiques et criminalité dans le midi (1789–1802)*. Ceyzérieu, 2016.

Staiano-Daniels, Lucian. "Masters in the Things of War: Rethinking Military Justice during the Thirty Years War." *German History* 39, no. 4 (2021): 497–518.

Staveley-Wadham, Rose. "Investigating Blackout Crime in the Second World War." *British Newspaper Archive*, Nov. 30, 2022. https://blog.britishnewspaperarchive.co.uk/2022/11/30/blackout-crime-in-the-second-world-war/.

Steedman, Carolyn. *History and the Law: A Love Story*. Cambridge, 2020.

Surkis, Judith. *Sex, Law, and Sovereignty in French Algeria, 1830–1930*. Ithaca, NY, 2019.

Tackett, Timothy. *The Coming of the Terror in the French Revolution*. Cambridge, MA, 2015.

Thénault, Sylvie. "L'état d'urgence (1955–2005): De l'Algérie coloniale à la France contemporaine; Destin d'une loi." *Le mouvement social*, no. 218 (2007): 63–78.

Thénault, Sylvie. "L'indigénat dans l'empire français: Algérie/Cochinchine, une double matrice." *Monde(s)* 12, no. 2 (2017): 21–40.

Thénault, Sylvie. *Violence ordinaire dans l'Algérie coloniale: Camps, internements, assignations à résidence*. Paris, 2012.

Thomas, Martin. *Empires of Intelligence: Security Services and Colonial Order after 1914*. Berkeley, CA, 2007.

Thomas, Martin. *Violence and Colonial Order: Police, Workers, and Protest in the European Colonial Empires, 1918–1940*. Cambridge, 2012.

Toureille, Valérie. *Vol et brigandage au Moyen Age*. Paris, 2006.

Verreycken, Quentin. *Crimes et gens de guerre au Moyen Age: Angleterre, France et principautés bourguignonnes au XVe siècle*. Paris, 2023.

Watson, Eric R. *Trial of George Joseph Smith*. Edinburgh, 1922.

Wilson, Peter H. "Warfare in Europe." In vol. 3 of *The Cambridge World History of Violence*, edited by Robert Antony, Stuart Carroll, and Caroline Dodds Pennock, 174–93. Cambridge, 2020.

Wright, N. A. R. "'Pillagers' and 'Brigands' in the Hundred Years War." *Journal of Medieval History* 9, no. 1 (1983): 15–24.

Mercy at War
Military Violence and the Politics of Royal Pardon in Fifteenth-Century France

QUENTIN VERREYCKEN

ABSTRACT   This article examines the construction of military criminality and the granting of pardons to soldiers in late medieval France. By the beginning of the fifteenth century, the offenses perpetrated by men of war were a recurrent problem of public order for royal government. Criminal records as well as narrative sources used a rich terminology to qualify the military abuses suffered by the population, which distinguished criminal soldiers from ordinary offenders. Although these abuses were repeatedly denounced by political literature and were supposed to be severely punished according to legislation, the king of France frequently granted pardon letters to soldiers, allowing them to escape criminal prosecution in exchange for the continuation of their services. Far from being simply the result of a lax attitude of the king, these pardons reflected the fragile balance of royal power in the fifteenth century, which required the king to conciliate the exercise of justice and the conduct of warfare. Exploring the politics of royal pardon toward criminal soldiers and the reactions they provoked, the article demonstrates how the French crown dealt with military offenders at the end of the Hundred Years' War and during its aftermath.

KEYWORDS   crime, France, Hundred Years' War, military violence, pardon letter

On September 25, 1523, King Francis I of France promulgated a royal decree known as the "ordinance against adventurers, pillagers, and people-eaters." This text provides a dramatic picture of the situation in the kingdom, as the troops raised by the crown to wage war against Emperor Charles V proved a major source of trouble for the French population. It explains that "due to the aforesaid wars, [there] have risen up some adventurers, vagrant people," and other "robbers, murderers, abductors and rapists of women and girls." The ordinance accuses these felons of "eating and devouring the people," by committing more atrocities than any other of the king's adversaries. Despite the appointment of provost marshals (*prévôts des maréchaux*) in every bailiwick to prosecute and execute these adventurers, royal justice had failed to prevent their proliferation, so it had become urgent to "purge this venom." By this royal decree Francis declared all

French Historical Studies • Vol. 47, No. 2 (May 2024) • DOI 10.1215/00161071-11025063
Copyright 2024 by Society for French Historical Studies

adventurers, plunderers, and other oppressors of the French people the enemies of the king and of the *chose publique*, urging his officers to apprehend and sentence them to death. More important, the king acknowledged that "without strong and violent antidote, such inconvenience cannot be cured," so he gave license to all his subjects to rob, kill, and tear apart these adventurers and their chiefs, without risking prosecution or having to apply for a royal pardon.[1]

In many ways, the royal ordinance of 1523, promulgated in the context of the Habsburg-Valois conflict, is a perfect illustration of the ideology of royal power that dominated in the late medieval and early modern periods.[2] In the preamble of the ordinance, Francis declares that God appointed him protector of the kingdom of France and of "the common and popular estate, which is the weakest, the humblest, and the lowest one." This solicitude of the king toward his most vulnerable subjects contrasts with the virulence with which he designates the adventurers and plunderers as public enemies and the targets of hatred. They are "cruel, inhuman, unmerciful," a group of "ravishing wolves created to harm everyone," "a cursed and serpentine seed widespread in our kingdom," so they deserve to be killed by anyone. Considering the king's duty to preserve his kingdom and subjects, such dramatic vocabulary shows that the enormity of the crimes committed by these felons against public order also constituted a direct offense against royal majesty itself. Yet, as Valérie Toureille remarks, the ordinance remains vague concerning the identity of the criminals targeted by royal justice and does not make a clear distinction between robbers and vagrants, former soldiers turned brigands, or those combatants in the king's service who also pillaged and plundered. They were all part of the same infestation that ruined the kingdom and persecuted its population, and as a result, they had to be eliminated.[3]

In late medieval and early modern France, it was not uncommon for soldiers to be perceived as a major source of disruption for society: they took food, goods, and accommodation by force, attacked and ransomed people, raped women, and caused various other damages—"they were all thieves and murderers, fire breathers, rapists of women," wrote the anonymous author of the *Journal d'un bourgeois de Paris* about a group of soldiers approaching Paris in July 1444.[4] In contrast to the ideal of the combatants as the loyal servants of their lord and the protectors of the community elaborated by medieval authors, the common opinion reported by chronicles was that soldiers were barely differentiable from other criminal figures that haunted the popular imagination. This

1. *Ordonnances de François Ier*, 3:298–304.
2. Babeau, *Les préambules des ordonnances royales*, 38–39.
3. Toureille, *Vol et brigandage*, 161.
4. Tuetey, *Journal d'un bourgeois de Paris*, 374–75.

negative perception of the military community, which still predominated in the sixteenth century due to the escalation of military brutalities during the Italian Wars and the Wars of Religion, was the result of a long process of criminalization of the abuses committed by soldiers since the beginning of the Hundred Years' War (1337–1453).[5]

The ordinance of 1523 was indeed the culmination of a series of royal decrees that, from the mid-fourteenth century on, severely punished the excesses committed by soldiers and progressively established the conditions for the legitimate exercise of armed force, in the service of the king and of the *chose publique*.[6] The purpose of this legislation was not only to better control the violence of soldiers but also to impose the king as the sole legitimate authority to raise armies, thus limiting the military agency of the princes who competed with royal power.[7] The outcome of these military reforms was the creation of a standing royal army known as the *compagnies d'ordonnance* in February 1445, which was justified in the royal legislation by the necessity to stop pillaging (*faire cesser de tous poins la pillerie*).[8] This transformation of French military institutions, arguably a premise of the so-called early modern military revolution,[9] was accompanied by the efforts of royal power to better enforce military discipline and coercion within the armies. The first part of the fifteenth century indeed saw a reinforcement in the administration of justice toward soldiers. Royal bailiffs and seneschals were commissioned to prosecute the crimes committed by soldiers that involved noncombatants, while the Parlement of Paris, the first sovereign court of justice in France, frequently ruled on these affairs on appeal. The parlement also judged in the first instance the military abuses that directly offended royal majesty.[10] In practice, however, royal justice rarely apprehended military offenders due to the mobility of the troops, the resistance of combatants, and the king's constant need of men to wage war against the English. Within the armies, the captain of each company was responsible for the crimes committed by the

5. Verreycken, "La criminalité militaire." See also Bowd, *Renaissance Mass Murder*; Carroll, *Blood and Violence*; Nassiet, *La violence*; and Potter, *Renaissance France at War*. In contrast, in sixteenth-century England soldiers were seen in a much more favorable light following their rehabilitation by Tudor propaganda: Grummitt, "Changing Perceptions," 197–202.

6. Bessey, *Construire l'armée française*; Cazaux, "Réglementation militaire royale."

7. Carbonnières, "Le pouvoir royal"; Firnhaber-Baker, *Violence and the State in Languedoc*.

8. Bessey, *Construire l'armée française*, 102. On Charles VII's military reform in 1445, see also Contamine, *Guerre, Etat et société*, 277–90; Hélary, "Effondrement et renaissance," 174–80; and Péquignot, "De la France à Barcelone."

9. For a more elaborated discussion on the military revolution and the contribution of the late medieval period to it, see Ayton and Price, *Medieval Military Revolution*; Parker, *Military Revolution*; and Rogers, *Military Revolution Debate*.

10. Bessey, *Construire l'armée française*, 94–95; Cazaux, *Les capitaines*, 225–43, 473–540. On the role of ordinary jurisdictions in prosecuting soldiers, see also Verreycken, *Pour nous servir en l'armée*, 196–202. For a comparison with English Normandy, see Rowe, "Discipline in the Norman Garrisons."

men under his command, and he had the obligation to bring them to justice. Military justice itself was originally in the hands of the principal officers in charge of commanding the royal armies, the constable and the marshal. However, they progressively abandoned the day-to-day application of military discipline in favor of a subordinate officer, the provost marshal, who was renowned for his severe and expeditious judgments but left us almost no record from his activities for the medieval period.[11]

Surprisingly, despite the multiplication of royal decrees and the strengthening of judicial coercion to severely punish military abuses, the king of France never ceased to grant pardons to soldiers, allowing hundreds of them to escape criminal prosecution in exchange for the continuation of their services. One of these soldiers, for example, was Roulant Raulete, a forty-year-old man-at-arms from the company of the bastard of Beaumanoir. In October 1441 he and his companions ransomed four merchants from Notre-Dame de Beauchêne in Poitou. Because of this act, he was captured by local justice and brought to royal prisons. Fearing that he would be fined or sentenced to a corporal punishment, he quickly submitted a written petition for pardon to Charles VII, in which he begged for the king's mercy. Raulete was right to be scared: ransoming the subjects of the king was indeed a serious crime that had been recently assimilated to *lèse-majesté* by a royal decree promulgated in the form of a pragmatic sanction in 1439, so the man-at-arms was potentially risking his life. To show that he deserved pardon, Raulete argued in his petition that he had ransomed these four merchants only to obtain food while traveling through the country. All the goods he took from the merchants had since been returned to them, while his own horses and possessions had been confiscated by royal justice. Finally, the man-at-arms appealed to the king's sympathy and described himself as a loyal soldier who, "dès le temps de son enfance" (since his childhood), had served Charles VII during his wars against the English and especially during the recent siege of the city of Pontoise between June and September 1441. Luckily for him, Raulete's request was not in vain. The king and his councillors promptly agreed to grant him a remission letter in December 1441, putting an end to the prosecution and freeing the petitioner from prison.[12]

The case of Roulant Raulete was hardly unique. In fifteenth-century France combatants usually represented between 2 and 15 percent of pardon beneficiaries, depending on the region and the period, which is an impressive figure given that,

---

11. Cazaux, *Les capitaines*, 243–58, 449–70; Contamine, *Guerre, Etat et société*, 515–32; Le Barrois d'Orgeval, *La justice militaire*, esp. 31–63; Schnerb, "Jurisdiction of the Constable and Marshals."

12. Paris, Archives Nationales (hereafter AN), JJ 176, fol. 270r, in Guerin and Celier, *Recueil des documents*, 8:130–31.

according to Philippe Contamine, royal armies barely reached 1.2 percent of the active masculine population at that time.[13] This may also appear paradoxical, considering the efforts of royal power to prosecute the very same soldiers. This situation has been severely judged by the early modern historiographer Charles Pinot Duclos, who noted in his *Histoire de Louis XI* (1745), "One cannot read without horror the letters of remission which were given in those times; there was hardly a man of war who did not need an abolition."[14] As the king of France was not the only monarch to favor combatants, the English crown has been similarly criticized by the modern historian Naomi D. Hurnard, who considers that due to the repeated issue of military pardons, "the king's prerogative of mercy, however worthy in conception, was certainly used to excess" and "in complete disregard of the need to maintain the deterrent force of prospective punishment."[15] This idea of a decline of law and justice in favor of military interests reflects a classical historiographical vision of the late Middle Ages as a period of structural crisis of public order, characterized by the incapacity of royal government to prevent the multiplication of crimes and violence generated by the Hundred Years' War. Largely dominant until the 1970s and 1980s, this impression has, however, been nuanced by historians of crime and criminal justice, who have shown that the fourteenth and fifteenth centuries represented a period of growth for royal government and judicial institutions, while the development of the power to pardon could ultimately serve the law enforcement.[16] My purpose in this article is therefore to understand why, in the context of increasing judicial coercion against soldiers, the king of France kept pardoning combatants throughout the fifteenth century. To do so, the article first examines how military criminality was gradually constructed as a political problem during the Hundred Years' War. It subsequently explores the politics of pardon toward soldiers during the reigns of Charles VII (1422–61) and Louis XI (1461–83), by studying which combatants benefited from the king's mercy and how these pardons served the interests of the French crown. I seek to demonstrate that, far from being the symptom of a failing and corrupted justice system that favored a culture of impunity among

13. See Cazaux, *Les capitaines*, 623–24; Contamine, *Guerre, Etat et société*, 317–18; Gauvard, *"De grace especial*," 533; Paresys, *Aux marges du royaume*, 29; Potter, "'Rigueur de Justice,'" 282, 289; and Sablon du Corail, "Naissance d'une frontière?," 74.

14. Duclos, *Histoire de Louis XI*, 1:8.

15. Hurnard, *King's Pardon*, vii. For similar comments, see also Kaeuper, *War, Justice, and Public Order*, 126–27. For a more recent and revisionist approach of English military pardons, see Lacey, *Royal Pardon*, 100–106; and Villalon, "Taking the King's Shilling."

16. Gauvard, *"De grace especial."* For a more complete historiographical survey, see Bove, *Le temps de la guerre de Cent Ans*, 573–626; and Verreycken, "Power to Pardon." Similar arguments on the role of royal pardon in restoring peace in sixteenth-century France during and after the Wars of Religion have been made by Frisch, *Forgetting Differences*, 26–62; Mellet and Foa, "Une 'politique de l'oubliance'"; Nassiet, *Guerre civile et pardon royal*; and Nassiet, *Les lettres de pardon du voyage de Charles IX*.

military offenders, the granting of pardon letters to soldiers in fact played an important role in the regulation of military criminality.

The Hundred Years' War and the Invention of Military Criminality

The attitude of medieval society toward violence in warfare has often been described as ambivalent.[17] On the one hand, the medieval nobility saw itself as a warrior elite and praised participation in warfare as a source of personal accomplishment and glory. The strongest manifestation of this military ethos was the development of chivalric culture, which not only valorized courtly manners or feats of arms in tournaments but also promoted recourse to violence to defend the honor of the knight or his lord.[18] The chivalric ideology therefore saw the pursuit of warfare and the use of violence as intrinsically positive when they were justified by the circumstances, as shown in this famous passage of Jean de Bueil's *Le Jouvencel* (ca. 1461–66): "War is a joyful thing! You hear and see many wonderful things and learn a lot of good lessons. When it's war in pursuit of a good cause, then you're the instrument of justice."[19] On the other hand, war and military violence were far from being unanimously accepted by medieval society. Predatory violence carried out in the context of warfare was frequently criticized by clergy and laity, especially when it was committed against churches, monasteries, and friendly populations. By the eleventh century seigneurial warfare had become so endemic that the church had created a mass peace movement known as the Peace of God, which proclaimed the immunity of peasants, clergy, women, and children (among others) in times of war, therefore providing a first legal framework for the distinction between combatants and noncombatants that was still operating in later medieval treaties such as *L'Abre de batailles* by Honoré Bovet (ca. 1387–89).[20]

The outbreak of the Hundred Years' War in 1337 marked a turning point in the perception of military violence. The *chevauchées* of Edward III's armies that devastated the French countryside during the first decades of the conflict shocked most chroniclers, who denounced this brutality.[21] Soldiers serving the king of France were considered hardly more respectable, because they regularly pillaged and ransomed allied populations. Another problem was the presence of mercenaries also known as *routiers* or *grandes compagnies* who, when they were not

---

17. Jamieson, "Sons of Iniquity," 91–92.

18. Kaeuper, *Chivalry and Violence*; Taylor, *Chivalry and the Ideals of Knighthood*.

19. Bueil, *Le Jouvencel*, 125.

20. Allmand, "War and the Non-combatant," 254–59; Malegam, *Sleep of Behemoth*, 27–31; Wright, "Tree of Battles," 18–19; Bovet, *L'arbre des batailles*, 202, 208. On seigneurial warfare and its regulation, see also Carbonnières, "Le pouvoir royal"; and Firnhaber-Baker, *Violence and the State in Languedoc*.

21. Wright, *Knights and Peasants*, 67–69. See also Rogers, "By Fire and Sword."

employed during truces, regularly plundered to survive.[22] These multiple acts of predation, combined with the extended duration of the conflict between France and England, considerably deteriorated the image of combatants in public opinion. As Christopher Allmand showed, these circumstances also prompted a broader intellectual debate about the restoration of the values of chivalry and the reformation of military institutions.[23] At the beginning of the fifteenth century, the conflict between Armagnacs and Burgundians (1407–35) only reinforced the negative reputation of soldiers, when chroniclers and propagandists reported rumors accusing combatants of the other side of committing acts of extreme—and sometimes imaginary—cruelty, to delegitimize the cause of the opponent.[24] A good example of this is the efforts of the Burgundian party to organize the excommunication of the Armagnac leaders and the combatants under their command, relying on Urban V's papal bull of 1365 against the great companies to justify the condemnation of the rebels.[25] Moreover, Luke Giraudet observed that, after the signature of the Peace of Arras in 1435, most of the negative attributes of the "Armagnac soldiers"—*larrons*, murderers, and the like—elaborated by the Burgundian propaganda were transferred to the *écorcheurs*, groups of disbanded soldiers who devastated multiple regions of France and neighboring principalities. Charles VII himself was criticized by authors in favor of the duke of Burgundy, who reproached him for his inability to provide for his armies and repress the *écorcherie*.[26]

Although the violence attributed to regular or unemployed soldiers was often exaggerated by fifteenth-century chroniclers and propagandists who accused their Burgundian or Armagnac opponents of the most terrible atrocities,[27] there is little doubt that the presence and circulation of combatants generated great fear for most of the population. Indeed, the negative reputation of soldiers was not only the product of rumors and propaganda but reflected the endemic nature of the offenses perpetrated by soldiers and registered in court and chancery records—including in remission letters. This concern was also expressed in the petitions submitted to the king by local communities through state

22. Contamine, "Les compagnies d'aventure"; Butaud, *Les compagnies de routiers*.

23. Allmand, "Changing Views of the Soldier." See also Allmand, "Des origines intellectuelles"; Cazaux, "Pour un droit de la guerre?"; and Grummitt, "Changing Perceptions of the Soldier."

24. Fargette, "Rumeurs, propagande et opinion publique"; Gauvard, "Rumeur et gens de guerre"; Giraudet, *Public Opinion and Political Contest*, 151–65.

25. *Ordonnances des roys de France*, 9:652–53. See also Giraudet, *Public Opinion and Political Contest*, 164.

26. Giraudet, *Public Opinion and Political Contest*, 165. About the *écorcheurs* and the *écorcherie* crisis, see Furon, *Les écorcheurs*; Toureille, *Robert de Sarrebrück*, esp. 127–32; and Tuetey, *Les écorcheurs*. For contemporary critics against Charles VII's treatment of the *écorcherie*, see La Marche, *Mémoires*, 1:243–45; and Tuetey, *Journal d'un bourgeois de Paris*, 355.

27. Bove, "Deconstructing the Chronicles."

assemblies, asking the monarch to make soldiers stop plundering.[28] There was, in other words, an urgent need to regulate military violence.

As a legal and political process, the criminalization of the abuses committed by soldiers in the late Middle Ages was complementary to the definition of the legitimate use of armed force. While the theory of the *iustum bellum* elaborated by medieval theologians and jurists after Augustine provided a moral and legal justification of the wars between Christians, the conduct of warfare itself was primarily ruled by the customs of war and the law of arms or chivalric law, which governed the actions of combatants in and outside the battlefield. This set of rules allowed soldiers to pillage and plunder in enemy territory or "pays de conqueste" to pay and supply troops. Despite the principles of the Peace of God movement, the customs of war offered little protection to noncombatants in enemy territory, especially during a siege, when the long-standing resistance of populations exposed them to a particularly devastating seizure by force: looting, massacres, rapes, and practically all forms of violence were permitted.[29] However, while the perpetuation of violence in enemy territory was tolerated and sometimes even encouraged by military commanders, the same actions were strictly forbidden when they were committed against allied populations or during truces. In other words, what defined the crimes committed by soldiers was not necessarily the nature of the offenses but, rather, the identity of their victims and the context of their perpetration. This is perfectly illustrated in a royal ordinance promulgated on March 3, 1357, which ordered the punishment of "any soldier from inside or outside the kingdom" who pillaged in France but also encouraged any subject "from any status, to take, gain, and pillage on the enemies of the kingdom."[30] For the monarchy, restoring public order therefore meant punishing attacks by soldiers on French subjects, rather than prohibiting any form of military violence.

From the mid-fourteenth century on, the kings of France repeatedly promulgated royal ordinances regulating the levy, structure, and discipline of the royal armies. As Loïc Cazaux points out, this military legislation fed into the construction of a "litany of royal discourses focusing on the repression of looting and disorders by men of war."[31] The offenses targeted by military legislation usually comprised pillage, ransom, rape, murder, robbery, arson, or destruction of houses and churches. This list also included some acts of indiscipline in the army that did not necessarily involve physical violence, such as desertion. In ordinance after ordinance, the repeated prohibition of these offenses shaped the

---

28. Cazaux, "Réglementation militaire royale," 95; Furon, "Gens de guerre en hiver," 91.
29. Keen, *Laws of War*, 103–8, 119–33. See also Russel, *Just War*.
30. *Ordonnances des roys de France*, 3:139.
31. Cazaux, "Réglementation militaire royale," 95.

contours of military criminality and the image of its perpetrators. Moreover, at the beginning of the fifteenth century, a particular vocabulary developed in the preambles of royal decrees, in the pleadings at the Parlement of Paris, and in pardon letters referring to the abuses committed by soldiers on the population as "dommaiges" (damages), "maulx" (miseries), "maléfices" (curses), "excès" (excesses), or "oppressions" that required a remedy from the king and justified the reformation of the royal military institutions. This terminology echoed the complaints in contemporary literature about the calamities of war and, as Cazaux and Pierre Prétou have shown, it was inspired by the notions of *enormitas* and *excessus*, two legal concepts from the Romano-canonical procedure, which designated the most serious offenses against public order.[32] Interestingly, a relatively similar vocabulary was still used a century later in legislation and criminal records to describe the "crimes exécrables" of soldiers during the Wars of Religion, such as rape, arson, and pillage.[33] By emphasizing the seriousness of these offenses committed by the combatants, these dramatic qualifications also provided a legal framework for the definition of public force and its limits, as military criminality was clearly differentiated from the crimes committed by the rest of the population and identified as a major threat to the kingdom's stability.

The sanctions delineated for each crime varied from one ordinance to another, ranging from the simple confiscation of pay and equipment to execution of the guilty party, as well as punishments at the captain's discretion. The disciplinary ordinance promulgated in the form of a pragmatic sanction by Charles VII on November 2, 1439, probably represented the culmination of this repressive policy.[34] Presented as the direct answer of the king to the complaints about the *écorcherie* crisis of the Estates General reunited in Orléans the previous month, this decree declared crimes of *lèse-majesté* plundering, ransoming, and robbing the king's subjects; confiscating their food or livestock without recompense; destroying their property and houses; and committing acts of brigandage on the roads. The culprits had to be imprisoned and their properties seized; they were deprived of any office they held and, ultimately, faced capital punishment. Moreover, almost a century before Francis I's ordinance against adventurers, the pragmatic sanction of 1439 gave permission to any subject to apprehend or kill any military offender.[35] Finally, Charles VII promised that "he [would] not give

---

32. Cazaux, *Les capitaines*, 528–32; Prétou, *Crime et justice*, 196–200. On the concepts of *enormitas* and *excessus* in the Middle Ages, see also Théry, "Atrocitas/enormitas."

33. Hamilton, "Adjudicating the Troubles," esp. 429–32; Hamilton, "Un 'cas exécrable' devant le Parlement de Paris."

34. Bessey, *Construire l'armée française*, 88–101.

35. A similar measure also appeared in the ordinance promulgated on March 28, 1431, for the repression of pillage in Poitou: Guerin and Celier, *Recueil des documents*, 8:1–7.

any remission" to the soldiers who committed one of the crimes listed in this ordinance, which made these military offenses virtually irremissible. Yet this last measure did not prevent the crown from continuing to pardon soldiers in the decades that followed.

Soldiers and the Medieval Power to Pardon

The right to remit crimes by issuing a charter of pardon was a common feature of royal and princely power in medieval Europe. In the kingdom of France, these charters took the form of a *lettre de rémission*, a letter patent issued by the royal chancery following a petition submitted by the supplicant to the king and his council, who decided whether the case was pardonable or not. There were also some variants to the remission letter, like the *lettre d'abolition*, which was generally granted not only to individuals but also to communities for crimes that affronted the royal majesty, such as treason, rebellion, or excesses in war. An abolition was also characterized by its having "abolished" the crime that was pardoned, which meant that it was erased from memory as if it never existed. As an instrument of oblivion, the abolition was therefore an important tool for the pacification and reconciliation of society, especially in a postwar context.[36] After the supplicant received his remission or abolition letter and paid the fees of 8 *livres* and 8 *sous parisis* for its sealing, a copy of the charter was recorded in the registers of the royal chancery, called the *Trésor des chartes* (see fig. 1). Subsequently, the supplicant was obliged to have his letter endorsed by a royal jurisdiction within a year and a day by means of a trial called *entérinement*; otherwise the royal pardon would not be considered valid. This procedure involved a new investigation by local officers to verify whether the supplicant had lied or withheld information in his petition, in which case the letter was declared *subreptice et obreptice* and the pardon canceled.[37] Finally, the trial also required the supplicant to conclude an arrangement with the victim party, called a *paix à partie*, which usually involved financial compensation. The ratification of the letter made the pardon permanent, restoring the supplicant's reputation (he was "remis à sa bonne fame et renommée," according to the formula in the charters) and allowing him to return to his former life.

One of the most remarkable characteristics of the French remission letters was their narrative content: the first part of each letter, based on the original petition submitted by the future pardon beneficiary, described in detail the circumstances of the crime. As Natalie Zemon Davis warned in her seminal study

36. Gauvard, "Pardonner et oublier"; Offenstadt, *Faire la paix au Moyen Age*, 50–55.
37. Gauvard, "Le roi de France," 393–99; Musin et Nassiet, "Les récits de rémission," 53–57; Otis-Cour, "Les limites de la grâce."

FIGURE 1 Remission letter recorded in the *Trésor des chartes*, December 1468 (Paris, Archives Nationales, JJ 195, fol. 46r). Manuscript digitized and made available online thanks to the support of the Archives Nationales and the HIMANIS European research program (JPI Cultural Heritage). https://bvmm.irht.cnrs.fr/iiif/23801/canvas/canvas-2347297/view (accessed July 25, 2023).

of sixteenth-century remission letters, these documents must be read cautiously because of the rhetorical and legal argumentation adopted by the suppliants and the chancery clerks who assisted them to make the case remissible.[38] Despite these legal and literary artifices that often make historians doubt the veracity of some aspects of the stories, remission letters remain a valuable form of documentation to study not only the discourses but also the daily lives and the social habits of late medieval people. The conflictual episodes described in the remission letters are strong indicators of the tensions that pervaded medieval society, how individuals interacted with each other, and how violence was perpetrated. The arguments used by suppliants to justify their actions, mitigate their responsibility, or shift the blame onto their victim also allow scholars to examine how the culture of violence operated in the late Middle Ages and how the use of force was justified or excused.

In the case of the remission letters granted to soldiers, they also enable us to observe multiple aspects of the military life—not only the extremely violent abuses committed in war but also more ordinary disputes in the armies or against the general population. The charter granted to the archer Jehan d'Estanchereux in October 1472, for example, is a good illustration of the conflicts of hierarchy that sometimes escalated into quarrels.[39] A month earlier the suppliant, who

38. Davis, *Fiction in the Archives*, esp. 15–25. See also Arnade and Prevenier, *Honor, Vengeance, and Social Trouble*, 13–18; and Verreycken, "'En Nous Humblement Requerant.'"

39. AN, JJ 195, fol. 182v.

was part of the company of the constable Louis of Luxembourg, count of Saint-Pol, guarding the Palace of Rouen in Normandy, witnessed a dispute between his captain and another soldier named Macé Valin. The captain was blaming Valin for not having performed his duty in guarding the palace's gate, with the soldier retorting "arrogamment" that he was doing the best he could (*il faisoit le mieulx qu'il povoit*) and should not receive such reprimands. Rankled by Valin's conduct, d'Estanchereux told him that the captain was right to talk to him like this and asked him why he did not come to keep watch. Valin again reacted angrily, arguing that he could have been killed by some enemy while doing his watch, to which d'Estanchereux responded: "You must not say anything unpleasant to the captain or anyone else, because if you do so, in this matter it would be enough to put your head in a ditch" (*Tu ne doiz point dire au cappitaine ne a aultre chose qui desplaire, car se tu le faisoies plus en telles matieres ce seroit assez pour toy envoyer la teste dedans les fossez*). The discussion continued to escalate, and Valin started to threaten the supplicant, drawing his dagger and telling him that he was no man for him (*tu n'estz pas homme pour moy!*). Perceiving himself to be in danger, d'Estanchereux drew his own dagger and struck his opponent on the head. Due to his "mauvais gouvernement" or lack of care, Valin died from his wound a month later, so the supplicant petitioned Louis XI for a remission letter, which he received in a matter of weeks.

Quite logically, the presence of combatants in the *Trésor des chartes* depended on the military activity of the crown. In the second half of the fourteenth century, the number of letters of remission granted to soldiers remained relatively limited but increased slightly in the 1360s after the Treaty of Brétigny and following Charles V's reconquest of territories previously lost to the English.[40] Comparatively, the reign of Charles VI (1380–1422) was characterized by a long period of calm in terms of military conflicts, at least until the beginning of the civil war in 1407; while the number of remission letters granted by the king during this period increased, the proportion of pardons delivered to soldiers declined sharply, and combatants represented only 1.4 percent of the supplicants.[41] In the 1420s and 1430s the irregularities in the records of the *Trésor des chartes* make it difficult to get an idea of the granting of pardons during the first two decades of Charles VI's reign. Nevertheless, the number of remission and abolition letters to soldiers appears to increase significantly during the 1440s, in the context of the troubles caused by the *écorcherie*. In the second part of the

40. Cazaux, *Les capitaines*, 629. No extensive study has been conducted on pardons for combatants in the first part of the fourteenth century, but at least fifty-six remission letters delivered to captains between 1314 and 1363 have been identified by Telliez, "Per potentiam officii," 298.

41. Gauvard, "De grace especial," 532.

fifteenth century, the reign of Louis XI was marked by the Franco-Burgundian wars and several other conflicts between the king and other princes of the kingdom, so no fewer than 13 percent of the remission letters (735 out of more than 5,600) were delivered to soldiers or men who had previously served the king in the armies.[42] The geographic distribution of the letters also reflects the concentration of combatants in border regions and highly militarized areas of France. For example, at the end of the first part of the fifteenth century, the region of Poitou had greatly suffered from the feudal revolt of the *Praguerie* in 1440 and by the presence of *écorcheurs* in the countryside, so 38.9 percent of the letters granted for a crime committed in the region between 1441 and 1456 were intended for soldiers.[43] Similarly, under Louis XI, most remission letters granted to combatants concerned crimes committed in Normandy (16.5 percent), Picardy (14 percent), or Artois (11.6 percent), three regions marked by several military conflicts or proximity to the Burgundian power.[44]

Soldiers seeking to secure a pardon usually introduced themselves at the beginning of their petition by giving their names, status, or the company in which they served: "The humble supplication of Olivier Clisson, squire, man-at-arms of our ordinance, under the charge of the count of Dammartin, great master of our hostel."[45] This gives us a little more information about the profiles of these combatants. A systematic study of the 735 remission letters granted by Louis XI to soldiers shows that most of these men of war were archers (37.7 percent) or members of the militia of the *franc-archers* (17.6 percent). There was also a significant proportion of men-at-arms (16.6 percent), who were professional and often noble combatants and formed the elite of the armies. On the other hand, only 1.7 percent of the pardoned combatants declared that they held a higher rank in the king's armies, such as lieutenants or captains—the latter usually petitioned only to obtain an abolition for rebellion.[46] Nevertheless, the nobility was widely represented among the troops, since 15.7 percent of the supplicants declared that they were squires and 1.3 percent that they were knights. The number of noblemen is also certainly underestimated, as more than half of the men-at-arms provide no information about their nobility. Among other notable information provided by the remission letters, about 130 supplicants

42. AN, JJ 194–226. See Verreycken, *Crimes et gens de guerre*, 50–65; and Sablon du Corail, "Naissance d'une frontière?," 74.

43. These letters have been edited in Guerin and Celier, *Recueil des documents*, vols. 8–9. See also Cazaux, *Les capitaines*, 622–28, 656–62; and Gauvard, "Pardonner et oublier," 28–29.

44. Verreycken, *Crimes et gens de guerre*, 98. Comparatively, between 13 and 15 percent of the letters of pardon granted in Picardy in the first part of the sixteenth century were delivered to combatants: Paresys, *Aux marges du royaume*, 29; Potter, "'Rigueur de Justice,'" 282, 289.

45. AN, JJ 195, fol. 273v.

46. Cazaux, *Les capitaines*, 669–75.

mentioned their age, of which the vast majority (67.9 percent) were between twenty and thirty years old, with 16.8 percent between thirty-one and forty years of age. Moreover, 10 percent of all the soldiers stated that they were married, and 10.4 percent also indicated that they had a profession outside the army (predominantly as valets or servants).

Finally, although most petitioners who introduced themselves as soldiers committed their crimes during their military service, a notable minority were not combatants when they perpetrated their offense. Indeed, during the reign of Louis XI, 2 percent of the remission letters were granted to supplicants who joined the armies only after they had committed a crime, in order to start a new life, escape local justice, and eventually obtain a royal pardon.[47] For example, in the early 1450s Jacotin de Flandres, a young unmarried man, fled Picardy after beating up Mathieu de Sarniel. He joined Charles VII's *compagnies d'ordonnance* and served the king in several military campaigns. For about seven years he never encountered any trouble from justice, until he decided to return to Picardy to visit some friends in Amiens; he was promptly captured by local officers. Jacotin, who claimed to be a clerk, was then transferred to the prisons of the bishop of Amiens, where he remained until he obtained a remission letter from Louis XI in September 1461.[48]

Conversely, 5.3 percent of these remission letters were addressed to men who had departed from military service and were endeavoring to resume their former occupations when they fell into crime. The letters in this last category consistently illustrate the financial difficulties faced by former soldiers, as they were six times more likely to be pardoned for theft than those who committed this crime during their military service (15 percent and 2.5 percent, respectively). To justify their actions, the supplicants argued that they had been impoverished by several years of military service and no longer possessed anything to spare for their lives. Occasionally, they also admitted that there was a sense of continuity between their attitude at war and the crimes they committed once they had finished their service. In one such remission letter, granted in 1472, Denis le Tavernier and Pierre Bullot explained that they had once served the king and "committed pillages, murders, and other crimes" at war. After they returned home, they realized that "they did not have enough to live on, or to pay the *taille* and

47. That fugitives would consciously turn to a military life to obtain a royal pardon has been particularly well documented for late thirteenth- and fourteenth-century England, where the king regularly proclaimed that he would pardon any offender who participated in his military campaigns. Similar proclamations occurred at least twice in the Low Countries under the dukes of Burgundy in the 1470s, but it has never been observed in France, to my knowledge. See Gribit, *Henry of Lancaster's Expedition*, 46–48; Lacey, *Royal Pardon*, 100–106; Verreycken, "Discipliner par la grâce," 25; and Villalon, "Taking the King's Shilling."

48. AN, JJ 198, fols. 144v–145r.

other charges," and as a result were compelled to steal sheets and money to support themselves.[49] Besides evading poverty, some veterans struggled to rid themselves of the bad reputation associated with combatants and faced the hostility of the population, like Person Blondel and Jehan Arnoul. After their company was disbanded in 1472, Blondel and Arnoul were insulted in a village in Champagne by a man named Jehan Lalemant who, as a supporter of the duke of Burgundy in his conflict with Louis XI, called them "villains gens de guerre."[50]

A typical portrait of the soldier in the remission letters emerges from these figures. The pardoned combatant was usually a man in his twenties, possibly married and with a family, and occupied another profession outside military life. These soldiers rarely occupied a high position in the armies, although they may well have included members of the lower nobility attracted by the prestige and prospects of social advancement offered by military service. Considering the humble origin of the supplicant, obtaining a remission letter was expensive: a French archer's monthly wage in the fifteenth century was between 3 and 7 *livres* 10 *deniers tournois*, whereas a man-at-arms was paid 10 or 15 *livres tournois*.[51] The purchase of a pardon, at 8 *livres* and 8 *sous parisis*, could therefore cost the supplicant several months of salary, but it was a necessity if he wanted to return home and reintegrate into society after he left military service, especially when he committed his crime close to where he lived and therefore risked being arrested by local authorities when he came back. Most supplicants (56.7 percent) indeed confessed to having fled the region in which they committed their crime to escape justice and argued that they risked falling into poverty if they did not obtain their remission: "The aforesaid Goulart and Colin have left our country and do not dare to converse or reside there anymore, unless our grace and mercy are bestowed on them."[52]

This last declaration also reminds us that the role of chancery conventions should not be underestimated here. The rules of the supplication as a literary genre required the petitioners to insist on their vulnerability, and as a result the information provided by the remission letter was primarily elaborated to elicit the king's pity, while those details that did not favor the supplicant's case were ignored.[53] Unsurprisingly, no soldier pardoned by Louis XI described himself as a brute or a thug; rather, he stood firm on his good reputation (22 percent of the cases) and his having never had any problem with justice before: "The aforesaid supplicant is a man of good life and honest conversation and has never

---

49. AN, JJ 197, fol. 86v.
50. AN, JJ 197, fols. 152v–153r.
51. Contamine, *Guerre, Etat et société*, 632–33.
52. AN, JJ 199, fols. 29r–31r.
53. Verreycken, "'En Nous Humblement Requerant,'" 5–10.

perpetrated or let perpetrate anything reprehensible."[54] Moreover, 23 percent of the combatants who received remission letters evoked their military service in their supplication as a justification for their pardon: "The aforesaid supplicant has always been in our service in the company of his aforesaid master and loyally fulfilled his duty during the aforesaid wars."[55] The granting of a royal pardon to military offenders was therefore presented as a reward for the loyalty and fidelity of the petitioner, which paradoxically reinforced the positive image of the combatant, who despite committing a crime remained a reliable servant of the king. Claude Gauvard saw in this repetition of military service another intervention of chancery clerks who, being well informed about the debates on the reformation of military institutions, "dreamed of an army at the service of the kingdom" and therefore encouraged the supplicants to embrace the royal ideology in their petitions.[56] This finally leads us to consider why the king of France frequently pardoned his soldiers and how these politics of pardon reflected the relationship between military order and royal authority.

War and the Politics of Pardon

In the late Middle Ages, the granting of remission letters to soldiers had to balance two fundamental attributions of royal power: administrating justice and waging war.[57] When he exercised mercy over combatants, the king of France acted both as the supreme judge of his kingdom and as the commander in chief of his armies, which made these pardons a manifestation not only of his judicial power but also of his relationship with his soldiers. As such, the mention of military service by the supplicants reflected their submission to the royal authority while at the same time making the pardon a form of reward for their efforts. But if the judicial and military attributions of the king obliged him to maintain peace and ensure public order within his kingdom, how could he justify regularly granting pardons to the combatants of his armies for attacking his subjects?

Following the dramatic descriptions of military violence in fifteenth-century chronicles and legislation, one may indeed expect remission letters granted to soldiers to be full of stories of pillaging, rape, and oppression. However, the letters preserved in the French *Trésor des chartes* reveal a more complex reality. The rise of the power to pardon in late medieval France was closely related to

54. AN, JJ 203, fols. 18v–19r.

55. AN, JJ 195, fol. 159r: "Ledit suppliant a esté tousiours en notre service en la compaignie de sondit maistre et s'est acquité loyaulement en notre service ou fait desdites guerres."

56. Gauvard, *"De grace especial,"* 859. See also Verreycken, "'En Nous Humblement Requerant,'" 14–15.

57. Deruelle and Verreycken, "Père du peuple ou roi de guerre?" See also Cornette, *Le roi de guerre*; and Krynen, *L'empire du roi.*

the development of royal justice and the criminalization of homicide during the thirteenth and fourteenth centuries. Under the principles of learned law, according to which the intent of the perpetrator takes precedence over the material consequences of his actions, the royal pardon distinguished accidental or excusable homicides (committed spontaneously, in anger, or in self-defense) from those aggravated by premeditation and dissimulation (murder).[58] Consequently, most remission letters issued by the royal chancery concerned homicide cases in which the supplicants explained that they had acted in self-defense or out of anger (*chaude cole*) in reaction to the insults and threats of their victim.[59] The charters of pardon granted to soldiers were no exception, though the proportion of blood crimes among them changed over time. At the beginning of the fifteenth century, the homicide rate in these letters was about 60 percent, according to Gauvard.[60] Fifty years later, during the reign of Louis XI, it reached 88.6 percent for remission letters concerning a crime committed during military service (see table 1).

TABLE 1. Pardoned crimes of soldiers during the reign of Louis XI, 1461–1483

Crime[a]	Frequency (%)
Homicide	88.6
Assault	0.8
Theft	2.5
Rape and/or elopement	2.2
Rebellion and/or treason	2.5
Other	3.5

[a] Crimes committed by soldiers enrolled in the armies ($n = 649$), therefore excluding offenses committed before or after military service.

In comparison, Gauvard estimates that at least 10 percent of the letters granted to soldiers under Charles VI covered pillages and plundering, which were, just after homicide, the most frequent pardoned crimes for soldiers.[61] However, this number falls to almost zero during the second half of the fifteenth century. Indeed, Louis XI granted only one abolition letter to a soldier of his armies who had "vescu sur le pays,"[62] plus a few more pardons to former soldiers of the duke of Burgundy who perpetrated diverse acts of violence in France when they were in the Burgundian armies.[63] To understand the reasons for the disappearance of the excesses of war in the *Trésor des chartes* in the second part of the fifteenth century, we must examine more closely the kings' politics of pardon toward their soldiers in the fifteenth century.

58. On the legal distinction between homicide and murder, see Skoda, *Medieval Violence*, 27–33.
59. Verreycken, "'En Nous Humblement Requerant,'" 15–21.
60. Gauvard, *"De grace especial,"* 529.
61. Gauvard, *"De grace especial,"* 529.
62. AN, JJ 203, fol. 27v.
63. AN, JJ 195, fol. 252v; JJ 203, fols. 101v–102r, 155v–156r; JJ 207, fols. 155v–156r.

After a relative period of calm in terms of military activity during most of Charles VI's reign, the rise of the civil war between the Armagnacs and the Burgundians in 1407 and the resurgence of the conflict with England in 1415 exposed the kingdom of France to the devastation caused by soldiers. During this period, the power to pardon proved an important instrument for the pacification and reconciliation of the kingdom, as the king occasionally granted abolition letters to declare oblivion on the crimes committed during this period. Provisions to this effect were included in the Treaty of Arras in 1435, in which Charles VII proclaimed the abolition of "all the cases that happened and all the aforesaid things accomplished and done on the occasion of the divisions and wars of this kingdom."[64] Yet we have seen that the end of the civil war was followed by the *écorcherie* crisis. For the Burgundian memorialist Olivier de La Marche, the person responsible for this situation was none other than Charles VII, who had been unable to maintain and pay his soldiers, which led them to pillage and cause more damages than during the civil war itself.[65] To put an end to the *écorcherie* phenomenon, the king subsequently promulgated the royal ordinance of 1439, in which he transformed excesses of war into crimes of *lèse-majesté* and rendered them irremissible.

In practice, however, the repression of military criminality was relatively limited. The analysis conducted by Loïc Cazaux of the criminal proceedings before the Parlement of Paris between 1420 and 1440 shows that soldiers who committed pillages, rapes, and other violence were rarely brought to the court, first because there were too many of them, and second because they easily evaded the authorities by moving from one region to another. It was mainly their captains, considered responsible for the misdeeds of their men, who were tried for excesses of war, but even in these cases the sentences pronounced by the judges of the parlement were rarely severe and usually consisted of paying financial compensations for the damages suffered by the population. As Cazaux argues, the imperative to wage war against the English made it difficult to severely punish military offenders, because it would mean losing more combatants who were indispensable for the defense of the kingdom. Consequently, instead of imposing severe sentences on soldiers, the purpose of the parlement was to promote norms from legislation on the limits of public force and obeisance to the king.[66]

Another idea behind the pragmatic sanction of 1439 was to establish a permanent royal army financed by a new regular tax. Yet this unpopular measure, combined with the king's claim to be the only authority entitled to raise troops

64. Cosneau, *Les grands traités*, 146.
65. La Marche, *Mémoires*, 1:243–45.
66. Cazaux, *Les capitaines*, 243–58; Cazaux, "Le connétable de France," 59–60.

in the kingdom, resulted in an almost immediate failure of the pragmatic sanction, followed in February 1440 by the *Praguerie*, a revolt of some of the great feudal lords and former captains of the king.[67] Despite the severe repression of this insurrectionary episode, the king was forced to temporarily abandon his project of a standing army, whereas he continued to regularly pardon *écorcheurs* and other soldiers to keep them at his service—including the rebels of the *Praguerie*, who benefited from an abolition in July 1440.[68]

Only after the Treaty of Tours had been signed with England on May 28, 1444, did Charles VII finally seize the opportunity to implement his military reforms and contain the *écorcherie*. Following the suspension of the conflict against the English, the king hired a large number of *écorcheurs* and, to keep them away from France, sent them in a bloody military campaign commanded by the Dauphin in Switzerland and Lorraine, where several thousands of them lost their lives.[69] Then in February 1445 he established his *compagnies d'ordonnance* and proclaimed a general abolition to the surviving *écorcheurs*, to integrate them permanently in this new military structure and ensure their obedience.[70] It was not the first time Charles VII granted such abolition specifically targeting soldiers. On April 9, 1431, twelve days after he had promulgated an ordinance prohibiting pillaging and plundering in Poitou, the king delivered a collective abolition letter to Jean de la Roche and the soldiers of his company, pardoning them the "grant quantité de roberies et pillories" they had committed in this region.[71] Although the text of the general abolition of 1445 has been lost, it appears that more than sixty individual abolition letters were granted to *écorcheurs* from 1445 to 1451 and recorded in the *Trésor des chartes*. The one obtained in August 1445 by Jean Marsillac, for example, explicitly refers to the "general abolition granted to the aforesaid men of war."[72] This letter abolished all the "cases, crimes, excesses, and other offenses" committed by the supplicant during the war against the English, with the notable exception of "all murders made of ambush, burning of fires, rape and abduction of women and girls, and the crime of sacrilege." Numerous other abolition letters granted during this period contain a similar clause, which excluded murder, rape, sacrilege, and arson from the abolition. As Gauvard pointed out, these reserved cases corresponded to the list of crimes that had been declared irremissible by the ordinance of reformation of 1357, which Charles VII probably brought up-to-date in

---

67. Lecuppre-Desjardin and Toureille, "Servir ou trahir."
68. Cazaux, "Les lendemains de la Praguerie," 365–66, 372–73.
69. Hardy, "1444–1445 Expedition of the Dauphin."
70. Toureille, *Robert de Sarrebrück*, 140–51. See also Péquignot, "De la France à Barcelone," 794–95.
71. Guerin and Celier, *Recueil des documents*, 8:1–20.
72. AN, JJ 177, fol. 124v; Guerin and Celier, *Recueil des documents*, 8:208–10.

his general abolition to not seem too indulgent about the most scandalous crimes committed by the *écorcheurs*.[73] Well informed of this clause, some soldiers therefore insisted in their supplications on their having never committed any of these unpardonable crimes, like Jehan de Fresneau in 1445, who declared that although some of his companions may have raped women, he had never been present or agreed about this (*aucuns ont violé femmes, non pas qu'il ait esté présent ne consentant à ce*).[74] Nevertheless, the king was not always observant of this clause, like when he granted an abolition letter in March 1446 to a squire named Jehan de Blanchefort, who let the soldiers under his command commit murders, arsons, rapes, and sacrileges.[75] For these soldiers, securing an individual abolition letter was a further guarantee that the general abolition proclaimed by Charles VII applied to them and that they would not be prosecuted for their crimes. This also means that many other combatants probably benefited from the general abolition, without trying to purchase an individual letter, and subsequently joined the newly established *compagnies d'ordonnance*. Royal pardon was therefore one of the key factors in the success of Charles VII's military reform, as well as in the decline of the *écorcherie*.[76]

During the first part of the fifteenth century, the practice of pardoning the excesses of war committed by French combatants was therefore primarily dictated by the necessity to pacify the kingdom and obtain the fidelity of soldiers. The granting of abolition letters was also the result of the incapacity of royal justice to efficiently prosecute and condemn the crimes committed by soldiers, which led the king to pardon military offenders in order to reestablish public order by decreeing that such crimes never existed.[77] Yet this indulgence of royal power could be only a short-term policy. After the taming of the last *écorcheurs*, Charles VII pursued the reconquest of the remaining French territories occupied by the English, whereas the number of abolition letters granted for excesses of war fell quickly during the relative period of peace of the 1450s, as the crown now concentrated its efforts on restoring the subjects' confidence in the royal justice system.[78] The study of English-occupied Gascony by Pierre Prétou offers a well-documented demonstration of this phenomenon: during the 1440s and 1450s, the use of royal pardon intensified to support the reconquest of the duchy, win the loyalty of Gascon subjects, and maintain the French military presence in this territory. For a time, the soldiers present in Gascony benefited

---

73. Gauvard, "Pardonner et oublier," 47; *Ordonnances des roys de France*, 3:129.
74. AN, JJ 177, fol. 65v; Guerin and Celier, *Recueil des documents*, 8:219.
75. AN, JJ 177, fols. 118v–119r; Tuetey, *Les écorcheurs*, 2:435–37.
76. Cazaux, *Les capitaines*, 649–51; Furon, "Les derniers feux de l'écorcherie."
77. Prétou, *Crime et justice*, 198–202.
78. See Schmit, *En bon trayn de justice*.

from a large number of remission and abolition letters for the crimes they committed in the duchy, and especially for excesses of war, but this pardoning policy changed at the beginning of the reign of Louis XI. The new king's tour of Gascony in 1462–63 marked a rupture with his predecessor and reconciled the Gascon people with the crown. During his voyage Louis XI granted remissions and abolitions for murder and rebellion but also for resisting and killing soldiers, whereas combatants were pardoned less and less often for excesses of war.[79]

The emergence, in chancery records, of soldiers being killed by noncombatants in the second part of the fifteenth century was not limited to the duchy of Gascony. In total, Louis XI granted about sixty such pardons in his whole kingdom between 1461 and 1483. Some of the cases covered by these remission letters relate to the classic scenarios of medieval conflictual sociability, such as tavern brawls and disputes between neighbors. However, a large number of letters also describe the distrust and resistance of populations toward soldiers. For example, on October 26, 1465, a *franc-archer* named Pierre Montredont, who was living "from the substance of the poor people" (*vivans de la substance du povre peuple*) in a village of Velay, entered the house of Bertholomi Bonnet to claim food. His son, François, answered that his father had already supplied other soldiers, which provoked the anger of Montredont, who confiscated a large quantity of hemp he found in the house. When François Bonnet protested, arguing that the *franc-archer* could not loot the house of his father because he did not reside in a *pays de conqueste*, Montredont reacted by drawing his dagger. Seeing the soldier approaching him angrily, François Bonnet took a staff and hit Montredont on the head and shoulder, resulting in his death the next day.[80]

There had been, in France, a long tradition of peasants' resistance against soldiers. We have seen that the 1357 ordinance authorized all subjects to defend themselves against the aggression of pillaging combatants and robbers, and in the pragmatic sanction of 1439 the king promised to grant pardon for any homicide committed against military offenders. As such, since the second half of the fourteenth century, peasants and villagers organized their defense by forming bands of armed men patrolling in the countryside, sometimes attacking on sight any soldier they found, including those who had not harmed them.[81] This practice did not disappear in the second part of the fifteenth century, but it was problematic when directed toward the king's soldiers and also potentially constituted an offense against the king, as only he could authorize the levy of troops. Yet Louis XI still showed some flexibility on such occasions. In July 1466

79. Prétou, "Abolir l'excès de guerre," 70–72; Prétou, *Crime et justice*, 307–17.
80. AN, JJ 204, fol. 25r–v.
81. Wright, *Knights and Peasants*, 80–95. See also Prétou, "Les voisins contre la route."

he granted an abolition letter to a group of people from Normandy who offended his royal majesty (*ayant grandement et en diverres manierres mespris et offensé contre nous en notre royal magesté*) because they armed themselves and robbed several soldiers from the duchy of Brittany, "to avenge and repel the insults, beating, pillages and pressures" (*pour eulx revenchier et repulser les injures, bateries, pilleries et oppressions a eulx faites*) committed by these combatants while they were supposed to fight for the king in the war of the public good.[82] Thus, while the king no longer tolerated the excesses committed by his soldiers, he agreed to pardon those who defended themselves against military abuses.

Another factor influencing the decline of abolition letters granted for excesses of war was the protests they aroused. Since the second part of the fourteenth century, royal pardon had been regularly criticized by humanist scholars, jurists, and theologians who claimed that it contributed to the weakening of the law, as it inculcated a sense of impunity among criminals.[83] One of those critics was the theologian Jean Courtecuisse, who in the context of the Cabochien revolt for the reformation of royal government in 1413, declared that "we call mercy pardoning the death of a wrongdoer and thus put in danger of death one hundred or one thousand men."[84] By denouncing the dangers of an excessive use of pardons, these intellectuals sought to strengthen the judicial system at the same time as they stoked fear of crime and reminded the king of his responsibilities. As a direct consequence of these debates, from the 1440s on, while the crown regularly granted abolition letters, the Parlement of Paris judged some of these "uncivil and unreasonable" and refused to endorse them. In particular, the judges of the parlement rejected those letters that pardoned crimes considered irremissible by the ordinance of 1357. Without questioning the king's right to grant pardons, the magistrates of the parlement considered themselves the guardians of the legislation that governed this power. By doing so, they reaffirmed the "boundaries of irremissibility,"[85] which forced the king and his council to be more careful before pardoning crimes that may be considered irremissible, including those committed by combatants. For the crown, responding to the demands for the restoration of public order meant establishing stricter military discipline and granting fewer pardons to his soldiers. "The good prince must proudly and boldly judge by rightfulness, authority, and lordship and avenge all the offenses committed by the knights; and he should not pardon to

---

82. AN, JJ 194, fol. 92r–v:.
83. Gauvard, "Les humanistes français et la justice."
84. Gauvard, *"De grace especial,"* 911.
85. Toureille, *Vol et brigandage*, 262. See also Gauvard, *Condamner à mort*, 202–9.

anyone his offense when it damages several others," proclaimed Louis XI in the *Rosier des guerres* (ca. 1481–82), a political treaty he dictated for his son, reflecting the idea that the excesses of war that threatened public order were no longer pardonable.[86]

This almost complete disappearance of abolitions for excesses of war during the reign of Louis XI does not mean that the new king did not care about his armies—quite the contrary: of more than 5,600 remission letters delivered during his reign, he granted about 735 pardons to soldiers and former combatants. As we have seen, most of these letters covered cases of homicide committed during a brawl. Moreover, in more than a third of the cases, the victim was a fellow soldier. Clearly, the population was not the only one to suffer from the crimes committed by combatants. Some letters even show soldiers coming to the rescue of noncombatants, like the one granted in March 1470 to Jehan Belymont. On February 19 of that year, this twenty-eight-year-old archer was staying in the village of Estrepieds in the *châtellenie* of Loudun, when a villager named Jehan Pichart came to him to complain about Estienne Maligneau, another soldier who had confiscated and held to ransom two pots belonging to Pichart. Belymont promptly mounted his horse and rode off to meet Maligneau, ordering him to return the pots, but the soldier refused and tried to flee. Belymont went after him and, in pursuit, struck him in the side with his javelin, which caused his death.[87]

The chronology of the remission letters granted by Louis XI (see fig. 2) also demonstrates the king's growing interest in his soldiers. The outbreak of the War of the Public Weal (1465) and the subsequent wars against Charles the Bold (1468–77), as well as the so-called War of the Burgundian Succession (1477–82), were all followed by an increase in the pardon activity of the king. This reflected the growing size of the royal armies: before the War of the Public Weal, the *compagnies d'ordonnances* were composed of about 1,706 *lances* of six combatants, which increased to 1,990 *lances* in 1470 and reached 4,000 in 1482.[88] The increasing military presence in the kingdom and the need to finance the armies only reinforced the burden of war for the French population, as soldiers passing through a region still frequently caused troubles that might require a pardon. Another indication of the king's growing interest in his soldiers was the increasing proportion of pardon letters granted to combatants annually: during the War of the Public Weal and until 1470, 11–12 percent of the remission letters

86. Paris, Bibliothèque Nationale de France, MS Fr. 17273, fol. 30r: "Le bon prince doit prendre fierté et hardement de juger par droicture, autorité et sagesse et de venger tous les meffaiz des chevaliers et ne pardonner à nul son meffait quant il touche plusieurs."

87. AN, JJ 196, fol. 152r–v.

88. Contamine, *Guerre, Etat et société*, 283; Lassalmonie, *La boîte à l'enchanteur*, 283, 520.

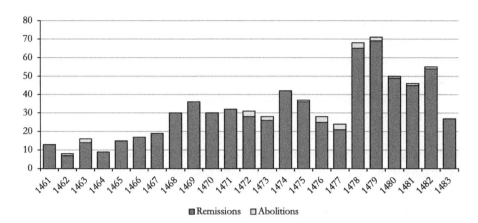

FIGURE 2 Remission and abolition letters to soldiers under Louis XI, 1461–1483 (Paris, Archives Nationales, JJ 194–226).

issued by the crown were granted to soldiers, but this rate then regularly exceeds 15 percent in the following decade and even reached 21 percent and 18 percent in 1478 and 1482, respectively. In this context, the large number of remission letters granted to soldiers, as well as the rapidity of the pardoning procedure itself (in 66 percent of cases, soldiers received their letter one to six months after their crime), shows how the king supported his troops and managed to protect them from the rigors of justice, as long as their crimes went beyond the limits of ordinary violence, that is, when they committed homicides. This resulted in a sort of "domestication" of the pardoned military criminality, which, in terms of the typology of crimes, was no longer different from that of the rest of population. This trend continued in the following decades, when the list of pardoned crimes was gradually restricted by royal legislation. As such, by the mid-sixteenth century it had become much rarer for soldiers and noncombatants alike to receive a pardon for anything other than homicide.[89]

While in the first part of the fifteenth century royal legislation and abolition letters promoted the notion of "excesses of war" to describe military criminality and assert its seriousness, the records of the *Trésor des chartes* from the latter half of the fifteenth century show that this category of crime was no longer tolerated and that soldiers were pardoned only when they committed offenses that were not condemned by military legislation. As such, the sudden rise and disappearance of the "excesses of war" in chancery records illustrate how the granting of pardons to soldiers ultimately supported the efforts of the crown to better control combatants. At the end of the Hundred Years' War, when Charles VII created his standing armies, the most undisciplined soldiers were offered a

89. Musin and Nassiet, "Les récits de rémission"; Nassiet, *La violence*, 25–27.

chance to join the *compagnies d'ordonnance*, but after the pacification of the kingdom in the 1450s and the disappearance of the *écorcherie*, there was no longer any justification for Louis XI to be so generous, so his soldiers had now to fall in line. Moreover, as the public debate on the dangers of an abusive royal mercy met the appeals to restore military discipline, the restriction of the pardoning policy toward soldiers was also the crown's response to the tension between, on the one hand, the necessity to maintain the cohesion of the royal armies and, on the other hand, the king's duty to appear as the protector of his whole kingdom and subjects and not only of his soldiers.

Conclusion

The pardon letters preserved in the French *Trésor des chartes* offer a nuanced perspective on military violence and how royal power dealt with the abuses committed by soldiers in fifteenth-century France. Although combatants were capable of extremely brutal actions such as pillaging and attacking noncombatants, only a minority of soldiers were actually pardoned for such cases, mainly during the late 1440s and early 1450s, in the context of the reform of the royal armies and the taming of the *écorcheurs*. Instead, most soldiers were pardoned for homicides committed in self-defense or in anger, like the rest of the subjects of the king of France. The circumstances of these crimes described in pardon letters provide precious information about everyday military life, the tensions that circulated in the armies, and the conflicts that arose between soldiers and the civilian population. The content of chancery records also reveals more about military offenders themselves, their social backgrounds, and how they constructed a positive image of themselves when petitioning for a pardon. Far from the stereotype of bloodthirsty brutes propagated by fifteenth-century chronicles, these soldiers tried to justify their actions and appear as good servants of the king, using rhetorical techniques suggested by the chancery clerks who assisted them in the drafting of their petitions.

Of course, the king of France and his counselors were not naive about these strategies; they consciously favored combatants to serve the interests of the royal government. For the French crown, the politics of pardon seem essentially pragmatic and guided by the political and military circumstances, but a closer examination also reveals that at the heart of the establishment of a sense of military remissibility was an ideological tension surrounding the king's authority as both the commander of his armies and the protector of his subjects. In the context of the end of the Hundred Years' War, the regular granting of remission and abolition letters to soldiers balanced the rightful application of justice and a need to maintain an army by offering a pardon to the soldiers in exchange for their submission to royal authority. Yet Charles VII's short-term strategy of erasing the crimes of the *écorcheurs* quickly met its limits due to the opposition it provoked. In the second half of the fifteenth century, the granting of remission letters to soldiers was still as frequent, but also much stricter, as Louis XI tried to maintain the discipline of his armies and no longer tolerated the molestation of his subjects by the soldiers.

This change in the pardoning policy did not mean that, in practice, the armies of Louis XI suddenly became well disciplined compared to those of his predecessors. Chroniclers, literary sources, and military legislation demonstrate that French soldiers continued to regularly commit pillages, ransoms, or rapes and that Louis XI himself encouraged such actions in enemy territories, especially during the invasion of the Burgundian principalities after the death of Charles the Bold in 1477.[90] During this period, the provost marshal became a key figure in the prosecution of the abuses committed by soldiers against noncombatants. Another endemic disciplinary problem that preoccupied the crown was the frequent unauthorized departures of soldiers within the royal armies. This led Louis XI to promulgate a decree in 1477 making desertion a crime of *lèse-majesté*, but he never granted any pardon letter for such crime.[91] Yet the lack of research on the appearance of combatants before courts in the second part of the fifteenth century[92] makes it difficult to estimate the extent of judicial repression against soldiers during this period, whereas the absence of pardons for excesses of war does not mean that these crimes were more frequently condemned. Following the outbreak of the Italian Wars, military violence toward noncombatants continued to increase, as illustrated by the ordinance of 1523. Throughout the sixteenth century, the king refused to grant remission letters for such crimes, but this did not prevent soldiers from occasionally attracting royal mercy, particularly during the Wars of Religion, when their exactions were covered by the proclamation of edicts of pacification and general amnesties.[93] More generally, in the context of the transformation of early modern European warfare, the abuses committed by soldiers and the strengthening of military discipline remained a major issue for rising absolutist monarchies.[94]

90. Scordia, "Entre guerre traditionnelle et sidération."

91. Vaesen and Charavay, *Lettres de Louis XI*, 6:204. See also Allmand, "Le problème de la désertion." Although no pardon letter was formally granted by Louis XI for the crime of desertion, a few soldiers who were pardoned for another crime admitted having fled the royal armies: Verreycken, *Crimes et gens de guerre*, 117–18.

92. With the notable exception of Cazaux, *Les capitaines*, 473–540, which focuses on the trials of French captains before the Parliament of Paris. Drewitt-Wex, "English 'Soldier,'" 159–96, also offers interesting points of comparison with the cases of English soldiers being tried before the King's Bench in 1442–56.

93. Carroll, *Blood and Violence*, 100; Nassiet, *Guerre civile et pardon royal*, xxvi, xliv.

94. Maffi, *Tra Marte e Astrea*; Meumann, "Civilians, the French Army, and Military Justice"; Wilson, "Warfare in Europe."

In these circumstances, it is difficult to conclude that the French crown's politics of pardon toward soldiers contributed to a decline in military violence in the fifteenth century, but was it ever their purpose? At the end and during the aftermath of the Hundred Years' War, the granting of charters of pardon to soldiers allowed the king of France to strengthen his control over his armies. In the long run, the use of remissions and abolitions to distinguish between acceptable violence and excesses of war—which could be pardoned on exceptional occasions only—together with the promulgation of legislation and the application of justice toward soldiers, helped better circumscribe military criminality and provided the legal tools to punish it.

QUENTIN VERREYCKEN holds a PhD in history from the University of Louvain and Saint-Louis University, Brussels, where he is a Fund for Scientific Research–FNRS postdoctoral researcher and a visiting lecturer. He is author of *Pour nous servir en l'armée: Le gouvernement et le pardon des gens de guerre sous Charles le Téméraire, duc de Bourgogne (1467–1477)* (2014) and *Crimes et gens de guerre au Moyen Age: Angleterre, France et principautés bourguignonnes au XVe siècle* (2023).

Acknowledgments

This article was made possible by a fellowship of the Fund for Scientific Research–FNRS in Belgium and a fellowship of the Käte Hamburger Kolleg "Legal Unity and Pluralism" at the University of Münster, funded by the Federal Ministry of Education and Research in Germany. The author would like to thank Claire Eldridge, Julie M. Powell, Luke Giraudet, Danielle Beaujon, Joseph Clarke, Angélique Ibáñez Aristondo, Andrew McKeon, Jessica Meyer, Chloë Pieters, Ariel Mond, and Katja Pyötsiä, as well as the two anonymous reviewers for their insightful feedback and comments.

References

Allmand, Christopher. "Changing Views of the Soldier in Late Medieval France." In *Guerre et société en France, en Angleterre et en Bourgogne, XIVe–XVe siècle*, edited by Philippe Contamine and Charles Giry-Deloison, 171–88. Lille, 1991.

Allmand, Christopher. "Des origines intellectuelles de l'armée française au Moyen Age." In *Un Moyen Age pour aujourd'hui: Pouvoir d'Etat, opinion publique, justice; Mélanges offerts à Claude Gauvard*, edited by Nicolas Offenstadt and Olivier Mattéoni, 47–56. Paris, 2010.

Allmand, Christopher. "Le problème de la désertion en France, en Angleterre et en Bourgogne à la fin du Moyen Age." In *Guerre, pouvoir et noblesse au Moyen Age: Mélanges en l'honneur de Philippe Contamine*, edited by Jacques Paviot and Jacques Verger, 32–41. Paris, 2000.

Allmand, Christopher. "War and the Non-combatant in the Middle Ages." In *Medieval Warfare: A History*, edited by Maurice F. Keen, 253–72. Oxford, 1999.

Arnade, Peter, and Walter Prevenier. *Honor, Vengeance, and Social Trouble: Pardon Letters in the Burgundian Low Countries*. Ithaca, NY, 2015.

Ayton, Andrew, and J. L. Price, eds. *The Medieval Military Revolution: State, Society, and Military Change in Medieval and Early Modern Europe*. London, 1995.

Babeau, Albert. *Les préambules des ordonnances royales et l'opinion publique*. Paris, 1986.

Bessey, Valérie, ed. *Construire l'armée française: Textes fondateurs des institutions militaires*. Vol. 1. Turnhout, 2006.

Bove, Boris. "Deconstructing the Chronicles: Rumours and Extreme Violence during the Siege of Meaux (1421–1422)." *French History* 24, no. 4 (2010): 501–23.

Bove, Boris. *Le temps de la guerre de Cent Ans (1328–1453)*. Paris, 2020.

Bovet, Honoré. *L'arbre des batailles*. Edited by Ernest Nys. Brussels, 1883.

Bowd, Stephen D. *Renaissance Mass Murder: Civilians and Soldiers during the Italian Wars*. Oxford, 2018.

Bueil, Jean de. *Le Jouvencel*. Translated by Craig Taylor and Jane Hilary Margaret Taylor. Woodbridge, 2020.

Butaud, Germain. *Les compagnies de routiers en France, 1357–1393*. Clermont-Ferrand, 2012.

Carbonnières, Louis de. "Le pouvoir royal face aux mécanismes de la guerre privée à la fin du Moyen Age: L'exemple du Parlement de Paris." *Droits* 46, no. 2 (2007): 3–18.

Carroll, Stuart. *Blood and Violence in Early Modern France*. Oxford, 2006.

Cazaux, Loïc. "Le connétable de France et le Parlement: La justice de guerre du royaume de France dans la première moitié du XVe siècle." In *Justice et guerre de l'antiquité à la Première Guerre mondiale*, edited by Marie Houllemare and Philippe Nivet, 53–62. Amiens, 2011.

Cazaux, Loïc. *Les capitaines dans le royaume de France: Guerre, pouvoir et justice au bas Moyen Age*. Paris, 2022.

Cazaux, Loïc. "Les lendemains de la Praguerie: Révolte et comportement politique à la fin de la guerre de Cent Ans." In *Lendemains de guerre . . . de l'antiquité au monde contemporain: Les hommes, l'espace et le récit, l'économie et le politique*, edited by François Pernot and Valérie Toureille, 365–74. Brussels, 2010.

Cazaux, Loïc. "Pour un droit de la guerre? La discipline militaire et les rapports entre combattants et non-combattants dans le *Livre des faits d'armes et de chevalerie* de Christine de Pizan." In *Une femme et la guerre à la fin du Moyen Age: "Le Livre des faits d'armes et de chevalerie" de Christine de Pizan*, edited by Dominique Demartini, Claire Le Ninan, and Anne Paupert, 89–102. Paris, 2016.

Cazaux, Loïc. "Réglementation militaire royale et usage de la force dans le royaume de France (XIVe–XVIe siècles)." *Inflexions*, no. 13 (2010): 93–104.

Contamine, Philippe. *Guerre, Etat et société à la fin du Moyen Age: Etudes sur les armées des rois de France, 1337–1494*. Paris, 1972.

Contamine, Philippe. "Les compagnies d'aventure en France pendant la guerre de Cent ans." *Mélanges de l'Ecole française de Rome, Moyen Age, temps modernes* 87 (1975): 365–96.

Cornette, Joël. *Le roi de guerre: Essai sur la souveraineté dans la France du Grand Siècle*. Paris, 1993.

Cosneau, Eugène, ed. *Les grands traités de la guerre de Cent Ans*. Paris, 1889.

Davis, Natalie Zemon. *Fiction in the Archives: Pardon Tales and Their Tellers in Sixteenth-Century France*. Cambridge, 1987.

Deruelle, Benjamin, and Quentin Verreycken. "Père du peuple ou roi de guerre? Arbitraire et arbitrage de la grâce des gens de guerre dans le royaume de France (1460–1559)." In *Arbitraire et arbitrages: Les zones grises du pouvoir (XIIe–XVIIIe siècles)*, edited by Benjamin Deruelle and Michel Hébert. Villeneuve-d'Ascq, forthcoming.

Drewitt-Wex, Thomas. "The English 'Soldier' c. 1400–1461: Perceptions of Professionalism and Criminality." PhD thesis, University of Winchester, 2019.

Duclos, Charles Pinot. *Histoire de Louis XI*. 3 vols. La Haye, 1745.

Fargette, Séverine. "Rumeurs, propagande et opinion publique au temps de la guerre civile (1407–1420)." *Le Moyen Age* 113, no. 2 (2007): 309–34.

Firnhaber-Baker, Justine. *Violence and the State in Languedoc, 1250–1400.* Cambridge, 2014.

Frisch, Andrea. *Forgetting Differences: Tragedy, Historiography, and the French Wars of Religion.* Edinburgh, 2015.

Furon, Christophe. "Gens de guerre en hiver: Le cas des écorcheurs durant l'hiver 1438–1439." *Questes*, no. 34 (2016): 85–118.

Furon, Christophe. "Les derniers feux de l'écorcherie: La Chevauchée de Robert de Flocques et Poton de Xaintrailles (printemps 1445)." *Bulletin du Centre d'études médiévales d'Auxerre* 26, no. 2 (2022). https://doi.org/10.4000/cem.19573.

Furon, Christophe. *Les écorcheurs: Guerre et pillage à la fin du Moyen Age, 1435–1445.* Paris, 2023.

Gauvard, Claude. *Condamner à mort au Moyen Age: Pratiques de la peine capitale en France, XIIIe–XVe siècle.* Paris, 2018.

Gauvard, Claude. *"De grace especial": Crime, Etat et société en France à la fin du Moyen Age.* Paris, 1991.

Gauvard, Claude. "Le roi de France et le gouvernement par la grâce à la fin du Moyen Age: Genèse et développement d'une politique judiciaire." In *Suppliques et requêtes: Le gouvernement par la grâce en Occident (XIIe–XVe siècle)*, edited by Hélène Millet, 371–404. Rome, 2003.

Gauvard, Claude. "Les humanistes français et la justice sous le règne de Charles VI." In *Pratiques de la culture écrite en France au XVe siècle*, edited by Monique Ornato, Nicole Pons, and Gilbert Ouy, 157–77. Louvain-la-Neuve, 1995.

Gauvard, Claude. "Pardonner et oublier après la guerre de Cent Ans: Le rôle des lettres d'abolition de la chancellerie royale française." In *Pardonner et oublier? Les discours sur le passé après l'occupation, la guerre civile et la révolution*, edited by Reiner Marcowitz and Werner Paravicini, 27–55. Munich, 2009.

Gauvard, Claude. "Rumeur et gens de guerre dans le royaume de France au milieu du XVe siècle." *Hypothèses*, no. 1 (2000): 281–92.

Giraudet, Luke. *Public Opinion and Political Contest in Late Medieval Paris: The Parisian Bourgeois and His Community, 1400–1450.* Turnhout, 2023.

Gribit, Nicolas A. *Henry of Lancaster's Expedition to Aquitaine, 1345–1346: Military Service and Professionalism in the Hundred Years' War.* Woodbridge, 2016.

Grummitt, David. "Changing Perceptions of the Soldier in Late Medieval England." In *The Fifteenth Century X: Parliament, Personalities, and Power: Papers Presented to Linda S. Clark*, edited by Hannes Kleineke, 189–202. Woodbridge, 2011.

Guerin, Paul, and Leonce Celier, eds. *Recueil des documents concernant le Poitou contenus dans les registres de la Chancellerie de France.* 14 vols. Poitiers, 1881–1958.

Hamilton, Tom. "Adjudicating the Troubles: Violence, Memory, and Criminal Justice at the End of the Wars of Religion." *French History* 34, no. 4 (2020): 417–34.

Hamilton, Tom. "Un 'cas exécrable' devant le Parlement de Paris à la fin des guerres de Religion (1599–1600)." *Criminocorpus*, January 20, 2023. https://doi.org/10.4000/criminocorpus.12196.

Hardy, Duncan. "The 1444–1445 Expedition of the Dauphin Louis to the Upper Rhine in Geopolitical Perspective." *Journal of Medieval History* 38, no. 3 (2012): 358–87.

Hélary, Xavier. "Effondrement et renaissance (1415–1453)." In *Histoire militaire de la France*, edited by Hervé Drévillon and Olivier Wieviorka, 153–80. Paris, 2018.

Hurnard, Naomi D. *The King's Pardon for Homicide before A.D. 1307.* Oxford, 1969.

Jamieson, Neil. "'Sons of Iniquity': The Problem of Unlawfulness and Criminality amongst Professional Soldiers in the Middle Ages." In *Outlaws in Medieval and Early Modern England: Crime, Government and Society, c. 1066–c. 1600*, edited by John C. Appleby and Paul Dalton, 91–110. New York, 2016.

Kaeuper, Richard W. *Chivalry and Violence in Medieval Europe.* Oxford, 1999.

Kaeuper, Richard W. *War, Justice, and Public Order: England and France in the Later Middle Ages.* Oxford, 1988.

Keen, Maurice H. *The Laws of War in the Late Middle Ages.* Oxford, 1965.

Krynen, Jacques. *L'empire du roi: Idées et croyances politiques en France, XIIIe–XVe siècle.* Paris, 1993.

Lacey, Helen. *The Royal Pardon: Access to Mercy in Fourteenth-Century England.* York, 2009.

La Marche, Olivier de. *Mémoires.* Edited by Henri Beaune and Jean d'Arbaumont. 4 vols. Paris, 1885.

Lassalmonie, Jean-François. *La boîte à l'enchanteur: Politique financière de Louis XI.* Paris, 2013.

Le Barrois d'Orgeval, Gabriel. *La justice militaire sous l'Ancien Régime: Le tribunal de la Connétablie de France, du XIVe siècle à 1790.* Paris, 1918.

Lecuppre-Desjardin, Elodie, and Valérie Toureille. "Servir ou trahir: La réaction des grands féodaux face aux innovations étatiques, au temps de la Praguerie." *Publications du Centre européen d'études bourguignonnes* 60 (2020): 7–14.

Maffi, Davide, ed. *Tra Marte e Astrea: Giustizia e giurisdizione militare nell'Europa della prima età moderna (secc. XVI–XVIII).* Milan, 2012.

Malegam, Jehangir Yezdi. *The Sleep of Behemoth: Disputing Peace and Violence in Medieval Europe, 1000–1200.* Ithaca, NY, 2013.

Mellet, Paul-Alexis, and Jérémie Foa. "Une 'politique de l'oubliance'? Mémoire et oubli pendant les guerres de Religion (1550–1600)." *Astérion*, no. 15 (2016). https://doi.org/10.4000/asterion.2829.

Meumann, Markus. "Civilians, the French Army, and Military Justice during the Reign of Louis XIV." In *Civilians and War in Europe, 1618–1815*, edited by Erica Charters, Eve Rosenhaft, and Hannah Smith, 100–117. Liverpool, 2012.

Musin, Aude, and Michel Nassiet. "Les récits de rémission dans la longue durée: Le cas de l'Anjou du XVe au XVIIIe siècle." *Revue d'histoire moderne et contemporaine* 57, no. 4 (2010): 51–71.

Nassiet, Michel, ed. *Guerre civile et pardon royal en Anjou (1580–1600): Lettres de pardon entérinées par le présidial d'Angers.* Paris, 2013.

Nassiet, Michel. *La violence, une histoire sociale: France, XVIe–XVIIIe siècles.* Seyssel, 2011.

Nassiet, Michel, ed. *Les lettres de pardon du voyage de Charles IX (1565–1566).* Paris, 2010.

Offenstadt, Nicolas. *Faire la paix au Moyen Age: Discours et gestes de paix pendant la guerre de Cent Ans.* Paris, 2007.

Ordonnances de François Ier. 9 vols. Paris, 1932–33.

Ordonnances des roys de France de la troisième race. 22 vols. Paris, 1723–1849.

Otis-Cour, Leah Lydia. "Les limites de la grâce et les exigences de la justice: L'entérinement et le refus d'entériner les lettres de rémission royales d'après les arrêts du Parlement de Toulouse à la fin du Moyen Age." In *Critères du juste et contrôle des juges*, 73–89. Montpellier, 1996.

Paresys, Isabelle. *Aux marges du royaume: Violence, justice et société en Picardie sous François Ier.* Paris, 1998.

Parker, Geoffrey. *The Military Revolution: Military Innovation and the Rise of the West, 1500–1800.* New York, 1988.

Péquignot, Stéphane. "De la France à Barcelone: Une version catalane de 'l'ordonnance perdue' de Charles VII sur les gens d'armes (1445)." *Revue historique*, no. 676 (2015): 793–830.

Potter, David. *Renaissance France at War: Armies, Culture, and Society, c. 1480–1560*. Woodbridge, 2008.

Potter, David. "'Rigueur de Justice': Crime, Murder, and the Law in Picardy, Fifteenth to Sixteenth Century." *French History* 11, no. 3 (1997): 265–309.

Prétou, Pierre. "Abolir l'excès de guerre: Le pardon royal face à la guerre de Guyenne, 1444–1463." In *Justice et guerre de l'antiquité à la Première Guerre mondiale*, edited by Marie Houllemare and Philippe Nivet, 63–72. Amiens, 2011.

Prétou, Pierre. *Crime et justice en Gascogne à la fin du Moyen Age*. Rennes, 2010.

Prétou, Pierre. "Les voisins contre la route: Réactions et imprécations communautaires en Gascogne face aux bandes armées pendant la guerre de Cent Ans." In *Routiers et mercenaires pendant la guerre de Cent Ans: Hommage à Jonathan Sumption*, edited by Guilhem Pépin, Françoise Lainé, and Frédéric Boutoulle, 133–45. Bordeaux, 2016.

Rogers, Clifford J. "By Fire and Sword: Bellum Hostile and 'Civilians' in the Hundred Years' War." In *Civilians in the Path of War*, edited by Mark Grimsley and Clifford J. Rogers, 33–78. Lincoln, NE, 2002.

Rogers, Clifford J., ed. *The Military Revolution Debate: Readings on the Military Transformations of Early Modern Europe*. Boulder, CO, 1995.

Rowe, B. J. H. "Discipline in the Norman Garrisons under Bedford, 1422–1435." *English Historical Review*, no. 182 (1931): 194–208.

Russel, Frederick H. *The Just War in the Middle Ages*. Cambridge, 1975.

Sablon du Corail, Amable. "Naissance d'une frontière? Louis XI et ses gens de guerre durant la guerre pour la succession de Bourgogne (1477–1482)." *Annuaire-Bulletin de la Société de l'histoire de France*, 2016 (2021): 71–95.

Schmit, Elisabeth. *En bon trayn de justice: Les grands jours du Parlement de Paris au lendemain de la guerre de Cent Ans*. Paris, 2022.

Schnerb, Bertrand. "The Jurisdiction of the Constable and Marshals of France in the Later Middle Ages." In *Courts of Chivalry and Admiralty in Late Medieval Europe*, edited by Anthony Musson and Nigel Ramsay, 143–56. Woodbridge, 2018.

Scordia, Lydwine. "Entre guerre traditionnelle et sidération des populations: Théories et pratiques de la guerre sous Louis XI." In *Le feu et la folie: L'irrationnel et la guerre (fin du Moyen Age–1920)*, edited by Laurent Vissière and Marion Trévisi, 81–99. Rennes, 2016.

Skoda, Hannah. *Medieval Violence: Physical Brutality in Northern France, 1270–1330*. Oxford, 2013.

Taylor, Craig. *Chivalry and the Ideals of Knighthood in France during the Hundred Years War*. Cambridge, 2013.

Telliez, Romain. *"Per potentiam officii": Les officiers devant la justice dans le royaume de France au XIVe siècle*. Paris, 2005.

Théry, Julien. "*Atrocitas/enormitas*: Esquisse pour une histoire de la catégorie de 'crime énorme' du Moyen Age à l'époque moderne." *Clio@Thémis: Revue électronique d'histoire du droit*, no. 4 (2011). https://doi.org/10.35562/cliothemis.1400.

Toureille, Valérie. *Robert de Sarrebrück ou l'honneur d'un écorcheur (v. 1400–v. 1462)*. Rennes, 2014.

Toureille, Valérie. *Vol et brigandage au Moyen Age*. Paris, 2006.

Tuetey, Alexandre, ed. *Journal d'un bourgeois de Paris, 1405–1449*. Paris, 1881.

Tuetey, Alexandre. *Les écorcheurs sous Charles VII: Episodes de l'histoire militaire de la France au XVe siècle d'après des documents inédits*. 2 vols. Paris, 1874.

Vaesen, Joseph, and Etienne Charavay, eds. *Lettres de Louis XI, roi de France*. 11 vols. Paris, 1883–1909.

Verreycken, Quentin. *Crimes et gens de guerre au Moyen Age: Angleterre, France et principautés bour-guignonnes au XVe siècle*. Paris, 2023.

Verreycken, Quentin. "Discipliner par la grâce: Les lettres de rémission aux gens de guerre dans l'Etat bourguignon au XVe siècle." *Crime, histoire et sociétés* 22, no. 1 (2018): 5–32.

Verreycken, Quentin. "'En Nous Humblement Requerant': Crime Narrations and Rhetorical Strategies in Late Medieval Pardon Letters." *Open Library of Humanities* 5, no. 1 (2019): 1–31. https://olh.openlibhums.org/article/id/4599/.

Verreycken, Quentin. "La criminalité militaire à la fin de la guerre de Cent Ans: Des violences extrêmes?" In *De la violence à l'extrême: Discours, représentations et pratiques de la violence chez les combattants*, edited by Benjamin Deruelle, Nicolas Handfield, and Philipp Portelance, 213–30. Paris, 2021.

Verreycken, Quentin. *Pour nous servir en l'armée: Le gouvernement et le pardon des gens de guerre sous Charles le Téméraire, duc de Bourgogne (1467–1477)*. Louvain-la-Neuve, 2014.

Verreycken, Quentin. "The Power to Pardon in Late Medieval and Early Modern Europe: New Perspectives in the History of Crime and Criminal Justice." *History Compass* 17, no. 6 (2019). https://doi.org/10.1111/hic3.12575.

Villalon, L. J. Andrew. "'Taking the King's Shilling' to Avoid 'the Wages of Sin': Royal Pardons for Military Malefactors during the Hundred Years War." In *The Hundred Years War (Part III): Further Considerations*, edited by L. J. Andrew Villalon and Donald J. Kagay, 357–435. Leiden, 2013.

Wilson, Peter H. "Warfare in Europe." In *The Cambridge World History of Violence*, edited by Robert Antony, Stuart Carroll, and Caroline Dodds Pennock, 174–93. Cambridge, 2020.

Wright, Nicholas A. *Knights and Peasants: The Hundred Years War in the French Countryside*. Woodbridge, 1998.

Wright, Nicholas A. "The Tree of Battles of Honoré Bouvet and the Laws of War." In *War, Literature, and Politics in the Late Middle Ages*, edited by Christopher Allmand, 12–31. Liverpool, 1976.

The Burning of Bédoin
Crime, Complicity, and Civil War in Revolutionary France

JOSEPH CLARKE

ABSTRACT   On May 28, 1794, a criminal investigation that had begun almost a month before concluded with the execution of sixty-three men and women, the imprisonment of fifteen more, and a few days later the destruction of an entire village. This article examines the burning of Bédoin, the crime that provoked it, and the judicial process that accompanied it, to explore the relationship between criminal cause and punitive effect during the Terror of year II. As a case study in revolutionary justice, this episode appears extreme, but this article argues that it allows us to interrogate the meanings that ordinary revolutionaries attached to terms like *crime* and *complicity* when the survival of the state seemed at stake. In looking beyond the Terror to the controversies that enveloped this village's destruction, this article also examines the aftermath of atrocity to consider how a society comes to terms with crime when both the definition of criminality and the identity of the criminal are in flux.

KEYWORDS   French Revolution, Terror, crime, atrocity, revolutionary justice

It was, according to the *représentant-en-mission* Etienne Maignet, "one of those crimes which calls forth all the vengeance of the laws."[1] Sometime during the night of 12–13 Floréal II (May 1–2, 1794), Bédoin's tree of liberty was uprooted and the copies of the Convention's decrees posted outside its *maison commune* torn down and "trampled in the mire."[2] In many respects, this was an unremarkable affair. Since its first appearance in 1790, the tree of liberty had become a ubiquitous emblem of revolutionary change. By 1794 Henri Grégoire estimated that sixty thousand had already been planted, and citizens discontented with the new regime frequently took an axe or a spade, possibly a little unsteadily after an evening in an auberge, to a beribboned sapling in the dead of

---

1. Paris, Archives Nationales (hereafter AN), AF/II/145, Maignet, *Au nom du peuple français . . . le 14 et 15 floréal*. From March 1793 the Convention delegated *représentants* like Maignet to oversee governance and repress revolt in the provinces. Armed with sweeping powers, they exercised significant autonomy in deciding the Terror's direction in areas under their authority. Biard, *Missionnaires de la République*.

2. AN, D/§1/29, Maignet to the Committee of Public Safety, 14 Floréal II (May 3, 1794).

French Historical Studies • Vol. 47, No. 2 (May 2024) • DOI 10.1215/00161071-11025055
Copyright 2024 by Society for French Historical Studies

night.[3] Just four kilometers from Bédoin, Crillon's liberty tree had suffered the same fate that March and, beyond the Vaucluse, inquiries into similar offenses were launched throughout France that spring, although they rarely resulted in convictions.[4] Evidence concerning these invariably nocturnal attacks was always elusive and, as Robert Allen has shown, revolutionary juries generally proved reluctant to convict in cases of this kind.[5] Indeed, even with a full confession, securing a conviction on a charge like this was not certain. Hauled before Paris's fearsome Revolutionary Tribunal in June 1794, twenty-two-year-old Antoine Dupris admitted taking his saber to a liberty tree, but he was still acquitted when he insisted that he loved the republic and had acted without malice.[6]

Bédoin's tree of liberty was different, however. While the tree was quickly found—tellingly, it had been dumped in the "pigs' meadow" outside the village—the culprit or culprits were not.[7] Yet, once word of this outrage reached Maignet, he set in motion a sequence of events that brought the full weight of the republic's political, judicial, and military authorities crashing down on Bédoin's two thousand inhabitants.[8] On May 28, when the criminal tribunal Maignet had dispatched from Avignon to investigate this offense concluded its deliberations, sixty-three villagers were executed, ten more outlawed, and another fifteen incarcerated, all in the space of a single afternoon. The executions done, the remaining residents were given twenty-four hours to evacuate their homes before, on Maignet's orders, the village was burned to the ground by the 250 soldiers who had invested it three weeks before.[9]

Something like this sketch may be familiar from various histories of the French Revolution. Rarely warranting more than a few sentences' summary, the burning of Bédoin has been enlisted by generations of historians to illustrate a range of perspectives on the revolutionary Terror. Some, like Donald Greer, have explained—or perhaps explained away—Bédoin's destruction by reference to a counterrevolutionary record supposedly stretching back years; others, like Peter McPhee and D. M. G. Sutherland, have cited it to illustrate the swingeing powers

3. Grégoire, *Essai historique et patriotique*, 23. On the tree of liberty, see Corvol, "Transformation of a Political Symbol"; and Pacini, "La Tigre Monarchique [et] l'Arbre de la République."

4. For Crillon, see Avignon, Archives Départementales de Vaucluse (hereafter ADV), 7L51, Procès-verbal de la commission Lego, 20 Floréal II. That same month two other *représentants*, Pierre Monestier and Nicolas Maure, launched inquiries into similar offenses in the Lot-et-Garonne and Seine-et-Marne, respectively. Aulard, *Recueil des actes du Comité de salut public* (hereafter CSP), 13:37–38, 726.

5. Allen, *Les tribunaux criminels*, 71, 206. See also Berger, *La justice pénale*, 73–77.

6. Wallon, *Histoire du tribunal révolutionnaire*, 4:294–95.

7. ADV, 7 L 51, Interrogation of Michel Rousseau, 6 Prairial II.

8. Bédoin's population stood at 2,026 in 1793. Avignon, Bibliothèque Municipale (hereafter BMA), MS 4204, fol. 1, District de Carpentras, "Tableau des communes, état de la population, dénombrement."

9. *Jugement rendu par le Tribunal révolutionnaire du département de Vaucluse.*

some *représentants* deployed in the departments under their jurisdiction.[10] By contrast, more recent scholarship, particularly that which Jeremy Popkin has provocatively described as the "Don't Say Terror school" of revolutionary historiography, has largely ignored Bédoin along with the wider repression Maignet orchestrated in the Vaucluse—an odd omission given the terrible death toll this department experienced in the summer of 1794.[11] For historians with a more local focus, by contrast, this episode has generally been viewed in terms of the precocious violence that engulfed Avignon and the Comtat Venaissin from 1790 on.[12] If the Midi was "the unquiet land of the Revolution," the former papal enclaves that fused to form the department of the Vaucluse represent some of its most turbulent terrain.[13] Site of the decade's first civil war, fought between pro-French forces and papal loyalists in 1790, and of its earliest prison massacre, the massacre de la Glacière in October 1791, the region had earned a reputation for violent extremes that persisted through the Federalist revolt of 1793, Maignet's mission the following year, and a vicious White Terror through the rest of the 1790s.[14] From its incorporation into France on, the specter of civil war loomed large in this divided *département*—the prospect of a second Vendée preoccupied Maignet from the moment his mission began there—and the violence visited on Bédoin is generally read in relation to these fractious local circumstances.[15]

That context constitutes an essential backdrop to the burning of Bédoin, but this article's approach to the archive these events generated is different. Rather than read these records as being so rooted in the politics of this very particular place as to appear atypical or even aberrant, my aim is instead to investigate what happened here as an example of what Edoardo Grendi described as the "exceptionally normal," an apparent anomaly that transcends its immediate context to reveal a range of wider attitudes and assumptions.[16] In this sense, the

10. See, e.g., Greer, *Incidence of the Terror*, 58; Martin, *Nouvelle histoire*, 437; Sutherland, *French Revolution and Empire*, 221; and McPhee, *Liberty or Death*, 261.

11. Popkin, review, 2. Despite overseeing a terror that in the space of just six weeks produced the eighth-highest number of executions in any department, Maignet seldom features in recent work on the Terror. When he is not mistaken for a mere "Jacobin in Valence" or relegated to a note as an aberration, his record in the Vaucluse rarely receives more than passing mention in this scholarship. For the execution rate in the Vaucluse, see Greer, *Incidence of the Terror*, 147. For some very summary references to Maignet, see Linton, *Choosing Terror*, 234; Jourdan, *La Révolution française*, 282; and Biard and Linton, *Terreur*, 285n18.

12. Le Gallo, "L'affaire de Bédoin"; Vaillandet, "L'affaire de Bédoin"; Moulinas, *Histoire de la Révolution d'Avignon*, 317–19; Lapied, *Le Comtat et la Révolution française*, 170–82.

13. Lucas, "Problem of the Midi," 2.

14. Lapied, "La crise fédéraliste dans le 'ci-devant' Comtat." On the White Terror, see Clay, "Vengeance, Justice, and the Reactions"; Vaillandet, "Après le 9 thermidor"; and Brown, *Ending the French Revolution*.

15. Maignet made this comparison repeatedly in his correspondence from the Vaucluse. See, e.g., AN, D/§1/29, Maignet to the Committee of Public Safety, 14 and 18 Floréal II (May 3 and 7, 1794).

16. Grendi, "Micro-analisi e storia sociale," 512.

burning of Bédoin, to borrow from another of the founding fathers of microhistory, Carlo Ginzburg, presents "small but significant clues" that reveal how ordinary revolutionaries understood criminality in a time of civil war.[17] More particularly, it suggests how they deployed one of the new regime's chief innovations in law, the offense of *lèse-nation*, to deal with those they deemed enemies of the people. This new criminal category had emerged early in the Revolution, and as Charles Walton and Jean-Christophe Gaven have shown, its conceptualization of crimes against the state owed much to earlier royal jurisprudence, but in defining certain kinds of speech and symbolic action as capital crimes, it became central to the republic's repressive arsenal.[18] Maignet viewed that liberty tree's uprooting in precisely these terms and wrote that it warranted spectacular punishment.[19] That instinctive identification is suggestive. When seen in this light, Bédoin's fate appears less a product of a polarized local politics and more a reflection of the preoccupations that defined the administration of justice in a time of civil war and state terror.

The burning of Bédoin is, in this sense, more emblematic than exceptional. This is not simply because there were precedents for everything that happened here in 1793–94. Maignet was not, for example, the only *représentant* to see to it that heads rolled because a tree of liberty was felled. His colleague André Dumont boasted of executions for the same offense in Beauvais that February, and the fact that Bédoin was renamed (twice) as a mark of its infamy is hardly unique.[20] Lyon, Toulon, Bordeaux, and Marseille had all endured that ignominy the year before. This was not even the first time the republic had resolved to wipe an entire community off the face of the earth. That Rubicon had already been crossed, albeit less comprehensively, when the National Convention decreed the destruction of Lyon on October 12, 1793.[21] Rather, the difference between what happened in Bédoin and these other examples is chiefly a question of scale. It reflects the fact that for an entire month the individuals and institutions that embodied law and order in year II could focus their investigative—and punitive—attentions on one village with the thoroughness that the authorities might aspire to but never achieved in cities or large towns. In a village this size revolutionary justice could proceed with few of the procedural checks or practical constraints that curtailed its application, even if only in part, in regular law courts or larger

17. Ginzburg, "Morelli, Freud, and Sherlock Holmes," 28.
18. Walton, *Policing Public Opinion*, 97–136; Gaven, *Le crime de lèse-nation*.
19. Clermont-Ferrand, Bibliothèque du Patrimoine, MS 360, fol. 131, Maignet to Lego, agent national of the district of Carpentras, 14 Floréal II (May 3, 1794).
20. Mavidal et al., *Archives parlementaires de la Révolution française* (hereafter *AP*), 86:9. Initially renamed "Bédoin the infamous," it became "Bédoin the annihilated" after its destruction. *Courrier d'Avignon*, 14 Prairial II (June 2, 1794), 156.
21. Herriot, *Lyon n'est plus*, 3:26.

urban centers. In this sense, the events that unfolded here exemplify revolutionary justice at its most intimate and invasive. Isolated it might be, but this village at the foot of Mont Ventoux allows us to look beyond Paris, its Revolutionary Tribunal, and the letter of the law, the perspectives that frame most studies of revolutionary justice, to interrogate the meaning of terms like *crime* and *complicity* when ordinary *révolutionnaires* were called on to put them to the test.[22]

If this case offers insights into the workings of justice in the new regime, its aftermath is just as revealing. After the Terror, Bédoin's destruction briefly became a cause célèbre, and that notoriety was international. Reports of the village engulfed by the republic's "avenging flames" were published throughout Europe, and the story lost nothing in the telling as it crisscrossed the continent.[23] In December 1794, for example, the *Annali di Roma* estimated the death toll there at a vastly inflated "twelve thousand," while William Cobbett's bestseller *The Bloody Buoy* included it among "the black list of enormities" the republic had committed.[24] Like an eighteenth-century Oradour-sur-Glane, Bédoin became an international byword for "the most horrible outrages against humanity," but the odium that enveloped its destruction was above all domestic.[25] As Republican politics pivoted after Thermidor II, the burning of Bédoin, rather than the act of vandalism that had provoked it, came to be seen as the real crime, and this poses the wider problem of how a society can come to terms with crime when both the definition of criminality and the identity of the criminal are in flux. From the autumn of 1794 on, demands that Maignet be held to account for "the terror he inspired"—and it would be "a difficult account," Louis-François Lefébure insisted—were regularly heard.[26] However, those calls were never acted on, and Maignet escaped any reckoning for his actions in the Vaucluse. On the contrary, he ended his days forty years later a respected, even revered, elder in his hometown in the Auvergne, where his popularity with the clergy of Restoration Ambert stands as a curious coda to the career of such a keen dechristianizer.[27]

22. For this predominantly Parisian perspective, see Boulant, *Le Tribunal révolutionnaire*; Eude, "La loi du 22 prairial"; Godfrey, *Revolutionary Justice*; Gueniffey, *La politique de la Terreur*; and Simonin, "Les acquittés de la Grande Terreur."

23. *Times*, June 3, 1794, 3. See also *Gazzetta universale* (Florence), Jan. 27, 1795, 58–59; *Walker's Hibernian Magazine* (Dublin), Jan. 1796, 57–63; *Ny Minverva* (Copenhagen), Apr. 1795, 124; and *Beiträge zur Geschichte der Französischen Revolution* (Leipzig, 1795), 3:152.

24. *Annali di Roma*, Dec. 1794, 228–29; Cobbett, *Bloody Buoy*, 21–22.

25. *Edinburgh Magazine*, Jan. 1796, 53–55. On Oradour-sur-Glane, see Farmer, *Martyred Village*.

26. A music master, botanist, and member of the Paris Commune in 1789, Lefébure returned to the Vaucluse in June 1793 as a *commissaire du pouvoir exécutif* charged with promoting agriculture and industry in the Midi. Denounced as a moderate in March 1794, he was arrested on Maignet's orders and, after three months in prison in Avignon, was transferred to Paris, where "the events of 9 thermidor saved me." Lefébure, *Justice contre Maignet*, 3, 8, 9.

27. In 1821 fifty-four local clerics signed a petition expressing "the esteem, confidence and public affection" Maignet inspired in Ambert. AN, F7/6714, "Certificat concernant M. Maignet," May 12, 1821.

Maignet's ability to ride out the storm after the Terror was far from unique. However, his example also complicates a recent theme in revolutionary historiography. Drawing an analogy with the waves of regime change that swept over Eastern Europe, Central and South America and postapartheid South Africa in the 1990s, historians have written of the period after Robespierre's fall as a time when something like "transitional justice" emerged in response to state terror. For Howard G. Brown, for example, the Thermidorians were "pioneers in the practices of transitional justice," while Corinne Gomez–Le Chevanton, Ronen Steinberg, and Loris Chavanette have analyzed the show trials that sent some former terrorists—Jean-Baptiste Carrier, Joseph Le Bon, and Antoine Fouquier-Tinville—to the guillotine in year III from a similar perspective.[28] This scholarship has unquestionably added to our understanding of France's reckoning with the Terror. However, part of its attraction undoubtedly lies in transitional justice's sheer elasticity as an idea, alongside, of course, its contemporary currency. As both concept and practice, transitional justice defies ready definition. Depending on the context, its priorities may be retributive or restorative or revolve around rehabilitation or remembrance, and elements of each of these themes surface in the account that follows.[29] Yet analyzing the 1790s in light of practices that evolved two centuries later inevitably involves some element of elision, particularly when the focus tends to fall on the handful of terrorists who did face justice in year III rather than the many more who did not. Indeed, there is a certain irony in the fact that the sixteen contributors to the most recent scholarly collection on transitional justice in year III outnumber the *conventionnels* who were convicted of capital crimes connected to the Terror.[30] If, as Ruti G. Teitel suggests of transitional justice's evolution since the mid-twentieth century, the judicial precedent set at Nuremberg has proved paradigmatic and, for better or worse, "punishment dominates our understanding of transitional justice," then its absence—the impunity men like Maignet ultimately enjoyed—is equally significant.[31] It obliges us to look beyond those rare instances when the republic did exact retribution for the wrongs of year II and consider what, to borrow

28. Brown, "Robespierre's Tail," 534; Gomez–Le Chevanton, "Juger Carrier"; Gomez–Le Chevanton, "Le procès Carrier"; Steinberg, "Terror on Trial"; Chavanette, "Le procès de Fouquier-Tinville." More generally, see the 2021 special issue of *Histoire de la justice* on transitional justice in the year III: Leuwers, Martin, and Salas, "Juger la 'terreur.'"
29. For a review of these practices across the former Soviet bloc after 1989, see Borneman, *Settling Accounts*.
30. Leuwers, Martin, and Salas, "Juger la 'terreur.'" Following the first executions of Robespierre and his allies on 10 Thermidor II, just five more deputies were executed for crimes connected to the Terror during the Convention's lifetime. Another five (the Montagnard "martyrs" of Prairial III) committed suicide on being sentenced to death on June 17, 1795.
31. Teitel, *Transitional Justice*, 27.

from Arthur Conan Doyle, "the dog that didn't bark" reveals about the nature of crime and the prospect of punishment in a republic at war with itself.

"This Abominable Crime"

Revolutionary justice, as Sutherland aptly remarks, "was not normal justice."[32] Its remit was political rather than judicial, the offenses it adjudicated were ideological rather than criminal in any conventional sense, and its object was to extirpate counterrevolution, however loosely defined that might be. Its institutions and procedures were framed accordingly. The men who manned revolutionary tribunals in year II were appointees rather than elected, as in the new regime's regular courts, and they were recruited on the strength of their political credentials rather than any legal experience. Their work also proceeded rapidly. Republicans' exasperation with the "eternal procedures" that delayed punishment of the guilty had whittled away the rights of the accused throughout 1793 in the belief that revolutionary justice, if it was to be effective, had to be seen to be swift, spectacular, and unsparing.[33] For one *conventionnel*, the former lawyer Claude Javogues, twenty-four hours seemed like a reasonable interlude between a suspect's indictment and execution, and while this kind of efficiency was not always possible, it was still something to aspire to.[34]

Etienne Maignet would hardly have disagreed. Another lawyer and a contributor to his home town's *cahier de doléances* in 1789, he rose to prominence in local politics in the Puy-de-Dôme before being elected to the Legislative Assembly in 1791 and the National Convention a year later.[35] There, he established a modest reputation as a conscientious member of the Comité des Secours Publics, but it was the time he spent away from Paris, as one of the Convention's proconsuls in the provinces, the *représentants-en-mission*, that ultimately defined his career. An industrious administrator—he later claimed to have drawn up over two thousand letters and as many decrees during his eight-month mission in the Midi—and a zealous dechristianizer, his initiatives on mission ranged from ambitious social engineering projects to promoting stodgily political plays for the edification of the masses.[36] However, the places his missions took him

32. Sutherland, *Murder in Aubagne*, 173.

33. Robespierre, "Pour la cloture des débats du Tribunal révolutionnaire," 160. On this acceleration of the legal process, see Godfrey, *Revolutionary Justice*; and Wallon, *Histoire du tribunal révolutionnaire*.

34. Lucas, *Structure of the Terror*, 245.

35. "Cahier des doléances de l'Assemblée générale du Tiers état de la ville d'Ambert," in Mège, *Les cahiers des paroisses*, 358–86. On Maignet, see Bourdin, "Maignet, Etienne Christophe"; and Guilhamou and Lapied, "La mission Maignet."

36. Maignet, *Compte rendu*, 4; Maignet, *Arrêté du représentant du peuple*. For the range of his activities, see BMA, 4º3862, "Recueil des arrêtés du représentant du peuple Maignet, envoyé dans le département des Bouches-du-Rhône, commencé le vingt un pluviôse an 2me de la République française, et fini le 29

to—Lyon in the autumn of 1793 and the Midi from January to August 1794—inevitably meant that the relationship between revolutionary justice and repression was never far from Maignet's mind. In October 1793 he had been instrumental, along with his fellow Auvergnat Georges Couthon, in establishing an extraordinary tribunal to prosecute Lyon's federalists. However, its lackluster performance, along with the deputies' failure to proceed with the demolitions decreed on October 12, led to their recall amid recriminations concerning the "execrable ci-devant Auvergnats'" lack of revolutionary rigor.[37] It is difficult to know whether this recall transformed Maignet's thinking—he was clearly shaken by criticism of his record in Lyon—or whether his ideas about repression simply evolved that winter.[38] But one thing seems clear: by the time his mission began in the Midi in January 1794, the reformer who had railed against ancien régime justice's unseemly "haste in sending men to their deaths" in 1789 was no more.[39]

If terror was, as Robespierre maintained that February, "nothing other than swift, severe and inflexible justice," Maignet's mission in the Bouches-du-Rhône and the Vaucluse reflected, and even anticipated, that agenda unswervingly.[40] Though conciliatory in some respects, Maignet was emphatic that revolutionary justice had to be remorseless and his *Instruction . . . on revolutionary government* of January 8 set the practicalities of this out from the start of his mission. Insisting that "death must always be the order of the day" for anyone plotting against the *patrie*, the *Instruction* was a call to judicial arms to deal with the "treason" and "civil war" of the previous summer. Given "the state of war in which we found ourselves," Maignet argued, the leisurely pace and legal niceties of the conventional courtroom could only "compromise public liberty," so in place of cumbersome procedures and querulous attorneys, "speed" and "severity" should be the judges' watchwords, "half-measures" and "false clemency" their foe.[41] A barrage of edicts amplified this advice that spring as powers of search and arrest were extended, public speech curtailed, and a tribunal installed to judge "révolutionnairement," that is, "without a jury or any recourse to an appeal."[42] Dismissing talk of an amnesty as a crime in itself, he launched a

thermidor même année [1794]"; and AN, AF/II/91, Missions des représentants du peuple: dossier 31, Maignet, Bouches-du-Rhône and the Vaucluse.

37. *CSP*, 8:121. For Javogues's jaundiced view of "the infamous Couthon and the scoundrel Maignet," see *CSP*, 10:697.

38. Months later Maignet was still busy refuting "calumnies" concerning his time in Lyon, and anxiety to prove his mettle to the Committee of Public Safety may have contributed to the hard line he adopted in the Midi. AN, D/§1/29, Maignet to the Committee of Public Safety, 28 Pluviôse II (Feb. 16, 1794).

39. "Cahier des doléances de l'Assemblée générale," 373.

40. Robespierre, "Rapport sur les principes de morale politique," 357.

41. Maignet, *Instruction du représentant du peuple français*, 3, 9.

42. Maignet, *Instruction du représentant du peuple français*, 3; Maignet, *Proclamation du représentant du peuple* (16 Ventôse II), 3. For the other measures, on 22 Pluviôse, 29 Ventôse, 5 and 23 Ventôse II, respectively, see BMA, 4⁰3862, Maignet, "Recueil des arrêtés du représentant du peuple Maignet."

"general purge" in Marseille and by February 25 was writing to Paris of "at least fifty" executions a day there, while "every night a neighborhood is purged; five hundred people have already been arrested."[43]

Having set revolutionary justice to rights in Marseille, Maignet did much the same in Avignon in April. His *Instruction* was reissued; proclamations defining the Revolution, in avowedly *robespierriste* terms, as a "war between crime and virtue, courage and cowardice" were published, and strict Republican morality was reasserted.[44] The latter seemed the most urgent task because, as Maignet repeatedly complained, the Vaucluse seemed both rotten to the core and on the brink of becoming another Vendée. In an implicit attack on his predecessor as *représentant-en-mission* there, the *roué*-turned-radical Joseph Rovère, Maignet's reports to Paris described a department where public opinion was thoroughly "perverted," the law either unknown or ignored, and royalist sympathies openly flaunted.[45] Worse still—and this was a frontal assault on Rovère and the patronage he had exercised in Avignon—public office appeared a haven for the corrupt and the counterrevolutionary, and only drastic measures, Maignet concluded, could deal with the crippling "moderatism that infects everything."[46] None of this would have been news in Paris. Local radicals had been bombarding the capital with identical complaints for months, and the Committee of Public Safety was already convinced the situation there was "extremely disquieting."[47] Yet Maignet's diagnosis of this department's "gangrenous" condition was different: it carried the imprimatur of his office and, more important, came with the authority to impose the "great remedies" this malaise required: a round of executions, "repeated every day for some time."[48]

From his arrival in Avignon, Maignet was convinced that the Vaucluse was both irredeemably corrupt and on the cusp of counterrevolution, and news of the attack on Bédoin's liberty tree on May 1–2 only confirmed those suspicions. However, if word of this outrage crystallized Maignet's already entrenched opinion of this "deplorable" department, it also catalyzed his sense that revolutionary justice should be both spectacular and unsparing.[49] As he wrote to the *agent-national* at Carpentras, Lego, on May 3, "One cannot give too much publicity to the prosecution of these crimes of lèse-nation," and this willingness to interpret

43. BMA, 4°3862, Maignet, *Proclamation du représentant du peuple* (19 Pluviôse II), 4; AN, D/§1/29, Maignet to the Committee of Public Safety, 7 Ventôse II (Feb. 25, 1794).

44. AN, AF/II/145, Maignet, *Proclamation du représentant du peuple* (21 Germinal II).

45. AN, D/§1/29, Maignet to the Committee of Public Safety, 26 Germinal and 3 Floréal II (Apr. 15 and 22, 1794).

46. AN, D/§1/29, Maignet to the Committee of Public Safety, 26 Germinal and 3 Floréal II (Apr. 15 and 22, 1794).

47. Committee of Public Safety to Robespierre le jeune, 20 Germinal II (Apr. 9, 1794), in *CSP*, 12:487.

48. AN, D/§1/29, Maignet to the Committee of Public Safety, 3 Floréal II (Apr. 22, 1794).

49. AN, D/§1/29, Maignet to the Committee of Public Safety, 26 Germinal II (Apr. 15, 1794).

an isolated act of vandalism as a crime against the state, along with the insistence that an example had to be made of it, set the tone for everything that happened that May.[50] This is not to suggest that the village's destruction was determined from the start. However, within twenty-four hours of that tree's uprooting, Maignet had dispatched the departmental *tribunal criminel* to investigate this "liberticide conspiracy" in situ, and ordered Lego, along with 250 soldiers from the ultraradical fourth battalion of the Ardèche, to Bédoin to enforce his instructions.[51] The population was to be disarmed, the local authorities detained as "presumed accomplices in this crime," and an investigation launched. Three days later, once he had decided that the villagers' "obstinacy" in refusing to name those responsible for "this abominable crime" was evidence of collective complicity, Maignet concluded that this was "enemy country which fire and the sword must destroy."[52] On May 6, four days before the *tribunal criminel* even arrived in Bédoin, the decree was issued to burn the village to the ground. Less a criminal process than a show of force to subdue a suspect department, the performative purpose of this entire *affaire* was writ large in the twelve thousand copies of these decrees printed and posted across the Vaucluse, all at the Bédoinais' expense.

Maignet took all these decisions without ever leaving Avignon—he never once set foot in Bédoin—but this is how terror tended to work in 1794. It was applied at one remove or, as Richard Cobb put it, by means of "an almost limitless laying on of hands," a process that delegated authority from the Convention to deputies on mission like Maignet and, beneath them, to militants they deemed up to the mark.[53] Ideally, those militants were outsiders: men like Lego, a Parisian notary who had taken up office in Carpentras in 1792, or Louis-Gabriel Suchet, the Lyonnais silk merchant's son who commanded the ardéchois soldiers sent to root the counterrevolution out of Bédoin.[54] Already battle hardened at the siege of Toulon, these troops seemed, some survivors later recalled, like foreign occupiers, but if outsiders were at the heart of what unfolded in Bédoin, there was a homegrown dimension to this terror too.[55] Proven local radicals like the public prosecutor from Carpentras, François Barjavel, brought an element of insider knowledge (and animus) to proceedings once investigations

50. Clermont-Ferrand, Bibliothèque du Patrimoine, MS 360, fol. 131, Maignet to Lego, agent national of the district of Carpentras, 14 Floréal II (May 3, 1794).

51. The troops were accompanied by a dozen gendarmes. Clermont-Ferrand, Bibliothèque du Patrimoine, MS 360, fol. 131, Maignet to Lego; and Maignet, *Au nom du peuple français . . . le 14 et 15 floréal*. On the Fourth Battalion of the Ardèche, see Vaschalde, *Les volontaires de l'Ardèche*.

52. BMA, MS 4203, fol. 80, Lego to Maignet, 17 Floréal II (May 6, 1794); Maignet, *Au nom du peuple français . . . 17 floréal II*.

53. Cobb, *Police and the People*, 188.

54. ADV, 7L 51, Procès-verbal de la commission Lego.

55. One petition compared the soldiers' behavior to that of "the ferocious Austrians and the vile English." *Ancien Moniteur* (hereafter *AM*), 17 Frimaire III (Dec. 7, 1794), 674.

began.[56] However, whether local or not, the men who invested Bédoin in the middle of the night on May 4–5 were endowed with all of the authority of the republic, and their arrival, as Lego gleefully informed Maignet, left "terror etched on every face."[57]

From this point on, Bédoin was effectively under martial law. Placed under curfew and cut off from the outside world—its perimeters were patrolled by Suchet's men—this was now a place where every seventh person was suddenly an outsider—a soldier, official, or magistrate—newly arrived, armed to the teeth, and empowered to arrest suspects, conduct searches, and undertake interrogations.[58] When Lego's initial demand that the villagers identify those responsible for the crime of May 1–2 yielded no results, the roundup began. The councillors, clergy, and *ci-devant* nobles that Maignet had marked out for special attention were the first to be detained, but the arrests continued long after that. By mid-May 113 villagers were already in custody, each of them piled, for want of a proper prison, into the former parish church, although the "dangerous, mephitic" conditions that developed there soon led to the opening of another makeshift jail. In the meantime, the municipality's papers were pored over, the registers of the surveillance committee and popular society scrutinized, and private houses ransacked, not simply to identify whose "sacrilegious hands" had uprooted the liberty tree but to obtain evidence of the wider counterrevolutionary conspiracy this outrage appeared to indicate.

As the investigation's remit expanded, so did its reach. By mid-May suspects were being shipped in from Avignon to face questioning just as property seized from detainees started moving in the opposite direction in anticipation of the village's destruction. Finding enough wagons to shift the 485 quintals of food, wine, fodder, and fuel that Lego seized on behalf of the republic proved a particular chore, although this was probably the least of his worries.[59] Daily reports had to be sent to Maignet, and his authorization was sought for every initiative, although this line of communication was never just one-way. Lego and Suchet were the men on the ground, and their damning verdicts on "this cursed country" helped intensify the repressive impulse: Lego even grumbled that the village's destruction "seemed too soft . . . given the enormity of the crime."[60]

56. Barjavel, *Mémoire justificatif.* The "six firm patriots" Lego imported from Carpentras to (briefly) replace Bédoin's municipality also fit this bill. BMA, MS 4203, fol. 80, Lego to Maignet, 19 Floréal II (May 8, 1794).

57. BMA, MS 4203, fol. 80, Lego to Maignet, 17 Floréal II (May 6, 1794).

58. This paragraph summarizes details drawn from ADV, 7L 51, Procès-verbal de la commission Lego.

59. BMA, MS 4203, fols. 82 and 88, Lego to Maignet, 24 Floréal and 9 Prairial II (May 13 and 28, 1794).

60. BMA, MS 4203, fols. 80 and 81, Lego to Maignet, 17 Floréal II (May 6, 1794) and 22 Floréal II (May 11, 1794).

However, if Lego had to account to Maignet for all his actions, Maignet was in turn answerable to Paris, and unlike some radical *représentants*, he rarely acted without informing the Committee of Public Safety first. As his mission to Lyon had already demonstrated, it was easy to fall foul of the committee, so he took care to ensure that it was aware of, and approved, all his plans here.[61] It was a kind of insurance policy, a hedge against being hauled over the coals for showing too much, or too little, enterprise, and this caution is part of the reason that Suchet's men had to wait to set fire to Bédoin. The decision "to make even the name of Bédoin disappear" was Maignet's idea, but it was encouraged from below and authorized from above.[62] Terror was, in every sense, a collaborative enterprise.

Maignet's anxiety to secure Paris's support for his plans partly explains why almost a month elapsed between the decree of May 6 and the first fires being lit on June 3. However, there are two other reasons why executing this exemplary punishment took longer than expected, and paradoxically, perhaps, both concern questions of procedural propriety. By the time the departmental tribunal arrived in Bédoin on May 10, its task had expanded exponentially, but its jurisdiction had also become much more problematic. Shortly before the justices reached Bédoin, the law of 19 Floréal conferred a monopoly in all cases of counterrevolution on the Revolutionary Tribunal and suppressed all special tribunals in the provinces.[63] It was part of the Convention's steady centralization of political prosecutions in the capital, a process that climaxed a month later with the law of 22 Prairial, but its implications for the judges' authority were immense. Having been sent to investigate a specific offense, they now found their remit had expanded to encompass a conspiracy supposedly involving over a hundred suspects, precisely the kind of case that should be tried in Paris rather than a provincial court. In the absence of any explicit authorization to pursue their inquiries, the judges' confidence in their jurisdiction evaporated the moment this legislation became known, and those doubts persisted, stalling any verdict until Maignet passed on confirmation from the capital that "the obstacles that momentarily hampered your progress are lifted" on May 23.[64]

61. For this regular back-and-forth between Maignet and the committee, see AN, D/§1/29, "Mission du citoyen Maignet . . . correspondence du représentant du 27 pluviôse an II au 2 fructidor." All *représentants* were required by the law of 14 Frimaire II to report to the Committee of Public Safety every *décade*, but not all deputies were as punctilious as Maignet in fulfilling this requirement.

62. AN, D/§1/29, Maignet to the Committee of Public Safety, 18 Floréal II (May 7, 1794).

63. *AM*, 20 Floréal II (May 9, 1794), 419. Derogations were possible but could be made only by the Committee of Public Safety.

64. The issue arose on May 16, when Lego expressed concern that the decree of 19 Floréal would "hinder the operations of the court and prevent it from avenging the outrage done to liberty," and was resolved only by Maignet's letter of May 23. BMA, MS 4203, fol. 83, Lego to Maignet, 27 Floréal II, and Maignet to the Tribunal, 4 Prairial II, in Fouque, *Mémoire justificatif*, 9.

Once that assurance was received, the tribunal swung into action. There was no trial to speak of in Bédoin, and certainly nothing comparable to the often-unpredictable courtroom spectacle the Revolutionary Tribunal presented. There were no defense attorneys present and no opportunity for the accused to dominate the courtroom as Georges Danton had in Paris that April; there was no jury to persuade in any case. On the contrary, the whole affair was conducted in camera, so when the end came on May 28 it was simply a matter of pronouncing a verdict reached after two weeks spent interrogating witnesses in private. That verdict was, in fact, the only public part of this entire process. With the whole village summoned to the market square (and surrounded by Suchet's men), the tribunal's president, Joseph Fouque, pronounced its findings at 2:00 p.m.[65] Fifty-two detainees were acquitted and released, albeit on punitive conditions—their innocence was evidently qualified—and fifteen custodial sentences were passed.[66] In verdicts entirely unrelated to the liberty tree's uprooting, a cobbler, Jacques Clop, got six years in irons for selling his wares at inflated prices, and François Constant received a year in jail for appearing in public without a tricolor cockade, while thirteen "suspects," mainly women, were sentenced to indefinite detention.[67] Having fled before the tribunal arrived, ten more locals were outlawed, effectively a death sentence as outlaws faced immediate execution under the terms of the *hors-la-loi* decree of March 19, 1793. Fouque's final verdict was, however, the most sweeping. A fortnight before the law of 22 Prairial prescribed a mandatory death sentence for all "enemies of the people," sixty-three "enemies of the Revolution" were convicted on a composite, catchall charge of having "attacked the liberty of the French people; encouraged the restoration of royalty in France; sought to pervert public opinion and hinder the progress of revolutionary government; [and] participated in federalist movements intended to overthrow the Republic by undermining its unity," and sentenced to death.[68] The executions began immediately. Thirty-five of those sentences were carried out on the guillotine that had been set up where the liberty tree had stood. Most likely to speed matters up, the remaining twenty-eight were shot on the spot by Suchet's soldiers, "in the presence of the people and before the Supreme Being," as the tribunal's secretary, Ducros, solemnly put it.[69]

65. Ducros, *Tableau de la situation politique*, 7.
66. Ducros, *Tableau de la situation politique*, 26.
67. *Jugement rendu par le Tribunal révolutionnaire du département de Vaucluse*, 24–26.
68. *Jugement rendu par le Tribunal révolutionnaire du département de Vaucluse*, 20.
69. Ducros, *Tableau de la situation politique*, 7; Suchet, *Patrie, égalité, liberté*, 5. The tribunal's verdict made no distinction between forms of execution, so it seems likely that these shootings were merely an attempt to expedite the executions, much as firing squads had been enlisted by the civil authorities when the guillotine proved too slow in Nantes, Toulon, and Lyon the previous winter.

This was state terror on a spectacular scale: the realization of a repressive vision that Maignet had set out in a letter to Couthon the month before: "We must terrify, and the blow is truly terrifying only when it is delivered before the eyes of those who have lived among the guilty."[70] In one afternoon those sixty-three executions more than doubled the number of death sentences the tribunal had passed in the seven months since its creation, and a few days later Maignet installed a *commission populaire* at Orange to dispense the same style of Republican justice throughout the Vaucluse. It sent another 332 people to the guillotine in just six weeks, although this fell far short of the "nine or ten thousand counterrevolutionaries" Maignet expected it to "purge" before 9 Thermidor cut short its work.[71] Yet Bédoin was different. Hundreds of executions drawn from across a department over a matter of months cannot compare to the death of 3 percent of one village's population in a single afternoon. No other commune in the Vaucluse came close to this level of repression that summer; the comparable figures for much larger towns like Avignon and Carpentras, for example, are just 0.21 percent and 0.32 percent.[72] This concentrated explosion of state-sanctioned killing marked Bédoin out, although in most other respects much of what happened here was characteristic of how the Terror functioned. The dead, like most of the Terror's victims, were mainly middle-aged men, although they also included seven women, and their ages ranged from the nineteen-year-old Marie Thomas to the octogenarian priest Joseph Constantin.[73] Socially, too, the toll was typical of the Terror as a whole: former nobles and religious were, as usual, overrepresented among the executed—six of each were killed. But otherwise the dead were a representative sample of village life. They included a dozen "men of property," rather more shopkeepers and tradesmen—bakers, weavers, potters, cobblers—a scattering of professionals, and some farmers; many had held public office in the past, but more had not.[74]

If Bédoin's dead appear unexceptional, so does the judges' willingness to dispense death sentences. While there are obvious differences in scale, a comparison with sentencing practices in the capital suggests that, once again, the proceedings in Bédoin were not radically out of step with how revolutionary justice worked in 1794. Just under half of those investigated by Bédoin's tribunal were sentenced to death (48.46 percent), a comparable figure to the Revolutionary

70. Maignet to Couthon, 4 Floréal II (Apr. 23, 1794), in *CSP*, 13:21.

71. Maignet, "Notes sur l'établissement du tribunal révolutionnaire," in Courtois, *Rapport*, 366, 369. For the executions in Orange, see Bonnel, *Les 332 victimes*.

72. For the execution rates elsewhere in the Vaucluse, see Lapied, *Le Comtat et la Révolution française*, 443.

73. *Jugement rendu par le Tribunal révolutionnaire du département de Vaucluse*, 20–24.

74. For the social profile of the Terror's victims nationally, see Greer, *Incidence of the Terror*, 154–60.

Tribunal's total of 52 percent, although the latter's death sentences were, of course, spread out over two years, not one day, and they included prisoners drawn from across France, not a single village. Indeed, one stood a slightly better chance of walking away a free man or woman in Paris than one did in Bédoin. While 42.5 percent of those who came before the Parisian tribunal were released without punishment, the figure here was just 37 percent, although in reality no one in Bédoin escaped punishment at all.[75]

If the number and nature of the executions here seem broadly typical, it was Maignet's decision to burn this "detestable" place to the ground that marked Bédoin out.[76] House razing had been an established, if rarely employed, punishment in medieval and early modern jurisprudence, but its use had effectively ended in France by the eighteenth century.[77] Under the ancien régime, the destruction of an offender's residence had been reserved for particularly heinous crimes, heresy and regicide especially, and it is a measure of how much the new offense of *lèse-nation* owed earlier ideas of *lèse-majesté* that republicans resurrected this archaic form of punishment to deal with criminals they considered particularly beyond the pale. However, the republic did not simply reinstate this anachronism; it extended its application from the individual offender to every member of a community tainted by the crime of *lèse-nation*. In decreeing the destruction of Lyon in October 1793, the Convention set a precedent for this, but if demolition could only ever be a symbolic gesture in a city of 120,000 inhabitants, it was a more manageable prospect in a village of 2,000. Here Maignet had an opportunity simultaneously to atone for his earlier inaction in Lyon, avenge an outrage done the nation, and, with an exemplary act of annihilation, send a striking message across the Midi. Bédoin's obliteration was, he informed the Committee of Public Safety, "the only way to preserve this whole region from the plots which have been hatched here."[78]

By most accounts, Suchet's soldiers did a thorough job. Writing his memoirs nearly thirty years later, Maignet tried to downplay the destruction, but contemporary sources are clear that this was no token gesture.[79] In letters to

75. For rates of execution, acquittal, and release in Paris, see Godfrey, *Revolutionary Justice*, 136–47.

76. AN, D/§1/29, Maignet to the Committee of Public Safety, 18 Floréal II (May 7, 1794).

77. Judicial house razing had all but ended in France by the late seventeenth century. Prior to the Revolution, its inclusion as a little-remarked rider to Robert-François Damiens's death sentence for attempted regicide in 1757 is the only recorded instance of its use in the eighteenth century. Friedrichs, "House-Destruction as a Ritual of Punishment."

78. AN, D/§1/29, Maignet to the Committee of Public Safety, 18 Floréal II (May 7, 1794).

79. Written to refute the "atrocious calumnies" leveled against him and insisting that "this mission marked the beginning of my woes," Maignet's memoirs alternate between defending what happened to Bédoin, trying to deflect responsibility for it, and downplaying its consequences, as in his questionable claim that "the destruction was limited to ten houses." BMA, MS 4368, fols. 155 and 180, "Mémoires inédits de Maignet."

Paris that June, the Avignon radical Agricol Moureau boasted that the blaze that consumed Bédoin could be seen from four leagues away, and the village, he glee-fully concluded, was "no more."[80] Shortly afterward the arrival of a small army of laborers tasked with sifting through the ashes to make saltpeter confirms this impression. They remained there all summer, and the records of their work, like the letters later written "from the ruins of Bédoin," make clear that little remained of what had once been over four hundred houses, several silk warehouses, and a newly built town hall.[81] There was even an iconoclastic edge to the soldiers' punitive zeal: Suchet's men mined the parish church with explosives, ensuring that it remained derelict for decades.[82] Whatever Maignet later maintained, Moureau was right: Bédoin was "no more," and it or, rather, its ruins were renamed "Bédoin the annihilated."[83] In a final flourish of retributive zeal, Maignet even ordered the surrounding fields sown with salt to ensure that Bédoin would remain a wasteland, its desolation a monument to "the nation's vengeance."[84]

This conflagration set Bédoin apart, but the criminal process it concluded was, in most other respects, unremarkable. As a trial, it exemplifies how the lan-guage of the law as it stood in 1794 did not so much distinguish guilt from inno-cence as describe a political space where this distinction almost ceased to exist. This poses the problem of the second procedural propriety that delayed the inevitable at Bédoin. However much these events were later condemned as an atrocity, the tribunal pursued its investigations conscientiously and in confor-mity with the law. From their arrival on May 10 to passing sentence on May 28, the judges were hard at work. Evidence was examined and suspects interrogated, 184 of them in total; searches were conducted and corroborating materials sought from neighboring municipalities. Bounties were even offered to inform-ers: Pierre Blauvac and Jean Pichot each received 100 livres for information lead-ing to the execution of two priests.[85] In this sense, the judges followed the letter of the law as they understood it, and this concern applied to the suspects before

80. Moureau to Claude-François Payan, letters of 16 and 18 Prairial II, in Courtois, *Rapport*, 387, 393.

81. ADV, 4L 180, "Atelier révolutionnaire de salpêtre de Bédoin: Recettes et dépenses"; Philippe Gou-pilleau to the Convention, 18 Brumaire III (Nov. 8, 1794), in *AP*, 102:73.

82. On the use of explosives in the church of Saint Pierre, see AN, F3/II/Vaucluse/4, "Rapport au Conseil des batiments civils par M. Rondelet, inspecteur général et membre du dit conseil sur un devis pour le rétablissement de l'église de la Commune de Bédoin," Apr. 1818.

83. *AM*, 17 Frimaire III (Dec. 7, 1794), 674.

84. Maignet, *Au nom du peuple français . . . le 17 floréal*, 3. The remaining residents were ordered to be distributed among, and kept under surveillance by, neighboring communes, but many took refuge in caves in the surrounding countryside instead. BMA, MS 4203, fol. 93, Lego to Maignet, 19 Prairial II; MS 4204, fol. 118, "Etat des habitants de ci-devant Bédouin annexes à la commune du Barroux."

85. François Imbert was acquitted on the strength of testimonials from the justice of the peace and popular society of his hometown, Caromb. ADV, 7 L 51, Interrogation of François Imbert, 26 Floréal II. For bounties, see ADV, 7L 5, "Jugement rendu par le Tribunal criminel du département de Vaucluse, séante à Bédoin l'infâme."

them as much as it reflected anxiety about their own jurisdiction. This was justice dispensed "révolutionnairement," without recourse to either the jury system established as "the jewel in the crown" of the early Revolution's legal reforms or any right to a defense, let alone an appeal, and it was all delivered at the point of a bayonet.[86] However, it was also quite legal. That is not to say that what happened here was in any sense impartial or just. On the contrary, the tiny guillotines François Barjavel doodled alongside some of the names in his trial notes suggest just how predetermined these death sentences were and how much the crime of May 1–2 was simply a pretext to purge a place that seemed a second "Sodom" in republican eyes.[87] Rather, it is to suggest that the definition of criminality under the law in 1794 was so capacious, the potential for self-incrimination so all-encompassing, and the rules of evidence so elastic that guilt was very easy to establish in a revolutionary court, particularly when an indictment was as accommodating as "hindering the progress" of the Revolution. A reflection of what Dan Edelstein has described as the "expansive nature" of legal language during the Terror, the proceedings at Bédoin are an object lesson in revolutionary law's capacity to incriminate by virtue of its sheer indeterminacy.[88]

The records of the tribunal's interrogations bear this out. From May 12 to 26 the judges spent day after day questioning detainees and listening to the denials, denunciations, and downright bewilderment one might have encountered in any village subjected to this kind of forensic scrutiny. Occasionally these interrogations proceeded at a gallop—up to twenty prisoners were examined on some days—but generally they advanced at a more measured pace as suspects were grilled about their record in public office, their personal finances, or their families' questionable connections. Some interviews were remarkably short. Pierre Brun was acquitted after just two questions prompted Barjavel to jot a brisk "ignorant" beside his name in his notes, but a short interrogation did not always bode well.[89] Pierre Martin was asked only four questions on May 26, but as an unrepentant refractory priest he was already guilty of a capital crime under the law of 29 Vendémiaire II, so further questioning was unnecessary.[90] Most suspects were asked if they knew who had upended the liberty tree, although many were

<hr />

86. Mason, "'Bosom of Proof,'" 36.

87. ADV, 7L 51, Barjavel, notes. The guillotines were drawn alongside the names of sixty-three-year-old Elénore-Françoise Raymond and her seventy-three-year-old husband, Joseph François Balbany de Vaubone, both former nobles. For the frequently repeated "Sodom" analogy, see AN, F7/4574, *Proclamation du Tribunal criminel du département de Vaucluse . . . 21 floréal II*.

88. Edelstein, *Terror of Natural Right*, 19.

89. ADV, 7 L 51, Interrogation of Pierre Brun, 26 Floréal II; Barjavel, Trial notes, Pierre Brun.

90. ADV, 7 L 51, Interrogation of Pierre Martin, 7 Prairial II. For this law's wider application, see Allen, *Les tribunaux criminels*, 249.

not, and some even volunteered the names of those they thought responsible. The *société populaire*'s president, Pierre Rousseau, featured repeatedly in these very speculative accusations, but this was never based on much more than a rumor that Rousseau had not slept at home on the night of May 1–2 and the fact that he was widely detested as a hypocrite and a thug.[91] This tittle-tattle persuaded Barjavel that Rousseau was probably the guilty party, but whoever did or did not uproot that tree was hardly the point.[92] Whatever else emerged from the tribunal's inquiries, their most striking feature is how little attention anyone actually paid the "abominable crime" that had ostensibly provoked this visitation of Republican wrath. Less an investigation than an inquisition, the tribunal's purpose was to probe the personal morality of the accused, to assess their political orthodoxy, and to determine whether and how far this deviated from the republican ideal.

In defining that ideal or, better yet, in deciding what deviance looked like, the tribunal took September 1793's Law of Suspects as its *vade mecum*. In distinguishing the true patriot from the potential counterrevolutionary, the tribunal's questioning focused on precisely those aspects of a detainee's character that law deemed decisive: their past conduct, connections, and words or writings, although the latter's relevance was probably moot given how many detainees could not sign the statements of their testimony. Everyone, for example, was asked to account for their financial means, just as article 2, subsection ii, of the law required, and the possession or acquisition of a *certificate de civisme* was always held up to scrutiny, again as the law specified. When particular issues were raised in light of the tribunal's trawl through the records, they were generally viewed through the prism of this legislation too. Ill-judged boasts or threats culled from the *comité de surveillance*'s files marked out those, like the Viau and Thomas families, who had backed the wrong horse politically over the past year. Misconduct in public office, both during Bédoin's brief flirtation with federalism in 1793 and more recently when the clique around mayor Silvestre Fructus and the Rousseau clan ran the municipality chiefly for their own profit, condemned many of the men who had held any form of office over the past two years. Their conspicuous failure to arrest enough suspects, misuse of public funds—too often spent in the auberge—and what was clearly a lively trade in *certificats de civisme* all contributed to the image

91. For examples of this rumor, see ADV, 7 L 51, Interrogations of Joseph Bernard, 24 Floréal II; Silvestre Fructus, 5 Prairial II; Dominique Nouvene, 6 Prairial II; Basile Tallene, 7 Prairial II. According to Jean-Joseph Branche, Rousseau was "a man who only wears the mantle of patriotism," while Marie Thomas described an earlier assault on her father as evidence of his violent character. ADV, 7 L 51, Interrogations of Jean-Joseph Branche, 5 Prairial, and Marie Thomas, 23 Floréal II.

92. ADV, 7L 51, Barjavel, notes.

of a community that fell far short of the law's ideal, a citizenry defined by its constant "devotion to the Revolution."[93]

The failure to live up to that exacting standard defined how criminality was determined that May. As the tribunal's terse memorandum of its investigations makes clear, guilt or innocence was often assigned on the basis of rumor, gossip, or one neighbor's account of another's alleged *propos inciviques*. These all sufficed for a conviction, but guilt was ultimately ascribed intuitively, according to the judges' assessment of an individual's moral character.[94] Thus a laconic "bad faith" summed up why Gabriel Bertrand was executed; a blunt "immoral" was the verdict on Thomas Rousseau, and "very negligent" sufficed to send the weaver François Jouve to the scaffold, despite his protests that "he thought he had done his duty, and if he failed in this it was out of ignorance."[95] These men's shortcomings seemed self-evident, but others were found guilty more by association than because of anything they had done or failed to do. The wrong family or friends invariably spelled trouble. The tribunal cut a swathe through Mayor Fructus's relatives along with the cronies who had enjoyed his hospitality at public expense, and the Rousseau clan fared just as badly. An émigré in the family was a predictably compromising connection. For Joseph Bernard, one son's presence in the army was no compensation for another who had fled France three years before, just as Marie Thomas's youth did not absolve her of her father's emigration. Others had simply kept the wrong souvenirs. Possession of the cache of "feudal records, fanatical seals and aristocratic letters" uncovered in Eléonore Raymond's home was a capital crime in itself, but it also reeked of intolerable nostalgia for the ancien régime, and that hastened her path to the guillotine alongside her husband, the *ci-devant* seigneur Balbary de Vaubone.[96] Like many who were put to death that afternoon, this elderly couple died because of who and what they were rather than anything they had actually done.

The image that emerges from these interrogations is overwhelmingly that of a community at odds with itself rather than in revolt against the republic. It is, unquestionably, an unattractive picture. However, as in the portrait of the "république au village" that Peter Jones sketched out in the southern Massif Central, these interrogations primarily suggest how little politics as it was understood in Paris or even Avignon mattered in places like Bédoin.[97] The tribunal's

93. Duvergier, *Collection complète*, 6:172. The misuse of public funds was a constant motif in the tribunal's questioning; see, e.g., ADV, 7 L51, Interrogations of Pierre Dauberte (5 Prairial), François Allemand (26 Floréal), Michel Fructus (25 Floréal).

94. ADV, 7 L51, Tableau des prévenus de la commune de Bédoin.

95. ADV, 7 L51, Tableau des prévenus de la commune de Bédoin; Barjavel, notes; Interrogation of François Jouve, 6 Prairial II.

96. ADV, 7 L51, Procès-verbal de la commission Lego, 22 Floréal II.

97. Jones, "*La République au Village*."

investigations reveal instead a tangle of conflicts concerning local power: who had it, who had lost it, and how it could be used or abused to advance private agendas or pursue family feuds. For all Roman Viau's reported bluster about playing boules with patriots' heads in 1793 or Mathieu Brun's boast that "the patriots were fucked" because the king was supposedly still alive, there was no vast counterrevolutionary conspiracy at work in Bédoin.[98] Rather, this was a place where ancient antagonisms endured in the guise of new political identities, where newly minted labels like *federalist* or *patriot* imparted an ideological veneer to the more intimate animosities of village life, and where public office was seen as an opportunity to settle old scores or make some money, but not a civic duty. Much of this behavior was unsavory and some of it certainly criminal, although imprisonment rather than execution should have been the corrupt *fonctionnaire's* fate according to September 1791's criminal code. Yet to men like Maignet, Lego, and Suchet, all this clannishness, cronyism, and chicanery signified something much more sinister than parochialism's enduring appeal. In their eyes, Bédoin represented not so much the reality of counterrevolution—and the ragbag of elderly aristocrats, retired clerics, and middle-aged tradesmen executed on May 28 hardly posed any meaningful threat to the state—as the irredeemable absence of Republican *vertu*. Suchet put it plainest of all when he insisted that "there is not the least spark of *civisme* in this commune," and in the summer of 1794 that alone warranted the "violent measures" he judged "indispensable."[99]

In Bédoin, politics was, to borrow from Stathis Kalyvas's account of civil war in the twentieth-century Argolid, thoroughly privatized: its aims, its institutions, even its language had been appropriated to serve predominantly personal, parochial ends, and for good Montagnards like Maignet, this perversion of the republic's purpose was anathema.[100] It constituted a moral cancer that had to be excised from the body politic, and a tribunal was the place to perform that surgery, an inferno the only way to cauterize the wound. Unrestrained by the strict rules of evidence that had guided the ancien régime's judiciary and unmoored from the jury system introduced in 1791, justice had become a means, as Maignet's friend Couthon put it two weeks later, "less of punishing [the enemies of the *patrie*] than of annihilating them."[101] Couthon announced that aim in proposing the law of 22 Prairial II (June 10, 1794) reorganizing the Revolutionary Tribunal. It was intended to expedite justice by, among other things, abolishing any right to a defense and permitting convictions on the strength of "either

98. Both were executed for these sentiments. ADV, 7 L51, Notes prises sur les registres du comité de surveillance.

99. AN, AF/II/145, Suchet to Maignet, 17 Floréal II (May 6, 1794).

100. On the "privatization of politics," see Kalyvas, *Logic of Violence*, 330–63.

101. *AM*, 24 Prairial II (June 12, 1794), 695.

material or moral proofs," and it is generally recognized as having transformed the Terror in the capital that summer.[102] However, it is clear from what happened in Bédoin that the men, means, and mentality required to commit judicial murder on a spectacular scale were in place in provincial France well before the Convention formally decided that the "enemies of the people" should be "exterminated" on the basis of purely "moral" certainty.[103]

"Justice and Humanity Must Be Promptly Avenged"

On May 17, 1794, Maignet's letter outlining his plans for Bédoin was greeted with lively applause in the Convention, and their execution appears to have had the desired effect in the Midi too.[104] In the weeks following Bédoin's destruction, the popular societies of the Bouches-du-Rhône and the Vaucluse vied with one another in applauding "the virtuous Maignet" as the savior of the south and acclaiming the "terrible but necessary example" made of this "sacrilegious commune."[105] The *sociétaires* of Sault's accolades were typical: "this dazzling act of justice" had worked wonders in the Vaucluse, transforming every local authority into "a sanctuary of every virtue and a formidable arsenal against every vice."[106] Such was the language of Republican orthodoxy in the summer of 1794. However, if the sincerity of these sentiments was impeccable, their timing was not. Sault's address arrived in the Convention on 9 Thermidor, and most deputies had other things on their minds that day. Robespierre's overthrow that evening and execution the next day—along with Maignet's closest associate on the governing committees, Couthon—began the tortuous reckoning with the Terror that made "horror," in Bronisław Baczko's terms, "the order of the day" for the rest of 1794.[107] As the press and pamphlet campaign against the Terror picked up after 9–10 Thermidor, shocking revelations of mass executions and individual atrocities from across France prompted, as Sergio Luzzatto has argued, the emergence of a new language to describe terror not simply as an injustice but as an attack on humanity itself.[108]

This reconceptualization of state terror as a crime against humanity began tentatively at first, with individual atrocities condemned as attacks "on humanity, on the French people and on the National Convention," but it gathered pace

---

102. Eude, "La loi de prairial"; Gueniffey, *La politique de la Terreur*, 277–301.

103. *AM*, 24 Prairial II (June 12, 1794), 695.

104. *La feuille de la République*, 29 Floréal II (May 17, 1794), 2; *AP*, 90:395.

105. "Adresse de la société populaire de Mormoiron," in *AP*, 92:21; also *AP*, 92:192, 256, 353.

106. "Adresse de la société populaire régénérée de la commune de Sault, le 16 prairial an II," in *AP*, 93:548.

107. Baczko, *Comment sortir de la Terreur*, 191–255. See also Brown, *Mass Violence and the Self*, 122–31; Vovelle, *Le tournant de l'an III*; Chavanette, *Quatre-vingt-quinze*; and Steinberg, *Afterlives of the Terror*.

108. Luzzatto, *L'automne de la Révolution*, 31.

that autumn.[109] A turning point came when the *conventionnels'* "search for a scapegoat" finally settled on Jean-Baptiste Carrier, the deputy who had overseen the *noyades* at Nantes a year before.[110] When the Convention voted to lift Carrier's immunity from prosecution, the final (almost unanimous) roll call was a litany of votes cast so "that outraged humanity may be avenged" or in disgust that a deputy had proved "the shame and scourge of humanity."[111] Carrier's long and painstakingly detailed trial—itself a deliberate contrast to the terrorists' summary justice—was, as Jean-Clément Martin has argued, supposed to distance the regime from its recent past and demonstrate that a republic governed by the rule of law had replaced one deformed by its abuse.[112] Yet its significance is probably more sweeping than this for two reasons. First, that prolonged process, stretching from the first denunciations in September to their inevitable dénouement on December 16, unleashed a press and pamphlet frenzy that firmly implanted the idea of state terror as a crime against humanity, a premeditated "populicide" even, in the public imagination.[113] Second and more immediately, Carrier's trial also inspired calls to arraign those responsible for other atrocities, and this quickly implicated many more *conventionnels*, men just like Maignet.

Carrier's trial whetted the public's appetite for justice, but it also demonstrates, almost by default, just how little inclination there was in the Convention to prosecute those responsible for these crimes. Denunciations continued to ring out across year III, and deputies who fell from grace were periodically purged by their colleagues—much as they had been in year II—but after Carrier's execution few of the Terror's principal protagonists ever stood trial.[114] The chief prosecutor of the Revolutionary Tribunal, Antoine Fouquier-Tinville, followed Carrier to the guillotine in May 1795, and Joseph Le Bon met the same fate five months later in Amiens.[115] That spring the "great guilty" quartet of Collot d'Herbois, Billaud-Varennes, Barère, and Vadier were impeached and exiled to what seemed certain death in Guiana, but only two of them were ever deported, and only Collot died there. In the provinces, some small-town functionaries did stand trial for

109. *Le mercure universel*, 2 Vendémiaire III (Sept. 22, 1794), 13.

110. Luzzatto (*L'automne de la Révolution*, 26) and Chavanette (*Quatre-vingt-quinze*, 119) both define Carrier's prosecution in this light.

111. *AP*, 102:105, 106, 108, 111, 114.

112. Martin, "Le procès Carrier."

113. Babeuf, *Du système de dépopulation*, 38, 53, 82. Parisians reportedly now spoke of the *terroristes* as "born enemies of the human race" or even, as one sail maker from Nantes put it, "the destroyers of the human race." *AM*, 23 Vendémiaire III (Oct. 14, 1794), 217; and *AM*, 16 Frimaire III (Dec. 6, 1794), 662. On that campaign more generally, see Brown, *Mass Violence and the Self*.

114. On those purges, see Harder, "Second Terror."

115. Chavanette, "Le procès de Fouquier-Tinville"; Steinberg, "Terror on Trial."

their role in the Terror, but convictions were, in general, few and far between. The rough justice meted out to former terrorists across the south in 1795 is a different matter but, in terms of due process, the pickings remained thin.[116] In sum, the judicial toll exacted for the Terror was modest enough, and that brings us back to Maignet. By the time Carrier went to the guillotine in December 1794, Maignet was widely reviled as a "monster" steeped in innocent blood, and Bédoin's fate was just as widely associated with the *robespierristes'* "system of arson and assassination."[117] Yet Maignet was never indicted, let alone convicted, and the reasons why suggest something of the difficulties involved in defining crime and culpability after the Terror.

Swept up in a mass recall of Montagnard deputies on mission a fortnight after 9–10 Thermidor, Maignet returned to Paris in September no longer the messiah of the Midi but a pariah.[118] That metamorphosis began slowly at first but gathered pace as allegations concerning mass arrests and arbitrary executions began to attach to his name that autumn. Claims that he was "Couthon's hired assassin" or, worse, Robespierre's "devoted executioner" were especially damaging at a time when copies of Jean-Claude Méhée's incendiary *La queue de Robespierre* were selling in their thousands.[119] In reality, though, there were bigger fish to fry than Maignet that autumn, and with public attention focused firmly on Carrier, he remained where he had been for most of his career in the Convention: in the shadows.

That began to change over the winter as several factors converged to focus public attention increasingly on the events at Bédoin. The first of these was circumstantial. If radicalism was in retreat in Paris, it was facing a rout in the Midi. In the Vaucluse, the arrival of a moderate *représentant*, Philippe Goupilleau, in August prompted a purge of Maignet's allies, the "maignetised authorities," and their public disgrace.[120] The men who presided over Bédoin's destruction, Lego, Barjavel, and Fouque, were all ousted from office that autumn, and the focus turned to Suchet's part in these "disgusting horrors" in October.[121] Claims that

116. On the White Terror, see Lucas, "Violence thermidorienne"; and Clay, "Vengeance, Justice, and the Reactions."

117. Lefébure, *Justice contre Maignet*, 3, 12.

118. His recall had to be reissued repeatedly. *CSP*, 16:77, 342, 664.

119. *Journal de la Montagne*, 6 Fructidor II (Aug. 23, 1794), 947; *AM*, 10 Fructidor II (Aug. 27, 1794), 1393. See also *AP*, 91:188, 315; 95: 471; *Journal de la Montagne*, 22 Fructidor II, 1073; 28 Fructidor II, 1117; 29 Fructidor II, 1128. On Méhée, see Biard, "Après la tête, la queue!"

120. Rovère, *Correspondance intime*, 119; Moulinas, *Histoire de la Révolution d'Avignon*, 331–37.

121. For Barjavel, see Barjavel, *Mémoire justificatif*. For Lego's dismissal, see BMA, MS 2529, fol. 163, "Arrêté de Goupilleau, du 19 brumaire an III, destituant Lego, agent national de Carpentras"; for Fouque, see ADV, 201 J12, Fouque to Goupilleau, 25 Vendémiaire III. For Suchet, see "La société populaire de Carpentras à la Convention nationale, le 14 vendémiaire an III," in *Le Républicain français*, 30 Vendémiaire III (Oct. 21, 1794), 2861.

this "abominable monster" had his men shoot prisoners in Bédoin for sport started to reach the Convention, and while nothing came of these attacks, Suchet still felt the need to respond in print with a lengthy *apologia pro vita sua*, complete with copious testimonials to his unimpeachable "civisme."[122] While he blankly denied the charge of cruelty, the crux of his defense concerned the legality of his actions. He had, he insisted, simply been doing his duty as an officer in obeying the orders he received: "I assisted with all my power the constituted authorities, under whose orders I found myself; faithful to his duty, what was the commander of an armed force to do? He had to obey the National Convention which sanctioned the measures at Bédoin, ensure its decrees were respected . . . and carry out orders emanating from a criminal tribunal."[123] Suchet survived this onslaught, but as the opprobrium engulfing his provincial protégés began to reach Paris, public attention increasingly turned to Maignet himself.

Joseph Rovère was crucial to this process. His correspondence with Goupilleau charts a comprehensive campaign to dismantle Maignet's legacy in the Midi and discredit his reputation in the capital.[124] The dismissal of the "maignetized authorities" was one strand of this crusade, but changing attitudes in the Convention was also critical, and Rovère spent much of the autumn reminding his colleagues of the "thousand horrors" men like Maignet were responsible for, and the risk they still posed, in the Midi.[125] That crusade intensified in November as scandalized petitions from the south, along with Goupilleau's moving appeals, evocatively written from "the ruins of Bédoin," called on the Convention to undo the crimes committed there and avenge "outraged humanity."[126] No longer "enemies of the Republic," Bédoin's dead were now its "victims," and this newfound status had important implications.[127] Whereas enmity had warranted extermination in Republican rhetoric, victimhood inspired empathy and conferred rights: a right to justice, certainly, but also a right to rehabilitation and redress. The Convention finally agreed to the latter on December 4, after Goupilleau made a dramatic return to the chamber, accompanied by a delegation of survivors from Bédoin. Their vivid, firsthand testimony of their plight, their insistence that this supposed stronghold of the counterrevolution had sent

122. "La société populaire de Carpentras"; Suchet, *Patrie, égalité, liberté*, 7.
123. Suchet, *Patrie, égalité, liberté*, 6.
124. Rovère, *Correspondance intime*.
125. *AM*, 2 Brumaire III (Oct. 23, 1794), 290–91. Rovère's campaign began shortly after 9 Thermidor. *AM*, 16 Thermidor II (Aug. 3, 1794), 379.
126. *Pétition à la Convention nationale des citoyens de la commune d'Avignon, victimes de la faction Robespierre, sur les atrocités commises dans cette commune et dans le département de Vaucluse*, Avignon, 1794, 5, 6; *AP*, 102:73–74.
127. For assertions of the villagers' victimhood, see *Pétition à la Convention nationale*; and AN, AF/ II/197, Goupilleau to the Committee of Public Safety, 18 Brumaire III (Nov. 8, 1794).

280 volunteers to fight for France, and above all, their demand that the republic be "severe toward crime and just toward the innocent" had an electric effect on the deputies.[128] Allied to the shrewd politics of their claim that Maignet's mission had been part of a plot to "establish Robespierre's throne in the south," the pathos of this appeal prompted speech after impassioned speech as deputies rose to distance themselves from "these atrocities" and demand that those responsible be punished. To keep silent when "justice demands swift vengeance," Louis Legendre insisted, "would be the greatest of crimes," while André Dumont, conveniently forgetting the executions he had applauded for the same offense that February, demanded that "justice and humanity must be promptly avenged" and called on the committees to arrest the "monster" responsible for "so many crimes."[129]

Action was immediately promised and, in one respect at least, promptly delivered. A week after the villagers' appearance—lightning speed by the Convention's standards—its committees agreed to send 300,000 livres south to help rebuild Bédoin, and by the end of the year the authorities in Carpentras had begun to distribute that aid.[130] Although well short of the 1.2 million livres the Abbé Sauve later estimated reconstruction would cost, it was a substantial sum and, in tandem with a temporary waiver on Bédoin's taxes, it represented some recognition that the villagers were owed redress.[131] The business of reintegrating Bédoin back into the republic gathered pace a month later when Goupilleau's successor, Jean Debry, reinstated its municipal authorities.[132] Bédoin's rehabilitation concluded, politically at least, a year to the day after its liberty tree had been torn down with a solemn ceremony marking the village's "resurrection."[133] After a procession through "the ashes and ruins" and a speech denouncing "the crime cloaked in patriotism" that had torn France apart throughout the Terror, Debry unveiled a small column commemorating Bédoin's "year of tears" (fig. 1).[134] That column still stands, and the panel on its pedestal still promises "the law restores justice / Take comfort, O unhappy people / since the scandal of the crime presages its punishment," but that promise was never kept. Bédoin was rehabilitated and its inhabitants received some redress, but the justice they

128. *AM*, 17 Frimaire III (Dec. 7, 1794), 676.

129. *AM*, 17 Frimaire III (Dec. 7, 1794), 676.

130. *Journal de Perlet*, 25 Frimaire III (Dec. 15, 1794), 115; BMA, MS 2529, fol. 335, "Arrêté du district de Carpentras pour l'exécution de la loi qui accorde un secours provisoire de 300 000 livres aux habitants de la commune de Bédoin, 9 Nivôse III." Notably, just 35,000 livres were set aside to support those left destitute by the destruction of their homes.

131. Sauvé in Berriat Saint-Prix, *La justice révolutionnaire*, 206; BMA, MS 4204, fol. 119.

132. *Journal de Perlet*, 25 Frimaire III (Dec. 15, 1794), 115; *CSP*, 19:669.

133. *Procès-verbal de la réhabilitation de Bédouin et de l'installation solennelle de sa municipalité et de la justice de paix du canton* (Avignon, an III), 2, 5.

134. *Procès-verbal de la réhabilitation de Bédouin*, 7.

FIGURE 1 "Monument élevé des ruines de Bédoin le 15 floréal an III . . . sur la place où fut égorgée une partie des malheureux habitants de cette infortunée commune" (1795). Courtesy of Avignon Bibliothèques, Est. Fol. 206/132.

demanded from the Convention, the justice pamphlets and petitioners called for that winter, never materialized. Maignet would be called to account for the destruction of Bédoin, but he would also be exonerated, and the reason why suggests something of the dilemmas that dealing with the crimes of the Terror posed.

With justice now "the order of the day," the Convention assured Bédoin's survivors on December 4 that those responsible for their suffering would pay for their crimes.[135] Matters came to a head the next month when Edme Courtois delivered his mammoth report on the papers found in Robespierre's lodgings after Thermidor. It was the most detailed investigation into the Terror to date, and though firmly focused on the Committee of Public Safety's leadership, it repeatedly implicated Maignet in their crimes.[136] When the Convention came to debate Courtois's report the following day (January 6, 1795), Maignet made one of his by now rare public appearances to refute these "diatribes" and called on the governing committees to clear his name.[137] Their response was immediate: speaking on the committees' behalf, Philippe Pons assured his colleagues that Maignet's case had been carefully examined and there was no reason to investigate his conduct any further.[138] Although Pons acknowledged that the burning of Bédoin was unquestionably a crime, what was at issue now was individual

135. *AM*, 17 Frimaire III (Dec. 7, 1794), 676.
136. Courtois, *Rapport*, 90, 91, 97, 365–77, 380–84.
137. *AM*, 20 Nivôse III (Jan. 9, 1795), 156.
138. *AM*, 20 Nivôse III (Jan. 9, 1795), 156. Pons claimed that the *comités* had reviewed Maignet's case over three sittings.

accountability, and the committees were unequivocal about that: Maignet was merely following orders when he had Bédoin burned down. As another of the Convention's legal experts, the author of 1793's Law of Suspects Merlin de Douai, explained: "The crime was committed in Paris, and Maignet did nothing but obey the edicts of the Committee [of Public Safety]. . . . Your committees have concluded that it is the leaders and not the led who ought to be struck down."[139] One after another the committees' members hammered this point home to their incredulous colleagues: this was not "Maignet's work but rather that of . . . the old Committee of Public Safety."[140] The message was clear: like all the other crimes committed in year II, Bédoin's destruction was down to the tiny cabal of *robespierristes* who had orchestrated tyranny from their rooms in the Tuileries until the daring patriots of the Convention overthrew them on 9 Thermidor. The Thermidorians had spent the last six months establishing this account of the Terror—the capital T was a very Thermidorian addition—and they were not about to see it unravel because of one village in the Vaucluse.[141]

The committees could not have been clearer, but many of their colleagues were unconvinced. Predictably, Rovère was incandescent, and the discussion grew increasingly heated until it fell to an unrepentant Maignet to deliver the coup de grâce.[142] Reviewing the correspondence he had sent north the previous summer, he read the letter he had sent the Convention itself, the letter describing the punishment planned for this "infamous commune," and with that the debate spluttered to a halt. A few diehards grumbled that Maignet remained guilty in their eyes, but after a brief "tumult" the matter was dropped and the Convention moved on with the order of business.[143] Maignet's insurance policy had paid off. In reading the correspondence he had sent the Convention, he reminded his colleagues of the one fact they had all chosen to forget: the "lively applause" that had greeted his plans and the decision to print his letter in the Convention's *Bulletin* the next day.[144] The memory of that applause was what determined the committees' decision not to take matters any further, and it decided Maignet's fate. He would not be charged with any offense because, as the response that letter had received suggested, if the burning of Bédoin was a

139. *AM*, 20 Nivôse III (Jan. 9, 1795), 157.

140. François Bourdon de l'Oise of the Committee of General Security, *AM*, 20 Nivôse III (Jan. 9, 1795), 157. From the same committee, Louis Legendre insisted that "the members of the old Committee of Public Safety were the sole authors of all these crimes." *AM*, 20 Nivôse III (Jan. 9, 1795), 157.

141. On that narrative, see Jones, *Fall of Robespierre*, 432–57.

142. *AM*, 20 Nivôse III (Jan. 9, 1795), 156.

143. *AM*, 20 Nivôse III (Jan. 9, 1795), 160.

144. *AP*, 90:395. Although this decision was widely reported in the press, Maignet's letter was not in fact published in the *Bulletin*. *La feuille de la République*, 29 Floréal II (May 18, 1794), 1–2.

crime then the whole Convention was complicit in it, and that was not a conclusion anyone in that chamber was prepared to accept.

Just as Suchet had argued in October, Maignet was only obeying orders, or at least that was the fiction the Convention settled on in January 1795. Charlotte Biggs, an astute observer of current affairs from her residence in Amiens, summed the situation up neatly that month. Maignet was, she wrote, a "source of considerable embarrassment," but once it became clear that he "was authorized by an express decree of the Convention, to burn Bedouin [sic], and guillotine its inhabitants, all parties were soon agreed to consign the whole to oblivion."[145] Biggs was right: Maignet was an embarrassment, but oblivion was not an option, at least not yet. The Convention's indignant rejection of Jacques-Antoine Boudin's call for a general amnesty a few days later suggests the deputies were not ready for any "law of forgetting and absolute silence" that January.[146] The threat of prosecution for crimes committed during the Terror remained too useful a weapon to wield against the Convention's radical rump to embrace Boudin's "salutary waters of oblivion" just yet. That would come later when, with their last act, the deputies issued their very selective amnesty for "acts purely related to the Revolution" on 4 Brumaire IV (October 26, 1795).[147] In the meantime, the Convention continued to punish individual offenders from within its ranks, just as it had in 1793–94, as political expediency required, with intermittent expulsions and periodic show trials. So, on April 1, 1795, after another *journée* prompted yet another purge, Rovère finally had his revenge and had Maignet included among the incorrigibles to be investigated for orchestrating the uprising of 12 Germinal III.[148] A warrant was issued for his arrest four days later, but by then Maignet, along with several of his co-accused, was nowhere to be found. Last seen leaving Paris by the Neuilly road on April 5, he remained in hiding until October's amnesty made further concealment unnecessary.[149] By the end of the year he was back in Paris, hobnobbing with what remained of radicalism's old guard in the café Chrétien and swearing "to avenge the death of Robespierre."[150]

145. Biggs, *Residence in France*, 2:338–39.

146. *AM*, 28 Nivôse III (Jan. 17, 1795), 222. On the wider politics of *oubli* in 1795, see Ozouf, "Thermidor ou la travail de l'oubli."

147. *AM*, 14 Brumaire IV (Nov. 5, 1795), 348–49. For that amnesty, see Brown, *Ending the French Revolution*, 26–29.

148. *AM*, 16 Germinal III (Apr. 5, 1795), 124; AN, F7/4443, "Pièces relatives à l'exécution du décret d'arrestation porté contre Cambon, Lecointre, Moïse Bayle, Grasset, Hentz, Maignet, Levasseur, Crassous, Thuriot."

149. On Maignet's departure on 16 Germinal, see AN, F7/4443, Rapport du c. Maingot, inspecteur de police, 18 Germinal an III.

150. Aulard, *Paris pendant la réaction*, 2:578.

Conclusion

A year after Maignet's reappearance in Paris, Louis Marie Prudhomme published his massive *General and Impartial History of the Errors, Offences and Crimes Committed during the French Revolution.*[151] Prudhomme was not the first writer to reckon with the violence of the Revolution, but his six-volume *History* was certainly the most ambitious attempt to count its cost in human life. Good journalist that he was, Prudhomme spared his readers nothing in this gruesome litany of "guillotinades, mitraillades, fusillades, foudroyades, noyades" and the burning of Bédoin features prominently here.[152] It first appears in a panel in volume 1's graphic "Tableau of Some of the Crimes Committed during the Revolution," and another engraving accompanies volume 6's detailed account of Maignet's mission in the Vaucluse (fig. 2).[153] Tell-

FIGURE 2 "Une jeune femme, accouchée depuis 4 jours. . . ." Prudhomme, *Histoire générale*, 6:174. Reproduced courtesy of the Board of Trinity College Dublin.

ingly, and uniquely in the *History*, both prints focus on the Terror as it was experienced by women and children. In the first, the foreground is dominated by families running helter-skelter through narrow streets as they flee the conflagration consuming their homes. The second builds on the pathos of that scene with a vignette of one young woman's attempts to haul her aged mother and children—unsuccessfully, we are told—from the flames engulfing their home. As an image of outraged innocence, of families violated and homes destroyed,

151. Prudhomme, *Histoire générale*. On the *Histoire*, see Zizek, "'Plume de Fer.'"
152. Prudhomme, *Histoire générale*, 1:lxxiv.
153. "Tableau d'une partie des crimes commis pendant la Révolution," Bibliothèque Nationale de France, coll. de Vinck, 6554. The burning of Bédoin is depicted in panel K along the bottom row of the print.

this is a portrait of state terror as an almost elemental force, a "catastrophe" where "insanity" and "atrocity" went hand in hand.[154]

The burning of Bédoin lived on in memory in publications like Prud-homme's *History*. However, if the village was rehabilitated and its destruction long remembered, there is little here that speaks of justice, transitional or other-wise, after the Terror. Decades later Bédoin was still in ruins; its public buildings were still derelict and its parish church unusable well into the 1820s.[155] If restor-ative justice was slow in reaching the Vaucluse, retribution proved even more elusive. For all year III's talk of justice, none of the men involved in this atrocity ever answered for their actions there. While Lego spent much of 1795 in prison awaiting trial for "the murder of sixty-three victims," the Convention's amnesty put an end to his incarceration, and he returned to Paris where, like Maignet, he resumed the legal career and family life he had left behind in 1792.[156] Joseph Fouque, too, escaped any reckoning with the verdicts he had delivered in Bé-doin. Following a bullish defense of his patriotic probity in October 1794, he sought sanctuary with the army in Liguria before returning to France and local politics; he ended his days a prosperous pottery manufacturer in Toulouse in 1829.[157] Suchet fared even better. His part in these events proved no brake on a career that climaxed under the empire as a marshal of France and duc d'Albu-féra, and his biographers have generally either ignored his actions in Bédoin or excused them as a youthful indiscretion, an episode of "regrettable, but pardon-able enthusiasm."[158] Only Barjavel ever mounted the scaffold he was so fond of doodling in his notes, but the cases he prosecuted in Bédoin had no bearing on his execution in June 1795.[159]

As after 1945, the experience of state-sanctioned violence on an unprece-dented scale forced the French—and wider western European opinion to some extent, too—to think about crime and criminality in new ways in the mid-1790s. Preexisting terms like *atrocity* and *massacre*—itself a product of an earlier French civil war—were reimagined and redefined, in what now appear preco-ciously modern terms, as crimes committed against humanity.[160] In place of the imprecision of these earlier terms—and *atrocity*, as Mark Osiel has noted, has

154. Prudhomme, *Histoire générale*, 6:177.

155. For the repeated requests for help rebuilding Bédoin's parish church, hospital, and town hall through the Empire and into the early 1820s, see AN, F3/II/Vaucluse/4, dossier Bédoin.

156. AN, F7/4774/13, dossier Lego.

157. ADV, 201 J11, 14, 20 and 24, Fouque papers; and Fouque, *Mémoire justificatif*. By 1798 Fouque's nomination as an elector in Apt was prompting anxious complaints that one "who delivered this land up to executioners and flames" was back in business politically. AN, AF/III/265, 56, Bose, commissaire près le tri-bunal correctionnel at Apt, to the Directory, 2 Germinal VI (Mar. 22, 1798).

158. Bergerot, *Le Maréchal Suchet*, 24.

159. Vaillandet, "Le procès des juges."

160. On massacre, see Greengrass, "Hidden Transcripts."

always lacked "clear conceptual edges" in law—this vocabulary helped, if not explain the Terror, then at least mark it out as something writers like Prud-homme felt obliged to bear witness to on behalf of "humanity, bloodied and torn, trembling beneath the demon of civil war."[161] However, if this kind of crime was radically reimagined after year II, the impunity Maignet and so many like him effectively enjoyed also suggests how limited this conceptual revolution proved in practical terms. And that should perhaps give us pause when speaking of "transitional justice" in the 1790s. Transitional justice is, by its very nature, imperfect. Its tribunals never prosecute every criminal, and its truth commis-sions leave most victims' voices unheard. In confronting past wrongs in some systematic form, however, it does, as Teitel suggests, "draw an important line between regimes," a line that declares the past passed and grounds a new regime's legitimacy in some commonly accepted sense of moral accountability, if not always of legal liability.[162] After the Terror the Convention repeatedly declared that line drawn, insisted that the rule of law had replaced the despotism of the *robespierriste* past, and even offered up the occasional scapegoat like Car-rier as evidence of how much the republic had changed. Yet Bourdon de l'Oise's ominous warning during the January 1795 debate on Maignet—"If we keep revis-iting the same facts, it is difficult to know where we will stop"—suggests the com-promises and contradictions this entailed, along with the unabashed emphasis on self-preservation that underscored so much of this talk of justice.[163] Declaring justice the order of the day may have allowed the *conventionnels* to distance themselves, and the republic, from the atrocities of year II, but accountability, whether moral or legal, remained rare in year III. On the contrary, Maignet's ability, like that of so many other terrorists, to get away with murder suggests just how entangled crime, punishment, and politics remained after the Terror, and that points toward another conclusion.

In May 1794 a liberty tree's uprooting had brought about the destruction of an entire community, not simply because that community appeared com-plicit in a crime but because it seemed to indicate a much wider conspiracy to overthrow the state. However, less than six months later it was the state's response to this act that inspired outrage, and it was the imposition of that collective punish-ment that seemed to signal (yet another) criminal conspiracy to undo the republic and install tyranny in its place. Those two diametrically opposed interpretations of the same event suggest the immense difficulties involved in defining what crime and criminality meant in a civil war context. As Georges Danton admitted in March 1793, "Nothing is more difficult than defining a political crime," but if

---

161. Osiel, *Obeying Orders*, 45; Prudhomme, *Histoire générale*, 1:v.
162. Teitel, *Transitional Justice*, 56.
163. *AM*, 20 Nivôse III (Jan. 9, 1795), 156.

Danton was willing to overlook that difficulty and sanction "terrible measures" in the name of public safety, the problem he identified remained.[164] Republicanism's response to that problem was a yearlong barrage of exceptional legislation that defined criminality in ever more elastic terms while steadily eroding individual rights in courts that routinely judged "révolutionnairement." After 9 Thermidor that system was quickly dismantled, and justice was solemnly declared "the order of the day." Yet justice was just as subordinated to partisan politics in year III as it had been in year II, and the *conventionnels*' punitive instincts remained just as acute as they had been during the Terror. Indeed, with the law of 10 Vendémiaire IV (October 2, 1795) decreeing that "every commune is responsible for crimes committed . . . on its territory," the Convention effectively extended the principles of complicity and collective punishment that Maignet had applied in Bédoin across the entire republic.[165]

Lynn Hunt has described legitimacy as a "general agreement on signs and symbols," and signs and symbols obviously matter, particularly in periods of revolutionary change.[166] They clearly mattered enormously in Bédoin, where an act of symbolic violence had been the starting point of this entire *affaire*, but more fundamental still, a state's legitimacy is predicated on the consent afforded its judicial function: the existence of some basic consensus as to what constitutes a crime, who should be held to account for it, and how and by whom it should be punished. If that consensus ever existed after 1789, the Franco-French conflict of 1793–94 tore it apart, and the language of the law—terms like *crime* and *complicity*, *innocence* and *accountability*—lost anything like a fixed meaning. Less a clearly codified judicial constant than an infinitely adaptable object of political convenience, crime—the laws that defined it and the institutions that adjudicated it—was instead weaponized in the service of factional strife in the Convention and internecine conflict in the provinces. In the process, justice became irretrievably divorced from the assumptions about the law and due process that had inspired the reforms men like Maignet demanded in 1789's *cahiers de doléances* and defined the National Assembly's judicial reforms in 1789–91. In the absence of anything like justice for the crimes of year II, as the Midi settled into a vicious cycle of retribution and revenge, the republic would live with the consequences of that divorce for the rest of the decade.

JOSEPH CLARKE is associate professor in history at Trinity College Dublin and author of *Commemorating the Dead in Revolutionary France: Revolution and Remembrance, 1789–1799* (2007).

164. *AP*, 60:62–63.
165. Duvergier, *Collection complète*, 8:370.
166. Hunt, *Politics, Culture, and Class*, 54.

Acknowledgments

The author wishes to thank Claire Eldridge and Julie M. Powell for organizing the workshop at which this special issue originated and for their feedback on earlier versions of this manuscript. Thanks are due, too, to Anne Dolan and the journal's anonymous reviewers for their helpful comments and suggestions on earlier iterations of this article. He is indebted to the archivists and librarians in Avignon, Clermont-Ferrand, and Paris who helped him track Etienne Maignet through the records, and to the dean of research at Trinity College Dublin for the funding award that made this research possible.

References

Allen, Robert. *Les tribunaux criminels sous la Révolution et l'Empire, 1792–1811*. Rennes, 2005.

Aulard, François-Alphonse, ed. *Paris pendant la réaction thermidorienne et sous le Directoire: Recueil de documents pour l'histoire de l'esprit public à Paris*. 5 vols. Paris, 1898–1902.

Aulard, François-Alphonse, ed. *Recueil des actes du Comité de salut public, avec la correspondance officielle des représentants en mission et le registre du conseil exécutif provisoire*. 33 vols. Paris, 1889–1951.

Babeuf, Gracchus. *Du système de dépopulation ou la vie et les crimes de Carrier. . . .* Paris, an III.

Baczko, Bronisław. *Comment sortir de la Terreur: Thermidor et la Révolution*. Paris, 1989.

Barjavel, François. *Mémoire justificatif pour François Barjavel, ex-accusateur public près le Tribunal criminel du Département de Vaucluse*. Paris, an II [1794].

Berger, Emmanuel. *La justice pénale sous la Révolution: Les enjeux d'un modèle judiciaire liberal*. Rennes, 2008.

Bergerot, Bernard. *Le Maréchal Suchet: Duc d'Albuféra*. Paris, 1986.

Berriat Saint-Prix, Charles. *La justice révolutionnaire à Paris, Bordeaux, Brest, Lyon, Nantes, Orange, Strasbourg*. Paris, 1861.

Biard, Michel. "Après la tête, la queue! La rhétorique antijacobine en fructidor an II—vendémiaire an III." In Vovelle, *Le tournant de l'an III*, 201–13.

Biard, Michel. *Missionnaires de la République: Les représentants du peuple en mission (1793–1795)*. Paris, 2002.

Biard, Michel, and Marisa Linton. *Terreur! La Révolution française face à ses démons*. Paris, 2020.

[Biggs, Charlotte]. *A Residence in France during the Years 1792–1793, 1794, and 1795: Described in a Series of Letters from an English Lady*. 2 vols. London, 1796–97.

Bonnel, Simeon. *Les 332 victimes de la commission populaire d'Orange en 1794*. Orange, 1888.

Borneman, John. *Settling Accounts: Violence, Justice, and Accountability in Postsocialist Europe*. Princeton, NJ, 1997.

Boulant, Antoine. *Le Tribunal révolutionnaire: Punir les ennemis du peuple*. Paris, 2018.

Bourdin, Philippe. "Maignet, Etienne Christophe." In vol. 2 of *Dictionnaire des conventionnels, 1792–1795*, edited by Michel Biard, Philippe Bourdin, and Hervé Leuwers, 784–88. Ferney-Voltaire, 2022.

Brown, Howard G. *Ending the French Revolution: Violence, Justice, and Repression from the Terror to Napoleon*. Charlottesville, VA, 2006.

Brown, Howard G. *Mass Violence and the Self: From the French Wars of Religion to the Paris Commune*. Ithaca, NY, 2019.

Brown, Howard G. "Robespierre's Tail: The Possibilities of Justice after the Terror." *Canadian Journal of History* 45, no. 3 (2010): 503–36.

Chavanette, Loris. "Le procès de Fouquier-Tinville, ou l'accusation de terreur en l'an II." In Leuwers, Martin, and Salas, "Juger la 'terreur,'" 47–59.

Chavanette, Loris. *Quatre-vingt-quinze: La Terreur en procès*. Paris, 2017.

Clay, Stephen. "Vengeance, Justice, and the Reactions in the Revolutionary Midi." *French History* 23, no. 1 (2009): 22–46.

Cobb, Richard. *The Police and the People: French Popular Protest, 1789–1820*. Oxford, 1970.

Cobbett, William [Peter Porcupine, pseud.]. *The Bloody Buoy, Abridged: Thrown Out as a Warning to Britons at the Present Important Period*. London, 1798.

Corvol, Andrée. "The Transformation of a Political Symbol: Tree Festivals in France from the Eighteenth to the Twentieth Centuries." *French History* 4, no. 4 (1990): 455–86.

Courtois, Edme Bonaventure. *Rapport fait au nom de la commission chargée de l'examen des papiers trouvés chez Robespierre et ses complices . . . dans la séance du 16 nivôse an III, de la République française une et indivisible*. Paris, an III [1795].

Ducros. *Tableau de la situation politique de la commune de Bédouin, département de Vaucluse*. Avignon, an II [1794].

Duvergier, Jean-Baptiste, ed. *Collection complète des lois, décret, ordonnances, règlements, avis du conseil d'état . . . de 1788 à 1830*. 37 vols. Paris, 1834–45.

Edelstein, Dan. *The Terror of Natural Right: Republicanism, the Cult of Nature, and the French Revolution*. Chicago, 2009.

Eude, Michel. "La loi de prairial." *Annales historiques de la Révolution française*, no. 55 (1983): 544–59.

Farmer, Sarah. *Martyred Village: Commemorating the 1944 Massacre at Oradour-sur-Glane*. Berkeley, CA, 1999.

Fouque, Joseph. *Mémoire justificatif pour Fouque, président, Faure, Boyer et Rémusat, juges, ci-devant au Tribunal criminel du département de Vaucluse, et Barjavel, Accusateur public, contre la dénonciation faite le 14 vendémiaire par la société de Carpentras*. N.p., an III [1794].

Friedrichs, Christopher R. "House-Destruction as a Ritual of Punishment in Early Modern Europe." *European History Quarterly* 50, no. 4 (2020): 599–624.

Gaven, Jean-Christophe. *Le crime de lèse-nation: Histoire d'une invention juridique et politique (1789–1791)*. Paris, 2016.

Ginzburg, Carlo. "Morelli, Freud, and Sherlock Holmes: Clues and Scientific Method." *History Workshop* 9, no. 1 (1980): 5–36.

Godfrey, James Logan. *Revolutionary Justice: A Study of the Organization, Personnel, and Procedure of the Paris Tribunal, 1793–1795*. Chapel Hill, NC, 1951.

Gomez–Le Chevanton, Corinne. "Juger Carrier, ou le droit à une vérité 'intentionnelle.'" In Leuwers, Martin, and Salas, "Juger la 'terreur,'" 35–46.

Gomez–Le Chevanton, Corinne. "Le procès Carrier: Enjeux politiques, pédagogie collective et construction mémorielle." *Annales historiques de la Révolution française*, no. 343 (2006): 73–92.

Greengrass, Mark. "Hidden Transcripts: Secret Histories and Personal Testimonies of Religious Violence in the French Wars of Religion." In *The Massacre in History*, edited by Mark Levene and Penny Roberts, 69–88. New York, 1999.

Greer, Donald. *The Incidence of the Terror during the French Revolution: A Statistical Interpretation*. Cambridge, MA, 1935.

Grégoire, Henri. *Essai historique et patriotique sur les arbres de la liberté*. Paris, 1794.

Grendi, Edoardo. "Micro-analisi e storia sociale." *Quaderni storici* 12, no. 35 (1977): 506–20.

Gueniffey, Patrice. *La politique de la Terreur: Essai sur la violence révolutionnaire, 1789–1794*. Paris, 2000.

Guilhamou, Jacques, and Martine Lapied. "La mission Maignet." *Annales historiques de la Révolution française*, no. 300 (1995): 283–94.

Harder, Mette. "A Second Terror: The Purges of French Revolutionary Legislators after Thermidor." *French Historical Studies* 38, no. 1 (2015): 33–60.

Herriot, Edouard. *Lyon n'est plus*. 4 vols. Paris, 1938.

Hunt, Lynn. *Politics, Culture, and Class in the French Revolution*. Berkeley, CA, 2004.

Jones, Colin. *The Fall of Robespierre: Twenty-Four Hours in Revolutionary Paris*. Oxford, 2021.

Jones, Peter. "*La République au Village* in the Southern Massif-Central, 1789–1799." *Historical Journal* 23, no. 4 (1980): 793–812.

Jourdan, Annie. *La Révolution française: Une histoire à repenser*. Paris, 2021.

Jugement rendu par le Tribunal révolutionnaire du département de Vaucluse qui déclare en état de contre-révolution la commune infame de Bédouin. Carpentras, an II [1794].

Kalyvas, Stathis. *The Logic of Violence in Civil War*. Cambridge, 2006.

Lapied, Martine. "La crise fédéraliste dans le 'ci-devant' Comtat." In *Les Fédéralismes: Réalités et représentations, 1789–1874; Actes du colloque de Marseille, septembre 1993*, edited by Centre Méridonal d'Histoire, 157–66. Aix-en-Provence, 1995.

Lapied, Martine. *Le Comtat et la Révolution française: Naissance des options collectives*. Aix-en-Provence, 1996.

Lefébure, Louis-François. *Justice contre Maignet, député à la Convention, destructeur de Bédoin*. N.p., n.d.

Le Gallo, Emile. "L'affaire de Bédoin." *La Révolution française* 41 (1901): 289–310.

Leuwers, Hervé, Virginie Martin, and Denis Salas, eds. "Juger la 'terreur': Justice transitionnelle et République de l'an III (1794–1795)." Special issue, *Histoire de la justice*, no. 32 (2021).

Linton, Marisa. *Choosing Terror: Virtue, Friendship, and Authenticity in the French Revolution*. Oxford, 2013.

Lucas, Colin. "The Problem of the Midi in the French Revolution." *Transactions of the Royal Historical Society* 28 (1978): 1–25.

Lucas, Colin. *The Structure of the Terror: The Example of Javogues and the Loire*. Oxford, 1973.

Lucas, Colin. "Violence thermidorienne et société traditionnelle: L'exemple du Forez." *Cahiers d'histoire* 20, no. 4 (1979): 3–43.

Luzzatto, Sergio. *L'automne de la Révolution: Luttes et cultures politiques dans la France thermidorienne*. Paris, 2001.

Maignet, Etienne. *Arrêté du représentant du peuple envoyé dans les départements des Bouches-du-Rhône et du Vaucluse, 9 germinal an II*. Marseille, 1794.

Maignet, Etienne. *Au nom du peuple français: Le représentant du peuple envoyé dans les départements des Bouches-du-Rhône et de Vaucluse . . . fait à Avignon, le 14 et 15 floréal*. Avignon, an II [1794].

Maignet, Etienne. *Au nom du peuple français—le représentant du peuple envoyé dans les départements des Bouches-du-Rhône et de Vaucluse . . . fait à Avignon, le 17 floréal*. Avignon, an II [1794].

Maignet, Etienne. *Compte rendu en exécution du décret du 21 nivôse, an III*. Paris, an III [1795].

Maignet, Etienne. *Instruction du représentant du peuple français, envoyé dans les départements des Bouches-du-Rhône et du Vaucluse, sur le gouvernement révolutionnaire*. Marseille, 1794.

Martin, Jean-Clément. "Le procès Carrier, un procès politique?" In *Les grands procès politiques: Une pédagogie collective*, edited by Emmanuel Le Roy Ladurie, 67–80. Paris, 2002.

Martin, Jean-Clément. *Nouvelle histoire de la Révolution française*. Paris, 2012.

Mason, Laura. "The 'Bosom of Proof': Criminal Justice and the Renewal of Oral Culture during the French Revolution." *Journal of Modern History* 6, no. 1 (2004): 29–61.

Mavidal, Jérôme, et al., eds. *Archives parlementaires de la Révolution française: Recueil complet des débats législatifs et politiques des chambres françaises.* 102 vols. Paris, 1875–2012.

McPhee, Peter. *Liberty or Death: The French Revolution.* New Haven, CT, 2016.

Mège, François, ed. *Les cahiers des paroisses d'Auvergne en 1789.* Clermont-Ferrand, 1899.

Moulinas, René. *Histoire de la Révolution d'Avignon.* Avignon, 1986.

Osiel, Mark. *Obeying Orders: Atrocity, Military Discipline, and the Law of War.* New York, 2017.

Ozouf, Mona. "Thermidor ou le travail de l'oubli." In *L'école de la France: Essais sur la Révolution, l'utopie et l'enseignement,* 91–108. Paris, 1984.

Pacini, Giulia. "'La Tigre Monarchique [et] l'Arbre de la République': Trees and the Body Politic in Revolutionary France." *Journal for Eighteenth-Century Studies* 41, no. 3 (2018): 407–25.

Popkin, Jeremy. Review of *La Révolution française: Une histoire à repenser,* by Annie Jourdan. *H-France Review* 23, no. 1 (2023). https://h-france.net/vol23reviews/vol23no1popkin.pdf.

Prudhomme, Louis Marie. *Histoire générale et impartiale des erreurs, des fautes et des crimes commis pendant la Révolution française à dater du 24 août 1787; contenant le nombre des individus qui ont péri par la Révolution.* 6 vols. Paris, an V.

Robespierre, Maximilien. "Pour la cloture des débats du Tribunal révolutionnaire après trois jours, 8 brumaire an II." In vol. 10 of *Œuvres complètes,* edited by Marc Bouloiseau and Albert Soboul, 159–61. Paris, 1967.

Robespierre, Maximilien. "Rapport sur les principes de morale politique." In vol. 10 of *Œuvres complètes,* edited by Marc Bouloiseau and Albert Soboul, 350–67. Paris, 1967.

Rovère, Joseph. *Correspondance intime du conventionnel Rovère avec Goupilleau (de Montaigu) en mission dans le Midi après la Terreur (1794–1795).* Edited by Michel Jouve. Nîmes, 1908.

Simonin, Anne. "Les acquittés de la Grande Terreur: Réflexions sur l'amitié dans la République." In *Les politiques de la Terreur, 1793–1794,* edited by Michel Biard, 183–205. Rennes, 2008.

Steinberg, Ronen. *The Afterlives of the Terror: Facing the Legacies of Mass Violence in Postrevolutionary France.* Ithaca, NY, 2019.

Steinberg, Ronen. "Terror on Trial: Accountability, Transitional Justice, and the *Affaire Le Bon* in Thermidorian France." *French Historical Studies* 39, no. 3 (2016): 419–44.

Suchet, Louis-Gabriel. *Patrie, égalité, liberté: L. G. Suchet, chef du quatrième bataillon de l'Ardèche à ses concitoyens.* Marseille, 1794.

Sutherland, D. M. G. *The French Revolution and Empire: The Quest for a Civic Order.* Oxford, 2003.

Sutherland, D. M. G. *Murder in Aubagne: Lynching, Law, and Justice during the French Revolution.* Cambridge, 2009.

Teitel, Ruti G. *Transitional Justice.* Oxford, 2002.

Vaillandet, P. "Après le 9 thermidor: Les débuts de la Terreur blanche en Vaucluse." *Annales historiques de la Révolution française,* no. 26 (1928): 109–27.

Vaillandet, P. "L'affaire de Bédoin." *Mémoires de l'Académie de Vaucluse* 30 (1930): 1–64.

Vaillandet, P. "Le procès des juges de la Commission populaire d'Orange." *Annales historiques de la Révolution française,* no. 32 (1929): 137–63.

Vaschalde, Henry. *Les volontaires de l'Ardèche, 1792–1793.* Paris, 1893.

Vovelle, Michel, ed. *Le tournant de l'an III: Réaction et Terreur blanche dans la France révolutionnaire.* Paris, 1997.

Wallon, Henri. *Histoire du tribunal révolutionnaire de Paris.* 6 vols. Paris, 1880–82.

Walton, Charles. *Policing Public Opinion in the French Revolution: The Culture of Calumny and the Problem of Free Speech.* Oxford, 2009.

Zizek, Joseph. "'Plume de Fer': Louis-Marie Prudhomme Writes the French Revolution." *French Historical Studies* 26, no. 4 (2003): 619–60.

"Brutal by Temperament and Taste"
Violence between Comrades in France's Armée d'Afrique, 1914–1918

CLAIRE ELDRIDGE

ABSTRACT   Central to the historiography of the First World War, scholarship on violence has focused on abstract and impersonal forms of violence between opposing forces or on more personal forms of violence between civilians and enemy combatants. In contrast, this article uses military justice archives to explore instances of serious interpersonal violence and sustained brutality between soldiers in the same combat unit. It provides a new vantage point to explore the complex entanglement of violence and camaraderie and how that played out in the specific context of France's multiethnic Armée d'Afrique. Unpacking the accusations, explanations, and justifications that emerge from multivocal military justice sources illustrates what it meant to commit and be criminalized for certain acts of violence in a context saturated with violence; how and where the line was drawn between acceptable and unacceptable conduct; and, most important, what violence reveals about individual combat experiences and relationships between comrades. Granting access to the perspectives and internal worlds of this diverse group of soldiers, many from racially and otherwise marginalized communities, military justice evidences a complicated and rich set of situational responses and social relationships that enhances our ability to reflect on the conflict's impact on the men caught up in it.

KEYWORDS   First World War, Armée d'Afrique, violence, military justice, empire

On the night of March 3, 1915, men from the Fifty-Fourth Company of the Second Régiment de Marche des Zouaves were trying to get some rest in their *cantonnement* or quarters. They were prevented from sleeping, however, by their intoxicated comrade, Lenhard, who was "causing a commotion." When their pleas to Lenhard to be quiet had no effect, the soldiers started throwing shoes and other objects at him. Things escalated rapidly, and officers were forced to intervene as Lenhard threatened those around him, stating his intention to take one particular *zouave* outside and slit his throat. In the *conseil de guerre*, or military tribunal, held in the wake of this incident, two *zouaves* testified that the initial "commotion" stemmed from them resisting Lenhard's attempt to force them to "commit acts against nature." Although he admitted being drunk and

French Historical Studies • Vol. 47, No. 2 (May 2024) • DOI 10.1215/00161071-11025079
Copyright 2024 by Society for French Historical Studies

that he might have "said a few stupid things," Lenhard, a European settler from the Algerian town of Oran, vehemently denied the accusations of sexual assault. Instead, he framed his behavior as part of normal banter between soldiers. The report submitted by his commanding officer painted a very different picture. "Brutal by temperament and taste," Lenhard was "the terror of his comrades," threatening them over the smallest matters, to the point that "they tremble before him." Not content with bullying his fellow soldiers, Lenhard also regularly menaced sergeants, captains, and other *gradés*. Indeed, since joining the military in 1906, Lenhard had accrued 260 days of punishments for minor offenses, mostly related to drunkenness and altercations with others, and had spent time in a disciplinary battalion, a rap sheet that would have done him no favors in the eyes of the tribunal judges. Found guilty of verbally assaulting and threatening his superiors, and of committing violence against a fellow *zouave*, Lenhard was sentenced to two years in a military prison.[1]

Using military justice archives, this article asks how we should situate and thus seek to comprehend the kinds of "brutal" behaviors of which Lenhard was accused, especially given the incredible levels of violence that formed the backdrop to his and other soldiers' daily lives between 1914 and 1918.[2] The multivocality of these sources, especially the inclusion of the voices and perspective of "ordinary" soldiers, enables the complexities of camaraderie to be explored in new ways, not least by thinking about how such relationships operated in the multiethnic divisions of France's Armée d'Afrique, where settlers like Lenhard served alongside metropolitan Frenchmen, naturalized Algerian Jews, and tens of thousands of colonized North Africans. Indeed, while the military understood and sought to deal with violence between their combatants in specific ways, the resultant judicial proceedings and associated documentation offer insights into a much broader spectrum of issues and behaviors. By granting access, often in unexpected ways, to the experiences and internal lives of this diverse group of combatants, many of whom came from racially and otherwise marginalized communities, military justice archives enable us to replace reductive characterization of men like Lenhard as simply "brutal by temperament and taste" with evidence of a complicated and rich set of situational responses and social relationships.

---

1. Service Historique de la Défense (henceforth SHD), GR 11 J 1548, Conseil de Guerre (henceforth CG), Lenhard, François Jean (2e bis RMZ, 45e DI).
2. Of an estimated 200,000 cases overall, 140,000 tribunal records survive. Organized by division, these sources constitute registers of "minutes" summarizing key information about the soldier, the crime, and the sentence passed. Each minute links to a *dossier de procédure* containing a more expansive set of paperwork generated during the *conseil de guerre* investigation and trial. Bach, *Justice militaire*, 155.

Conflict, Camaraderie, and Colonialism

The ferocious violence of the First World War is starkly visible in the conflict's statistics: of the 8.4 million men mobilized by France, some 1.3 million died, representing 3.4 percent of the entire French population. There were more than 3.5 million documented wounded, many of them injured more than once, while a million men faced the postwar world with some form of permanent disability.[3] The early stages of the fighting were the most brutal. During the first forty-five days, some six hundred thousand men were killed, wounded, imprisoned, or missing.[4] This figures included twenty-seven thousand soldiers killed on Saturday August 22, 1914, the bloodiest day in French military history up to that point.[5] That there was a "clear spatial, temporal and social structure to the exercise of lethal violence," meaning that these elements were not the same for all soldiers at all moments, does not alter the overriding point that this was, to use Anne Duménil's words, "a war of infinite violence."[6] Although initially notable for its absence from histories of the conflict, especially among scholars who were also veterans, violence is now firmly established within the historiography of the First World War. This scholarship has primarily focused on abstract, impersonal forms of violence between opposing forces or on more personal manifestations between civilians and enemy soldiers.[7] Almost no attention has been paid to violence between individuals in the same combat unit.[8] Indeed, the opposite of violence toward the enemy is often considered violence against the self, rather than against one's comrades.[9] Of course, no one has claimed the French Army was free from conflict. Tensions were inevitable given the conditions in which men from disparate social, cultural, and geographic backgrounds were forced to

---

3. Prost, *In the Wake of War*, 44–45; Delaporte, "Mutilation and Disfiguration."

4. Attal and Rolland, "La Justice militaire en 1914–1915," 134.

5. Saint-Fuscien, "End of the Great Military Leader?," 64.

6. Ziemann, *Violence and the German Soldier*, 21; Duménil, "Soldiers' Suffering and Military Justice," 44.

7. Among this vast literature, some particularly useful entry points for the French case are Audoin-Rouzeau and Becker, "Violence et consentement"; Cochet, *Survivre au front*; and Geyer, "Violence et expérience de la violence." For a broader overview, see Bourke, *Intimate History of Killing*. For literature on violence toward civilians, see Harris, "'Child of the Barbarian'"; Connolly, *Experience of Occupation in the Nord*, 37–66; and Audoin-Rouzeau, *L'enfant de l'ennemi*. The legacies of this violence have been explored most notably through critical engagement with George L. Mosse's theory that European societies were "brutalized" by the First World War, as argued in *Fallen Soldiers*. The most pertinent critiques of Mosse's work, for the purposes of this article, are Prost, "Les limites de la brutalisation"; Hassett and Moyd, "Introduction"; and Edele and Gerwarth, "Limits of Demobilization."

8. There has, however, been some work on violence, specifically interracial violence, between civilians on the same side, notably Tyler Stovall's investigation in "Color Line behind the Lines" of violence between metropolitan French and colonial workers on the home front.

9. See, e.g., claims made in Becker and Rousso, "D'un guerre l'autre," 71.

live and fight. Examples of the quotidian expressions of such frustrations litter the letters, diaries, and memoirs of metropolitan French soldiers that form the backbone of scholarship on camaraderie in the trenches.[10] Yet for all it is common to acknowledge that the French Army was "not a peaceful and harmonious institution" but rather one that "experienced outbursts, violence and threats, some of which were tacitly tolerated and others severely punished," the nature and implications of those "outbursts, violence and threats" and the military's reaction to them have yet to be explored in depth.[11]

Also frequently missing from the literature is a consideration of how interactions might have functioned when the language, religion, ethnicity, and relationship to "Frenchness" of the comrades in question differed from that of most combatants.[12] This is why it is particularly instructive to look at the three infantry divisions that made up France's Armée d'Afrique (the Thirty-Seventh, the Thirty-Eighth, and the Forty-Fifth). Normally garrisoned in North Africa, these divisions comprised European settlers, naturalized Algerian Jews, and colonized North African subjects alongside metropolitan Frenchmen. Recruits with French citizenship, including settlers and Algerian Jews, mostly served in *zouave* regiments, while colonized subjects were placed into *tirailleur* units, albeit with a centrally mandated quota of white French officers to oversee them. In the military, as in the empire, the subject/citizen distinction was used by the French Republic as a proxy for racial differentiation. The legal designation *colonial subject* should therefore be understood as referring to Arab or Berber combatants from North Africa, unless otherwise specified.

Contact between different Armée d'Afrique formations, on and off the battlefield, was not uncommon, especially following the creation of "mixed" *zouave* and *tirailleur* regiments from mid-1915. Much valuable work exists exploring the everyday impact of this imbrication of metropole and empire on colonial combatants. While the source base underpinning these studies is varied, incorporating postal censorship records, the press, and oral histories (albeit mainly focused on West African troops), the written words of French officers, colonial officials, and colonial politicians tend to feature prominently, which, given the imbalances

---

10. Such work was pioneered by Jacques Meyer in *La vie quotidienne des soldats pendant la Grande Guerre*. More recent examples include Maurin, *Armée, guerre, société*; Lafon, *La camaraderie au front*; Mariot, "Social Encounters in the French Trenches"; and Mariot, *Tous unis dans la tranchée?*

11. Cazals and Loez, *Dans les tranchées*, 226.

12. Often colonial troops are simply not discussed in the literature on camaraderie, where the default assumption remains that "the soldier" was a white, metropolitan Frenchman. On the rare occasions when combatants from the empire are mentioned, it is usually very briefly and as a category apart. For an example of the latter, see Alexandre Lafon's tellingly titled chapter "Des 'autres' comme camarades? Coloniaux, alliés et ennemis," in *La camaraderie au front*, 181–87.

in the records available, is understandable.[13] It is important to take these official and institutional perspectives into account, and much can be gleaned from attentive and critical readings of such top-down sources, as the extant scholarship demonstrates. But there are also limits, particularly in terms of what we can learn from, rather than simply about, colonial soldiers.

Military justice archives equally contain these kinds of top-down institutional documents that reflect what those in charge deemed a priority to prosecute and punish more than behavior on the ground. However, the inclusion of often extensive transcripts of interviews with and/or statements from the accused, victims, and witnesses gathered at different stages of the judicial process—during initial questioning at the moment of arrest and/or in the accused man's unit to establish what happened, as part of the inquiry to determine whether the soldier should be prosecuted, and as part of the tribunal itself—draws in an alternative set of perspectives. This makes military justice a valuable and underused source that amplifies a particularly unheard subset of voices: colonized combatants serving in the Armée d'Afrique. My approach to these documents owes much to the *monde du contact* paradigm advanced by Emmanuel Blanchard and Sylvie Thénault and to recent work on "contact zones" by Santanu Das, Anna Maguire, and Daniel Steinbach.[14] In contrast to the latter's focus on literary sources, however, the use of military justice sources expands the field of possible voices specifically to illiterate and non-French speaking soldiers. As I have argued elsewhere, these sources, although always mediated to some degree, especially in the case of soldiers who were illiterate and/or forced to communicate through an interpreter, still provide valuable insights into lives of colonized and otherwise marginalized soldiers who left almost no other firsthand documentation.[15]

Tracing the complex entanglement of violence and camaraderie articulated via military justice sources using units whose roots lie in the empire thus brings into conversation these three previously quite separate strands of historiography. Centering instances of serious interpersonal violence, such as assault and murder or sustained brutality, like that displayed by Lenhard, in the ranks of

---

13. Fogarty, *Race and War in France*, 13. Fogarty's work is a crucial reference point in an expanding body of literature exploring the French empire in the First World War. Other notable works include Andrews and Kanya-Forstner, "France, Africa, and the First World War"; Meynier, *L'Algérie révélée*; Michel, *L'appel à l'Afrique*, reprinted as *Les Africains et la Grande Guerre*; Echenberg, *Colonial Conscripts*; Lunn, *Memoirs of the Maelstrom*; Frémeaux, *Les colonies dans la Grande Guerre*; Mann, "Not Quite Citizens"; Recham, *Les Musulmans algériens*; Mann, *Native Sons*; and Hassett, *Mobilising Memory*.

14. Blanchard and Thénault, "Quel 'monde du contact'?"; Das, Maguire, and Steinbach, *Colonial Encounters*, esp. 1–34; Maguire, *Contact Zones of the First World War*.

15. Eldridge, "Conflict and Community in the Trenches." The best data on the socioeconomic profile of men brought before a *conseil de guerre* can be found in Emmanuel Saint-Fuscien's detailed statistical breakdown of the Third Infantry Division in *A vos ordres?*, 134–38.

men supposedly on the same side allows us to think through three interrelated questions: what it meant to commit and be criminalized for certain acts of violence in a context saturated with violence; how and where the line was drawn between acceptable, tolerable, and unacceptable conduct; and, most important, what violence reveals about individual combat experiences and relationships between comrades. Unpacking the accusations, explanations and justifications that emerge, essentially reading these official archives "against the grain," reveals the conditions, emotions, and experiences of serving soldiers, including information about metal health and same-sex sexual relationships that are difficult to find for soldiers in general but particularly scarce for colonized combatants. Surfacing material relating to the internal emotional worlds of colonized subjects broadens and deepens our historical portrait of "the soldier," contributing to the process of writing back in a group of combatants who are still largely considered a category apart, when they are considered at all.[16]

The article begins by mapping how unsanctioned violence in the French Army was defined, assessed, and prosecuted (or not) by military authorities during the Great War and the role that race and racialized thinking played in those processes. It demonstrates both how intersecting privileges associated with race, rank, and class worked to justify certain acts of violence and exonerate their perpetrators and how passive colonial knowledge was put into active practice to condemn other behaviors and other kinds of soldiers. Constructions generated "from above" by commanding officers and officials involved with military justice are then juxtaposed with the picture presented "from below" through the testimonies of men involved in altercations to show what happened when the complicating and messy categories of race, religion, and sexuality collided with apparently clear-cut military hierarchies and judicial categories and processes in highly pressured situations. What emerges from the case studies in the second half of the article, which focus on alcohol consumption, mental health, and same-sex sexual relationships among colonized soldiers, is that behaviors the military authorities were quick to attribute to innate character flaws might be better understood as situational responses to an incredibly stressful and violent daily environment that enhance our understanding of soldierly endurance and its limits. As well as offering a direct challenge to racialized understandings of colonized combatants, these records demonstrate that violent episodes the military dismissed as having "no motive" were in fact rooted in complex sets of

---

16. In addition to the texts cited above with respect to the French empire and the First World War, see Michelle Moyd's innovative work on the German East African context, particularly *Violent Intermediaries* and "Color Lines, Front Lines."

emotions and experiences that become visible as the soldiers in question were called on to explain themselves and their actions.

Defining the Boundary between Acceptable and Unacceptable Violence

The fundamental purpose of military justice was to maintain order, discipline, and thus cohesion under fire by prosecuting and punishing behavior that violated military norms and rules. What constituted a "crime" in the eyes of the French armed forces was outlined in the Code of Military Justice.[17] Minor infractions and petty offenses were dealt with internally by the soldier's unit, while more serious crimes and *délits* were brought before a *conseil de guerre* or tribunal. Conduct warranting a tribunal appearance covered acts that were crimes in civilian life, such as theft, assault, rape, and murder, as well as offenses specific to military life, such as refusing to obey an order, abandoning a post, and desertion.[18] Cases could be dismissed during the investigative stage before reaching a tribunal by way of a *non-lieu* decision. When it was deemed necessary to proceed to a full *conseil de guerre* hearing, a guilty verdict required a majority vote by at least three of the five judges, all of whom were serving officers of varying seniority. As in the civilian justice system, punishments ran the full gamut up to the death penalty, although most of those found guilty were given custodial sentences ranging from a few months to many years. France's acute manpower needs, however, meant that increasing numbers of these sentences were suspended to allow convicted men to return to the front lines, often presented as an opportunity for them to "redeem" themselves (*racheter la faute*).[19] Nonetheless, the stakes were high for soldiers, and prosecutions instilled considerable fear, as the military intended. These proceedings also represented a very public othering of the combatant, placing him outside the dominant norms of duty, honor, and self-sacrifice that were integral to military life and regimental reputations.[20]

17. First compiled in 1857, the code was not substantially altered until April 1916, when the introduction of "extenuating circumstances" and suspended sentences made the system more flexible. For the 1916 version of the code, see https://gallica.bnf.fr/ark:/12148/bpt6k6108631j.r=code%20de%20la%20justice%20militaire%201916?rk=42918;4.

18. Saint-Fuscien, "La justice militaire française," 116; Suard, "La justice militaire française," 149.

19. It is estimated that because of suspended sentences (*sursis*) and other changes introduced in 1916 only 10 percent of condemned men completed all or part of their sentences. Saint-Fuscien, *A vos ordres*, 189, 227.

20. In addition to André Bach's key reference text, *Justice militaire*, scholarship on this topic has been led by Saint-Fuscien, among whose many works "Juger et être jugé" and "Pourquoi obéit-on?" particularly inform my thinking here. Cases of *fusillés* (men executed by firing squad) and the campaigns to rehabilitate them are addressed in Bach, *Fusillés pour l'exemple*; Offenstadt, *Les fusillés de la Grande Guerre*; and Le Naour, *Fusillés*. For questions of authority and obedience, see Saint-Fuscien, *A vos ordres?*; and Smith, *Between Mutiny and Obedience*. On the 1917 mutinies, see in particular Pedroncini, *Les mutineries de 1917*; Loez, *14–18, les refus de la guerre*; and Rolland, *La grève des tranchées*. For a highly critical view of military justice, see Roux, *La Grande Guerre inconnue*, 216.

When defining violence, the military authorities made a clear distinction between the controlled and disciplined collective violence of the battlefield directed toward a common aim (the defeat of Germany) and the uncontrolled, unsanctioned violence of individual soldiers that threatened order, hierarchy, morale, and thus the effective functioning of a unit. However, this latter category encompassed a broad spectrum of behaviors, from the spontaneous physical articulation of daily frustrations, usually in the form of a punch, kick, or slap, all the way up to the taking of a human life in a premeditated fashion. Violence could be accidental, incurred while subduing an unruly or drunk comrade or when carrying out routine duties like cleaning a rifle, or committed in self-defense. The focus here is on serious forms of interpersonal violence covering the military justice charges of assault (*voies de fait*), aggravated assault/battery (*coups et blessures*), manslaughter (*homicide involontaire*), homicide (*homicide/ homicide volontaire*), murder (*meurtre*), and premeditated murder (*assassination*).[21] Excluded from the data set are threats (*outrages*), unless they also entailed the enactment of physical violence. Because this is a study of violence between comrades, cases of sexual assault or indecency (*viol* or *attentat à la pudeur*) against civilians are not considered, but accusations between soldiers are analyzed. Far less prevalent than prosecutions for the two dominant crimes of desertion or abandoning a post, the charges associated with violence listed above accounted for just over 4 percent ($n=245$) of *conseil de guerre* cases in the Armée d'Afrique between 1914 and 1919; in 40 percent of these cases the accused soldier(s) were colonized combatants. In terms of the severity of the violence, 8.7 percent of the altercations that were prosecuted involved the deliberate taking of another life.[22] Most incidents took place behind the lines, reflecting the overall distribution of crimes in both the Armée d'Afrique and the army more broadly.[23] Unsurprisingly, despite all these clearly defined categories, rules and procedures, the

21. For the punishments associated with these different crimes, see the post-1916 Code de Justice Militaire pour l'armée de terre: https://gallica.bnf.fr/ark:/12148/bpt6k6108631j?rk=300430;4.

22. There is some variation across the three divisions of the Armée d'Afrique, with charges associated with violence accounting for 5.94 percent of cases in the Thirty-Seventh Division, 3.88 percent in the Thirty-Eighth Division, and 3.67 percent in the Forty-Fifth Division. The overall figure for the Armée d'Afrique is 4.16 percent. There is also racial variation, with colonized soldiers accounting for 58 percent, 49 percent, and 26 percent, respectively in the Thirty-Seventh, Thirty-Eighth, and Forty-Fifth divisions. Excluded from these statistics are *non-lieu* cases that were investigated but dismissed before they reached the tribunal stage. These figures are based on as complete a survey of the archives as possible, but limitations on access to military justice files at the SHD since 2020, caused by the pandemic and other factors, may have kept me from identifying a few cases.

23. In his work on the Third Infantry Division, Saint-Fuscien estimates that in 1914 at least 80 percent of men were judged for crimes in the combat zone, such as "abandoning a post in the presence of the enemy." In 1918 the opposite was true, with at least 75 percent of tribunal decisions concerning actions in noncombat zones. The *cantonnement* and its environs were the prime locations for rule breaking. Saint-Fuscien, "Pourquoi obéit-on?," 9; Saint-Fuscien, *A vos ordres*, 102–7.

actual application of military justice was context dependent and subjective, not least because many of the relevant decisions were made by officers who were also serving at the front.[24] Exploring the gap that often existed between the letter of the law, as set down by the Code of Military Justice, and how things operated on the ground reveals what behaviors were and were not considered acceptable and under what circumstances. Central to such determinations were perceptions of the accused as articulated by those with higher ranks—assessments that, in turn, highlight the priorities and concerns of military authorities at particular moments in the conflict.

At the most basic level, what was tolerable remains invisible, the incidents and infractions never written up. Accused of striking an inferior he deemed to have been insubordinate, Corporal Gibergy was asked if there were a lot of "troublemakers" (*mauvais têtes*) in his company of *zouaves*. Gesturing to this invisible hinterland of behavior that was challenging but not sufficiently serious to warrant further measures, Gibergy replied, "There are a great number, and the exercise of command is therefore made very difficult."[25] Gibergy's case equally points to one of the most obvious lines between acceptable and unacceptable behavior: violence that violated the military hierarchy.

The 1857 Code of Military Justice, which remained in force until 1916, was founded on the "full submission" of the soldier to an order, any order, emanating from a superior without hesitation or murmur as their first duty and the sine qua non on which the strength of the army rested. From the moment they enlisted, and long before they reached a battlefield, all recruits were thus subjected to extremely severe discipline designed to ensure they accepted the constraints and rigors of military life.[26] Given the sanctity of command structures and the imperative to maintain respect for this fundamental martial principle, violence committed by rank-and-file soldiers against their superiors was thus regularly and harshly punished. Such transgressions were compounded, in the case of the Armée d'Afrique, by the intersection of racial and military hierarchies that frequently created scenarios in which colonized subjects were accused of attacking white European officers. Returning to quarters for evening roll call on June 21, 1915, the *tirailleur* Bouhaka, who had been drinking—although not, he claimed,

24. With respect to the British and German armies, there is some excellent work on these issues, such as Duménil, "En marge du combat?"; Jahr, "War, Discipline, and Politics"; and Jahr, "Désertion et déserteurs."

25. SHD, GR 11 J 1322, CG, Gibergy, Léon Alexis (3e RMZ, 37e DI), "Procès verbal d'interrogatoire: Gibergy, Léon Alexis," Jan. 28, 1916. Gibergy was found not guilty.

26. Roynette also notes, however, that the military, although the most severe institution, was not the only one in the Third Republic to pursue such a philosophy (*Bons pour le service*, 343). Schools also had very coercive and harsh disciplinary regimes, as did many workplaces.

to the point of being inebriated—got into a fight with another *tirailleur*. Stepping in to separate the two men, Corporal Mariano received several blows. The corporal presented this as an attack on him by Bouhaka, whereas the *tirailleur* stated that in the melee Mariano struck him on the nose and he returned the blow "instinctively," without knowing exactly whom he was hitting. Found guilty of battery, assault against a superior, and "obvious and public drunkenness," Bouhaka was sentenced to eight years' hard labor, a strikingly harsh sentence, even considering the long list of minor punishments he had incurred since enrolling with the army in 1904.[27]

More complex were cases of violence committed by superiors against men under their command. While officers were within their rights to chastise their men, and even to "strike" (*frapper*) an inferior in defense of the self or others, to "rally" deserters, or prevent acts of pillage, clear limits were placed on such behavior, at least in theory.[28] Prosecutions for breaking these rules were certainly rare, and even when brought to a *conseil de guerre*, the superiors in question were almost never convicted. The *adjudant* Sarrazin, for example, was found not guilty of assault despite admitting to caning a soldier, who refused to undertake a work detail behind the lines, so hard he was incapacitated for more than thirty days.[29] However, references by soldiers to the use of physical force by their superiors were commonplace. Multiple dossiers mention blows distributed when issuing orders and ensuring these were carried out, or as an accompaniment to verbal warnings about behavior. Soldiers also reported being manhandled to hurry them along during marches and work tasks, or as they were transported to disciplinary spaces. Rank-and-file soldiers accused of insulting or assaulting a superior often stated in their defense that the officer in question had struck them either first or as well. Writing to the commander of the Forty-Fifth Division on March 27, 1915, about an assault charge brought against the *tirailleur* Mohamed for attacking his superior, the quartermaster Déguero, the tribunal's *commissaire rapporteur* noted that the accused *tirailleur* claimed he had been kicked and punched by Déguero after he stopped to adjust his uniform while en route to his work duties. The *commissaire* then asked the general if "it might be a good idea" to also charge the corporal in accordance with the military code. Clearly the general agreed, as Déguero, a settler from Algiers, was subsequently found guilty and sentenced to two months in prison. But without the intervention of the *commissaire*, this act would likely have gone unpunished.[30] Indeed, this is

27. SHD, GR 11 J 1550, CG, Bouhaka, Bouzira ould Mohammed (1er RMTA, 45e DI).
28. SHD, GR 19 N 298, n. 3190, "Du général commandant en chef à M. le général de l'armée," Sept. 1, 1914. Quoted in Saint-Fuscien, *A vos ordres?*, 210.
29. SHD, GR 11 J 1568, CG, Sarrazin, Louis (3e BMILA, 45e DI).
30. SHD, GR 11 J 1548, CG, Déguero, François (1er RMTA, 45e DI), "Le Capitaine Cusa, commissaire rapporteur près du Conseil de guerre de la 45e Division à M. le Général Commandant la 45e Division," Mar.

the only example I have found in the Armée d'Afrique where accusations of violence by a superior raised by an already accused inferior were followed up. Normally, any such claims arising from soldiers' testimonies were discredited, discounted, or simply ignored in reports by commanding officers and in the *commissaire rapporteur*'s summative "report of the affair."[31]

A key consideration for the military authorities when deciding where to draw the line between acceptable and unacceptable behavior was the perceived character of the accused. Being deemed a "good" soldier was a clear asset in the military justice process. In several cases, soldiers accused of violent acts were found not guilty or had their cases dismissed before they reached the tribunal stage based on previous or subsequent bravery in battle. Such acts were taken as evidence of the accused soldier's willingness to "redeem their fault" and their ability to be reintegrated back into the unit.[32] One of the most explicit statements of the logic underpinning such decisions can be found in the not-guilty verdict handed to the aforementioned Corporal Gibergy who was charged with striking an inferior, a *zouave* named Latil. On January 21, 1916, a soldier from another section came to distribute packets of tobacco. As leader of his unit, Gibergy was asked how many packets of tobacco were required. When he answered eleven, Latil interrupted to say that the section had only ten men. Furious at the intervention, Gibergy slapped Latil with the back of his left hand. Latil went straight to the captain to report the incident, which Gibergy immediately admitted to. Expressing regret, Gibergy described the slap as "an almost unconscious gesture" prompted by Latil's "habit of meddling in an irritating manner" and compounded by the fact that Latil's words "made me out to be a thief." At the time of the incident, Gibergy continued, Latil happened to have his head bent toward him, which favored a "brusque movement" that he was "not able to repress."[33]

27, 1915. Déguero appears variously in the file as Déguiro and Séguiro. Mohamed was ultimately acquitted of "violence against superiors." SHD, GR 11 J 1548, CG, Ahmed ben Mohamed (6e RMT, 45e DI).

31. Based on his study of the Third Infantry Division, Saint-Fuscien argues that before spring 1916 there were "no mentions of 'punches' or 'shoves' by superiors in court martial records" and that defendants never complained about such acts, which were never cited in their defense. He attributes the shift in 1916 to changing norms surrounding the role of the officer in the face of lengthy, arduous, and costly offensives and mounting concerns regarding the morale of the troops. While traditional martial masculine traits such as courage and sangfroid remained in place, these were now supplemented by the requirement that officers show care and concern for their men if they wished to retain their respect and obedience. This timeline does not hold for the Armée d'Afrique, as demonstrated by the cases of Gibergy (Jan. 1916) and Déguero (Mar. 1915), among others. While this does not necessarily undermine Saint-Fuscien's wider claim that brutality by officers became less acceptable as the war progressed, it is a useful reminder that each division possessed its own culture, of which discipline was part. See "End of the Great Military Leader?," 68–70.

32. See, e.g., SHD, GR 11 J 1320, CG, Pipi, Marcel François Auguste (2e RMZ, 37e DI). This was also a feature of German military justice, as outlined in Duménil, "En marge du combat?," 105–8.

33. SHD, GR 11 J 1322, Gibergy, "Procès-verbal d'interrogatoire: Gibergy, Léon," Jan. 28, 1916.

In his report of the incident, Captain Richardot accepted that the violence displayed by Gibergy was "obviously condemnable," even more so because Latil was "a good soldier . . . a peaceful and calm man." Nonetheless, Richardot asserted, "mitigating circumstances are clearly present." These included testimonies expressing surprise that Gibergy was being held in detention over this incident since he did not have a reputation for mistreating his men; Gibergy's almost entirely clean rap sheet save for one minor punishment from November 20, 1914, prior to his promotion to corporal; and Latil's own statement that he wished he had not filed a complaint "especially as the corporal is a brave and energetic man who has proven himself." This final point was clearly pivotal since, having outlined the extenuating factors, Captain Richardot added that even if Gibergy had shown himself to be "brutal" in this instance, "his violent nature may have been (let us not forget) a factor in the ferocious bravery with which he has already fought and which has earned him a *médaille militaire*."[34] This decoration and the accompanying citation, in Richardot's eyes, shed a "singular light" on Gibergy's temperament, leading him to conclude that "in this hand-to-hand [*coups-à-coups*] war of the trenches, when the often indomitable tenacity that must be deployed to take or keep a piece [of territory] requires true savagery, temperaments like Corporal Gibergy's deserve their share of consideration."[35]

Obliged by procedural rules to refer the incident to a *conseil de guerre*, Richardot nonetheless made an explicit case for leniency toward Gibergy. This suggests a tacit admission by the military of the brutalizing nature of fighting in the trenches, an admission that, since the army needed men willing to use violence, they also had to accept that sometimes those behaviors would spill out beyond the battlefield, including among those with the challenging task of maintaining order in the ranks in the midst of these very difficult conditions. Although we do not have access to the deliberations of the tribunal judges, their unanimous not-guilty verdict indicates they found Richardot's entreaties persuasive. Gibergy's case thus demonstrates that a soldier's perceived value to the military effort could redefine the boundary between acceptable and unacceptable violence and take precedence over rendering justice to a victim. Consideration was given bravery and good conduct prior to and immediately following a violent offense, because this suggested the potential for the accused soldier to (re)conform to the dominant masculine martial tropes of courage, self-discipline—or at least a militarily

34. Gibergy received not only a *médaille militaire* but also a *croix de guerre* with distinction (*palmes*) for bravery, including lack of concern for his own safety, during combat on February 17–18, 1915.

35. SHD, GR 11 J 1322, Gibergy, "Rapport du Capitaine Richardot, Commandant la 4e Compagnie de 3e Régiment de Zouaves," n.d. The mitigating evidence Richardot mentioned is drawn from "Procès-verbal d'information: Sotton, Pierre," Jan. 28, 1916; "Relevé des punitions: Gibergy, Léon"; and "Procès-verbal d'information: Latil, Emile," Jan. 28, 1916.

valuable loss of self-discipline in the case of Gibergy's "ferocious bravery" in battle—and a willingness to risk one's life for the *patrie*.[36]

Although not explicitly named, race, alongside other structural privileges, almost certainly shaped how Gibergy's violence was perceived. The "savagery" for which he was praised would likely have been read very differently had he not been a white, metropolitan Frenchman from Allevard, near Grenoble. As the existing scholarship has demonstrated, acknowledgment of praiseworthy masculine battlefield virtues sat alongside racist fears that the supposed "barbarity" of "uncivilized" African combatants—which made them such effective fighters, according to dominant ideologies—could be turned against the French at any moment unless carefully controlled and appropriately directed at all times.[37] As a result, judgments regarding violence involving colonized soldiers could be particularly charged.

Although the precise impact of race can be difficult to parse, especially in terms of causality, because it was one of multiple intersecting factors in any given scenario, a set of case studies that usefully point to how race informed military thinking as well as judicial processes and outcomes is violence perceived to be connected to same-sex sexual relations. We can see this in the case of the *tirailleur* Moktar, for example, who was tried for one count of premeditated murder and two charges of attempted murder. Although the tribunal could not determine unequivocally the precise relationship between the men involved, Moktar's reputation as an "impure [*immonde*] individual" and an "inveterate pederast" (a term used frequently by the military at this time as a synonym for *homosexual*) played a significant role in awarding the harshest possible punishment: military degradation and the death penalty. The strength of the tribunal's feeling was underlined by the *commissaire rapporteur*'s summary report, which, unusually, included the personal comment that he was "entirely in agreement" with the view expressed by the judges. The *commissaire* went on to specify that "human life is too valuable, above all in times of war, to defer to filthy passions," before concluding that "an act of this nature risks being badly interpreted by our indigenous troops."[38]

Sex between men was not a crime, either in civil society or in the military, sodomy having been decriminalized in 1791 by the Revolutionary Constituent

36. A similar set of logics and outcome can be found in the case of Lieutenant Jean Beaudemoulin, whose "abuse of authority" accusation was dropped before it reached the tribunal stage. See SHD, GR 11 J 1350, Non-lieu (henceforth NL), Beaudemoulin, Jean (2e RMZ, 37e DI).

37. The most famous text to articulate this view is Mangin, *La force noire*. For a more extensive discussion of these ambiguities, see Fogarty, *Race and War in France*, 55–96.

38. SHD, GR 11 J 1323, CG, Moktar, Salem ben Tidjani (2e RMTA, 37e DI), "Rapport sur l'affaire," July 3, 1916.

Assembly. Military justice therefore became involved only in instances of sexual assault or indecency, or when (accusations of) same-sex sexual relationships led to some form of violent altercation. In the latter case, which was much more common, it was the rule breaking associated with the violence that was prosecuted, the purported relationships serving as explanatory or background context, as the example of Moktar illustrates.[39] This encapsulates the ambiguity in the military's stance toward same-sex sexual relationships. As in wider society, homosexuality remained highly stigmatized in the French armed forces in the early twentieth century, particularly because of its association with "feminine" characteristics that stood in direct opposition to martial masculine ideals, rendering the soldier in question a "suspect comrade" on multiple levels.[40] What military authorities feared most was the supposed contagious potential of homosexuality to "infect" "normal" soldiers and thus undermine the morale, cohesion, and effectiveness of their troops, as alluded to in the *commissaire*'s comment about the risk of Moktar's actions being "badly interpreted by our indigenous troops." At the same time, the military could not stop such relationships from forming. Indeed, the social promiscuity of these intense, all-male environments may have actively facilitated them, producing a fluid and porous spectrum of behaviors that stood in contrast to the binary categories that structured dominant societal norms. Jason Crouthamel's argument that comradeship in the German army functioned as an "umbrella concept under which men with different perceptions of emotional and sexual norms found inclusion" is thus equally applicable to the French context.[41] Nor did the French Army show much zeal in punishing such practices, generally preferring to turn a blind eye, certainly during wartime when more urgent matters took priority[42]—until, that is, these sexual encounters disrupted the normal functioning of the unit, at which point soldiers like Moktar and their behavior crossed the line from tolerable to unacceptable.[43]

What the *commissaire* also made explicit in his report was the racialized framing of Moktar's behavior through his assertion that "the nationality of the

39. Data from the Armée d'Afrique bear out Saint-Fuscien's observation that crimes concerning morals were rare at the level of the *conseil de guerre* (*A vos ordres?*, 140–41). Across the three divisions there is only one case of a prosecution for indecent assault (*attentat à la pudeur*) in which the victim was a fellow soldier; the charge was dismissed by means of a *non-lieu* decision. See SHD, GR 11 J 1348, NL, Brahim, Ben Ali (2e RMT—Brigade du Maroc, 37e DI).

40. For examples of this stigmatization in practice, see Revenin, *Homosexualité et prostitution masculines à Paris*, 136. For an alternative perspective, Florence Tamagne in *Histoire de l'homosexualité en Europe* argues that homosexuality acquired a new and more positive visibility during the First World War as part of the "fraternity of the trenches."

41. Crouthamel, *Intimate History of the Front*, 3, 46–61.

42. For further discussion, see Tamagne, "Guerre et homosexualité," 124, 127.

43. Jackson, *One of the Boys*, makes a similar argument with respect to homosexuality in the Canadian military in the Second World War.

accused [who was Tunisian] cannot be an attenuating factor since Arab law punishes masturbation with the death penalty."[44] This statement gestures to the contradictory colonial beliefs that homosexuality was endemic among North African Muslims yet also forbidden by a religion whose concept of "justice" was brutal, irrational, and excessive, in implicit contrast to the French system. The link between sexual licentiousness and the empire, in which hot climates were deemed to provoke sexual "excesses," was firmly embedded in the French cultural imaginary by 1914. Practices such as sodomy, often referred to as the "Oriental vice," were especially strongly associated with France's North African territories and with the Armée d'Afrique garrisoned there. Robert Aldrich opens his book on colonialism and homosexuality by noting that "in French slang, *'faire passer son brevet colonial'* . . . meant to initiate [a soldier] into sodomy."[45] Much ink was spilled by military officials and medics over the potential for French soldiers to be corrupted by the supposed sexual deviancy of Arab men, especially given the lack of European women in these colonial spaces, and the risk of such contagion spreading to the metropole. The Armée d'Afrique's infamous disciplinary battalions and colonial prisons or *bagnes*, known colloquially as *biribi*, served as a prominent focal point for such anxieties.[46]

As men of their time and milieu, officers like the *commissaire rapporteur* cited above were impregnated with these ideas and associated racial stereotypes, which in turn shaped how they understood and judged the behavior of soldiers in the Armée d'Afrique. While same-sex sexual relations occurred between soldiers of all races and ethnicities, and indeed, ranks, in the army, it is telling that all but two of the *conseil de guerre* cases in the Armée d'Afrique where this is a factor pertain to soldiers who were colonized subjects.[47] Moreover, the two exceptions involving French citizens relate to the Algerian-born settler Lenhard, whose story opened this article, and a naturalized Algerian Jew.[48] This implies a

---

44. SHD, GR 11 J 1323, Moktar, "Rapport sur l'affaire," July 3, 1916.

45. Aldrich, *Colonialism and Homosexuality*, 1.

46. For further discussion of these ideas and their prevalence, see Joly, "Sexe, guerres et désir colonial"; Aldrich, "Colonial Man"; and Kalifa, *Biribi*, esp. 265–86.

47. Perceptions and judgments regarding homosocial relations between soldiers were inflected by class as well as race, with different standards applied to officers and the rank and file. Perhaps the most obvious and commented-on example is Marshall Hubert Lyautey, who served as resident-general of Morocco (1912–16, 1917–25) and minister of war (1916–17). His sexual proclivities were endlessly speculated on without apparent detriment to his military career.

48. Neither man was brought up on a sexual assault charge. Instead, both were accused of violence against a fellow *zouave*. The purported sexual advances that apparently underpinned this violence emerged only through reports and testimony. SHD, GR 11 J 1548, Lenhard; SHD, GR 11 J 1555, CG, Chouraqui, Abraham (3e bis RMZ, 45e DI).

certain instability between citizenship status and identity, particularly regarding perceptions of "Frenchness" that applied to combatants who were colonial citizens (as opposed to colonized subjects) from North Africa.[49] Given that bodies are prime sites through which "imperial and colonial power was imagined and exercised," cases like Moktar's also demonstrate the complex intersections of race, masculinity, and empire.[50] By attesting to the perceived inability of soldiers from North Africa to master their "baser" instincts and control their behavior more generally, *conseil de guerre* prosecutions both reflected and reinforced existing notions that "French" masculinity existed on a higher plane "shaped by civilization as well as racial superiority."[51] Military justice records thus offer a valuable perspective on how passive colonial knowledge was put into active practice as decisions were made about where to draw the line between acceptable and unacceptable violence.[52]

Moktar's actions were presented as deriving from innate "flaws" linked to his racial identity, demonstrating that when deciding which violations of the rules and norms could be tolerated and which had to be punished, the man mattered as much as, and sometimes more than, the crime. Gibergy's slap could be dismissed by the military authorities as an isolated incident, an aberration amid an otherwise correctly directed (as in toward the enemy) and therefore militarily valuable enactment of violence, an interpretation shored up by Gibergy's race and rank. In contrast, unsanctioned violence among ordinary soldiers stemming from "pathologies," like those attributed to Moktar, was deemed much more threatening because it was thought to be rooted in a "degeneracy" that suggested the soldier in question was irrecuperable. Habitually violent soldiers like the "brutal by temperament and taste" *zouave* Lenhard, who bullied and terrorized both his comrades and his superiors equally, fell into this category, as did men who persistently abused alcohol.[53] But how did the soldiers themselves understand and seek to explain the violent acts they were accused of committing, and what do their explanations tell us about their experiences more broadly?

49. Among the literature on this subject, see in particular Zack, "French and Algerian Identities in Formation"; Sivan, "Colonialism and Popular Culture in Algeria"; Yedes, "Social Dynamics in Colonial Algeria"; and Eldridge, "'The Forgotten of This Tribute.'"

50. Burton and Ballantyne, "Introduction," 6. Although Foucault omitted the colonial from his analysis (*La volonté de savoir*), the other obvious reference point here is his concept of biopower.

51. Aldrich, "Colonial Man," 125, 135.

52. Steinbach, "Between Intimacy and Violence," 100–101.

53. Terms such as *pathology* and *degeneracy* occur frequently in medical and judicial discussions from this era, particularly in connection with soldiers deemed in some way failing to fulfill their duties. See, e.g., Porot and Hesnard, *L'expertise mentale militaire*; Roux, "Les mutilations volontaires par coup de feu"; and Brousseau, "Essai sur la peur aux armées."

Situational Responses and the Toll of War

Generally absent from the military's assessments in cases like those outlined above was any acknowledgment that the conditions under which combatants lived might play a role in their violent acts, any suggestion that the triggers for their behaviors might be, at least in part, situational rather than simply inherent and immutable. Yet if we switch from a top-down to a bottom-up perspective on violence and center the voices and perspectives of the soldiers themselves, a different picture emerges. By paying attention to the testimonies of those most directly implicated, we get a sense, albeit mediated and imperfect, of their experiences of and responses to war. Using testimonies gathered from the accused, victims, and witnesses at the different moments in the investigative process, we can see how soldiers framed and justified their actions, often challenging externally imposed characterizations in the process. Whereas military authorities rarely linked violent behavior to the stresses and strains of sustained and extremely violent warfare, the impact of the wider conflict on their well-being and their everyday relationships features prominently in accounts from accused men. Their testimonies thus provide valuable insights into the complex social and emotional worlds of combatants, particularly colonized North Africans for whom, as already noted, we lack the kind of textual first-person narratives available for many other groups of combatants.

The atrocious conditions of trench warfare, the stress associated with the near-constant risk of death or injury, and the constraints exercised by the endless rules and tasks imposed by the military hierarchy created an ideal breeding ground for friction between soldiers. It was therefore not uncommon for tempers to flare, such as when the *zouave* Quevauvilliers struck his corporal in the face after the latter refused to return a nail file Quevauvilliers claimed belonged to him.[54] Incidents of momentary aggression could equally occur between friends. During a "brawl" among a group of drunken *zouaves*, the nineteen-year-old soldier Bertin was hit twice in the side by his otherwise close friend Navas, a settler from Algiers. Dismissing the incident as just a couple of punches, Bertin took himself off to bed. Only the next morning did he realize that Navas had stabbed him. Bertin downplayed the incident, possibly to protect his friend, stressing that "my wound wasn't serious," since despite having to see the medic, he could resume his duties immediately. He concluded his testimony by asserting, "Now, Navas and I, who have always been good comrades, we've reconciled."[55] Tensions

---

54. SHD, GR 11 J 1370, CG, Quevauvilliers, Georges (4e RMZT, 38e DI).

55. SHD, GR 11 J 1319, CG, Navas, Georges (9e RMZ, 37e DI), "Procès-verbal d'information: Bertin, Eugène," Apr. 5, 1915. Bertin's testimony probably contributed to the not-guilty verdict handed down by the tribunal, especially as it countered assertions by Navas's commanding officer that he was a quarrelsome drunk unable to "let a meal pass without getting himself into a drunken state." But other contextual information would have played a part, including the fact that Navas was also deemed someone who "has always

could be especially pronounced in colonial units because military authorities assumed a homogeneity among colonized soldiers from North Africa that ignored the many social, political, ethnic, and linguistic differences between these combatants. Furthermore, such units were often led by officers with little to no knowledge of the religious customs, languages, and cultures of the men under their command whom they viewed simply as "Arabs" or "Muslims."[56] "Tempers might have been improved," David Englander suggests, "had the *poilu* been better able to get away from it all." But leave allocations rarely functioned smoothly or regularly and were, in any case, applied differently to troops from North Africa.[57]

Even if some soldiers came from worlds in which physical violence was an accepted way of settling disagreements,[58] what raised the stakes, very considerably, between 1914 and 1918 was their easy access to deadly weaponry. Minor altercations over mundane things could thus escalate rapidly, sometimes with tragic consequences. The indigenous sergeant Smizzi, for example, almost lost his life when the *tirailleur* Maoui fired his rifle at him in retaliation for breaking up a card game earlier in the day.[59] The *tirailleur* Belhacène had a similarly lucky escape after being shot at by his comrade Kaddour when a prior dispute, once again over a card game, was reignited by Belhacène helping himself without permission to food Kaddour had prepared for himself.[60] During a discussion over whose turn it was to undertake guard duty, the *tirailleur* Aoujène suddenly took a knife from his pocket and struck the *tirailleur* Chériti near his heart.[61] Chériti survived, but his fellow *tirailleur* Boualeg bled out instantly after he was stabbed in the chest by the soldier Guendouze, who took exception to a casual comment Boualeg made about the difference between their respective time at the front line.[62] In these and many other instances, the aggressiveness of the response from the soldier in question appears disproportionate to the initial trigger, suggesting men struggling to cope. Indeed, one way of interpreting the willful infliction of violence on fellow soldiers is to see it as evidence of the tendency of soldiers

given satisfaction and completed his duties as a liaison agent with zeal" and that no one actually saw him use a knife on Bertin.

56. Meynier, *L'Algérie révélée*, 448; Dean, "French Colonial Army and the Great War," 491–93.

57. Englander, "French Soldier," 57. The most detailed account of leave policies and their application can be found in Cronier, *Permissionnaires dans la Grande Guerre*. For a discussion of the specificities of leave for colonial combatants, see Eldridge, "Absence, Agency, and Empire."

58. Cochet, *Survivre au front*, 35–37.

59. SHD, GR 11 J 1547, CG, Maoui, ben Ali Zirda (3e RMZT, 45e DI).

60. SHD, GR 11 J 1325, CG, Kaddour, Sayah (3e RMTA, 37e DI).

61. SHD, GR 11 J 1319, CG, Aoujène, Mohamed ben Belkacem (2e RMTA, 37e DI).

62. SHD, GR 11 J 1321, CG, Guendouze, Mezeghiche (3e RMTA, 37e DI). Counterintuitively, Guendouze was the more experienced soldier, and Boualeg seems to have been simply speculating on how much longer it would take him to acquire the same degree of front-line knowledge.

to become emotionally numb and indifferent, even fatalistic, as a psychological response to their daily conditions, especially as the war lengthened.[63]

Excessive alcohol consumption was ubiquitous in these kinds of cases of violence between soldiers. Drinking was a staple feature of French life prior to the First World War, particularly among rural and urban working-class communities.[64] Although forbidden by the Qur'an and socially frowned on, alcohol was equally present in North Africa, again especially among young men in urban settings.[65] Accustomed to alcohol in their civilian lives, many soldiers, including colonized Muslim combatants, continued to drink after their incorporation into the army. Indeed, the military actively supplied their troops with alcohol in various guises and in progressively greater quantities. Wine, especially the lower strength *pinard*, was considered a hygienic beverage and constituted a particular dietary staple.[66] Military authorities believed that alcohol served a range of beneficial, even necessary functions, such as combating cold, fear, or boredom; lowering inhibitions and thus encouraging aggressivity during assaults; and bolstering morale. Soldiers fully agreed that alcohol was vital to their service, and much has been written about the symbolic and material significance of *pinard* to the *poilu* identity.[67] Comforting, ritualistic, and easily shared, alcohol facilitated sociability, helping build comradeship and thus undergirding soldierly endurance.[68] Yet it equally caused tensions and even broke relationships between men. Asked why, "out of the blue," he had hit a fellow *tirailleur* several times in the head with the foot of a bedstead, the *tirailleur* Bouhamla replied: "I was taken with drink. . . . He owed me 10 francs for some time. I very much regret my act."[69] Bouhamla's victim required hospital treatment, but he was luckier than the *tirailleur* Bettioni, who was killed when a bayonet, wielded by his comrade Boussebie, struck him in the region of his heart. Despite proroguing the original *conseil de guerre* so more information could be collected, the

63. Crouthamel, *Intimate History*, 58.

64. Between 1910 and 1913 the average annual consumption of wine in metropolitan France was estimated to be 128 liters per person, rising to 200 liters for urban and working-class *départements* like the Seine. This was alongside an average annual consumption of 33 liters of beer, 34 liters of cider, and just over 4 liters of spirits. Lucand, *Le pinard des poilus*, 19; Nourisson, *Le buveur du XIXe siècle*, 24–27.

65. For discussion of drinking culture in North Africa, see Znaien, "Les territoires de l'alcool à Tunis et à Casablanca"; White, *Blood of the Colony*; Pinaud, *L'alcoolisme chez les Arabes en Algérie*; and Sheikh and Islam, "Islam, Alcohol, and Identity."

66. Starting at one-quarter liter a day for men at the front lines, the ration was extended six months later to soldiers behind the lines. In 1916 the ration was increased to half a liter, rising again in January 1918 to one liter, half of it provided free and half sold to the soldier at a price below the going rate. Fillaut, "Lutte contre l'alcoolisme," 144.

67. In addition to the already cited works, see Ridel, *L'ivresse du soldat*; Cochet, "1914–1918"; and Zientek, "Wine and Blood."

68. Lucand, *Le pinard des poilus*, 18, 77.

69. SHD, GR 11 J 1322, CG, Bouhamla, Abdallah ben (2e RMTA, 37e DI). Found guilty of "aggravated assault," Bouhamla was sentenced to one year in prison.

tribunal could not get to the bottom of the quarrel between the two men that had led to the fatal stabbing. All parties concerned, however, agreed that Boussebie was drunk and that, although generally a good soldier and "not mean," "he frequently got drunk and in those moments he was violent and quarrelsome."[70]

Drinking undoubtedly fueled altercations. Yet alcohol, and particularly the abuse of it, was also a response to the environment in which soldiers found themselves, a sign of men seeking to anesthetize themselves against conditions they found difficult to endure. As the author of a postal control report from November 1916 wrote: "The habit of getting drunk in the *cantonment* is general. . . . It seems that the men console themselves for everything with *pinard*."[71] Christophe Lucand goes further, arguing that alcoholism was one of the major factors in the triggering of mental disorders among soldiers, even if neither medical nor military personnel were willing to acknowledge this at the time.[72] Indeed, any suggestion that the imbrication of inebriation and violence might be driven by contextual factors is striking by its absence from reports penned by officers in military justice files. The *tirailleur* Lakdar, for example, was given five years of hard labor for threatening to kill his indigenous sergeant following a reprimand for the state of his uniform; the fact that he was preparing to load his rifle as he issued this threat undoubtedly contributed to the long sentence. Lakdar's claim that he was drunk and did not recall what had taken place evidently did not win him any sympathy.[73] Writing up the incident, the captain of his company offered the following damning comment:

> Lakdar is a bad soldier. An inveterate drinker—he is completely irascible in character and becomes intractable as soon as he has drunk, all are afraid—he is a raging [*furieux*] alcoholic.
>
> All means were used to soften him up, gentleness, severe punishments, nothing has any effect on him. I consider him a dangerous individual, his physical strength and his violent character making him feared by his comrades and even by his officers.[74]

70. SHD, GR 11 J 1328, CG, Boussebie, Ali ould Benziane (2e RMTA, 37e DI), "Procès-verbal d'information: Boudjemane, Mohamed ben Mohamed," Feb. 6, 1916. Found guilty but with extenuating circumstances, Boussebie was given a two-year suspended sentence.

71. SHD, 16 N 1484, "Rapport sur la correspondance des troupes du 10 au 25 novembre 1916," quoted in Saint-Fuscien, *A vos ordres?*, 106. Although the report was written in relation to the Third Division, its findings are generalizable across the army.

72. Lucand, *Le pinard des poilus*, 91.

73. SHD, GR 11 J 1364, CG, Lakdar, Belgacem ben (4e RMZT, 38e DI), "Procès-verbal des déclarations reçues par l'officier de police judiciaire: Lakdar, Belgacem ben," Dec. 9, 1915.

74. SHD, GR 11 J 1364, Lakdar, "Rapport du Capitaine Ciambelli, Commandant la 24e Cie," Nov. 25, 1915. Despite these apparently serious character flaws, Lakdar's sentence was suspended, and he was put back into service.

Similar comments were made about the *tirailleur* Asnaoui, who "in a state of drunkenness" threatened to hit several comrades with whom he had been playing cards earlier in the day. In the scuffle to subdue Asnaoui, the indigenous sergeant Amor was punched. Once again, the character assessment provided by the commanding officer was highly condemnatory: "Incorrigible drunkard, argumentative player, [Asnaoui] is a deplorable example to the company. Very strong, he is feared by his comrades whom he does not hesitate to brutalize. This black sheep must be gotten rid of immediately."[75] Admitting that he had drunk "more than necessary" (two liters of wine, according to witnesses), Asnaoui defended his actions by arguing that if he drank and was a little difficult, "it is because I was not well-treated and I was often brutalized. In addition, I haven't had leave since March 1916 [Asnaoui's crime took place in July 1917] and I could never get to go."[76] Challenging his superior's reductive reading of him as "incorrigible," Asnaoui's account provides a more multifaceted set of explanations for his actions, one that contextualizes his drunkenness and associated aggression as a response both to violence he experienced at the hands of others and to the impact on his emotional well-being of prolonged exposure to the war without respite.

Behavior that military authorities were quick to dismiss as stemming from innate character flaws might therefore be better understood as situational responses to the war, indicative of individual suffering and distress.[77] This can clearly be seen in the case of the Algerian *tirailleur* Bonnebal who was brought before a *conseil de guerre* accused of murder. On October 6, 1916, at around 8:00 p.m. in the *cantonnement* where his company was billeted, Bonnebal took his rifle, placed a cartridge in it, and fired at the *tirailleur* Saïbi, who was sitting a few feet away from him chatting with another soldier; Saïbi died instantly. Having joined the company only hours earlier, Saïbi had never spoken to Bonnebal. Despite interviewing multiple witnesses, Captain Belhomme was at a loss to explain this act committed "without any apparent provocation." Bonnebal's own testimony, provided through an interpreter, was "incoherent," leading the captain to speculate that he was suffering from a "persecution complex" (*la folie de la persecution*) and might not have been "in possession of all his faculties"; either "mad or faking madness."[78] Bonnebal's comrades concurred, stating that he seemed "ill" (*un malade*). Indeed, on several occasions between October 1 and 5,

75. SHD, GR 11 J 1377, CG, Asnaoui, Larbi ben Amar ben (8e RMTA, 38e DI), "Rapport du Capitaine Filio, Commandant la 19e Cie du 8e Tir.," July 24, 1917.

76. SHD, GR 11 J 1377, Asnaoui, "Procès-verbal de première comparution," Aug. 31, 1917.

77. Anne Duménil offers a thought-provoking discussion of suffering as a motive for military crimes, specifically in relation to soldiers who fled the battlefield, in "Soldiers' Suffering and Military Justice," 45–50.

78. SHD, GR 11 J 1327, CG, Bonnebal, Mohammed (2e RMTA, 37e DI), "Rapport du Capitaine Belhomme, Commandant la 14e Compagnie," Oct. 6, 1916.

Bonnebal had sought refuge near his officers asserting that another comrade had threatened to kill him, even though the officers in question saw no evidence of mistreatment toward Bonnebal. He also claimed a letter had been sent to his superiors from a sergeant in another company ordering him to be killed.[79] However, a medical examination on October 12, 1916, concluded: "No mental trouble. To rejoin his corps under escort." A more detailed assessment by the head of the neuropsychiatric wing of the Bar-le-Duc military hospital similarly asserted that it was "impossible" to "detect in him a real delusion of persecution or other mental disorders characterizing a clearly determined psychosis," although the difficulties of communicating with Bonnebal through an interpreter were noted.[80]

In view of these difficulties and seemingly unconvinced by the two medical opinions, the tribunal judges refused to deliver a verdict, requesting further evidence. This led to Bonnebal being placed under observation in a different psychiatric hospital on November 27. Over the next three weeks Bonnebal remained "somber, suspicious, mute," staying in bed all day and not engaging in communal life. The medical team even brought in "another Arab who speaks French to sleep next to him to serve as an interpreter for us," but Bonnebal "energetically refused" to converse with this man even to exchange the most banal pleasantries. Things changed dramatically, however, on December 22, when an external interpreter, holding the rank of captain, visited the hospital and spoke with Bonnebal. At this point the *tirailleur* "revealed his delirium": "I have been hurt for a long time. I took revenge because I suffered a lot. They insulted me, they threatened me, you know very well that I am within my rights. Besides, they'll kill me if we're alone."[81] Accepting the diagnosis that Bonnebal was an "alienated person" (*un aliéné*) suffering from delusions of persecution with "dangerous reactions," a second tribunal in July 1917 declared the *tirailleur* not guilty. Following the hospital's recommendation, they agreed that Bonnebal could no longer serve in the military and should be discharged and confined to an asylum.

Although it is not possible to determine whether Bonnebal's mental health issues predated the war, they were evidently exacerbated by his daily environment and underpinned his act of sudden violence. Bonnebal's case was unusual in the lengths to which the military went to clarify his mental state, but the result is a rich trove of documents that humanize "the accused" and place his act

79. SHD, GR 11 J 1327, Bonnebal, "Procès-verbal des déclarations reçues par l'officier de police judiciaire: Bonnebal, Mohamed," Oct. 10, 1916.
80. SHD, GR 11 J 1327, Bonnebal, "Certificat de visite," Oct. 12, 1916; "Examen mental du Tirailleur BONNEBAL, Hôpital Centrale, 2e Armée, Place de Bar-le-Duc," Oct. 17, 1916.
81. SHD, GR 11 J 1327, Bonnebal, "Compte rendue médicale concernant le tirailleur Bonnebal Mohamed, inculpé de meurtre, Service neuro-psychiatrique, Hôpital du Collège, St Dizier," Dec. 23, 1916.

of apparently unprovoked violence in its wider and more complex context. This offers a different lens through which to explore the impact of the conflict on specific individuals. Such insights have relevance for ongoing debates about soldierly endurance, adding nuance to our understanding of what it meant to cope (or not) during the First World War. Evidence from this and the previously cited examples thus complement more established bodies of scholarship on phenomena such as shell shock, desertion, and mutiny by pointing to the other ways that combatants' limits to coping might manifest and be traceable. Centering cases involving colonized subjects allows us to integrate the experiences of this group of soldiers into these literatures while highlighting the potential to build on work examining mental health among colonized populations in the empire by considering the treatment of such men when transplanted to the metropole.[82]

The Social and Emotional Worlds of Soldiers

Conseil de guerre files equally provide compelling glimpses into the complex social and emotional worlds of the rank and file, particularly in terms of their relationships to one another. Acts of violence that superior officers described as having "no motive" or whose origin they deemed trivial or incomprehensible (especially common in cases involving colonized combatants), on closer inspection, turn out to pertain to issues that mattered deeply to the soldiers concerned. Military justice thus offers a good example of how prosecuting certain acts, in this case violence, can open a vista onto other, often hidden, subjects, behaviors, and experiences. This can be illustrated by returning to prosecutions for violence that feature accusations or suspicions of same-sex sexual relationships, this time considering them from the soldiers' rather than the authorities' perspective.

Evidence of sexual practices is notoriously hard to locate and complicated to assess, especially in terms of disentangling perception from experience and identity.[83] Analysis is further complicated in this context by the contemporary stigmas surrounding homosexuality, the pressures imposed by dominant notions of (martial) masculinity, the unequal power relationships at play in the *conseil de guerre* process, and the stakes (judicial but also reputational) for all implicated parties, not just the accused. Cases involving same-sex sexual relationships were typically characterized by confusing and often contradictory sets of testimony that military officials tried to disentangle and then reassemble into what they

82. See, e.g., Keller, *Colonial Madness*; Edington, *Beyond the Asylum*; and Bullard, "Truth in Madness."

83. For a more in-depth discussion of these challenges, see Crouthamel, *Intimate History of the Front*, 10–11; Ross, "Sex in the Archives"; Herzog, "War and Sexuality in Europe's Twentieth Century"; and Clark, *Desire*, 1–15. Although dealing with a different chronological period, I also found it useful to think with Hamilton, "Sodomy and Criminal Justice."

deemed the most coherent and plausible narrative. Yet what was a problem for military justice, which focused on determining the "facts," is an asset for the historian. Offering multiple perspectives on the same set of events, these sources through careful reading can tell us much about soldiers' perceptions and their constructions of situations and of themselves. The frequency and forcefulness with which denials about same-sex relationships were issued, for example, tells us much about the strength of the culture of opprobrium surrounding homosexuality in the military and the cultures from which these men came. Even those who were called simply as witnesses were often reluctant to admit to knowing that such things happened in their unit, let alone the specific circumstances being invoked, lest they be tainted by association. As part of denying that sexual relations had played any part in his decision to kill his close friend Cheniki, the *tirailleur* Benchelighem told the tribunal: "No, I never had relations against nature with him. But since they claimed that, I told him [Cheniki] to distance himself from me."[84]

A more extreme example of the urge to distance oneself from any association with such behavior was provided by the *tirailleur* Boughazi, who freely admitted killing Corporal M'Bareck with a shot to the heart at 4:00 a.m. on April 9, 1915, but stated that he had done so because the corporal had attempted, several times, to commit "acts against nature" with him. Boughazi not only admitted to the murder but, in the immediate aftermath, fetched the duty sergeant to show him what he had done. In his testimony Boughazi stated that the first time the corporal made such advances, he told him to leave him alone; the second time, he warned M'Bareck that if he did it again, he would kill him; the third time, he loaded his rifle and fired. "Boughazi finds the crime he committed totally natural," reported the *tirailleur*'s commanding officer; "the corporal wanted to abuse him; he [Boughazi] showed that he was a man of honor by killing him." This assessment was undoubtedly informed by Boughazi's own statements when he was questioned in his unit. Asked why he did not simply report M'Bareck's behavior to his officers, he replied, "A complaint would have made me look like a woman in the eyes of the whole company; I preferred to kill M'Bareck."[85] This was also what he told an older comrade, Kaddour, in whom he had confided. When Kaddour encouraged Boughazi to report the harassment, the latter refused on the grounds that, in Kaddour's words, "he

---

84. SHD, GR 11 J 1326, CG, Benchelighem, Messaoud ben Belkacem (3e RMTA, 37e DI), "Interview with Benchelighem," n.d.

85. SHD, GR 11 J 1319, CG, Boughazi, Bouazza ould Mohammed (2e RMTA, 37e DI), "Rapport du Capitaine Ducastel, Commandant la 16ème Compagnie du 2e Régiment de Marche de Tirailleurs Indigènes," Apr. 9, 1915; "Procès-verbal d'interrogatoire: Boughazi, Bouazza ould Mohammed," Apr. 15, 1915.

would be suspected of having unnatural morals."[86] What seems to have been at stake for Boughazi was his sense of both honor and masculinity. Indeed, it is telling that on the third occasion when M'Bareck tried to assault him, Kaddour, wakened by the noise, lit a candle to see what was going on, in the process making public M'Bareck's effort to open Boughazi's trousers. Quickly extinguishing the light, Kaddour testified that Boughazi's shot rang out moments later. What is also interesting about this case, in terms of the military's attitude toward same-sex relationships, is the response from the tribunal judges, all five of whom declared Boughazi not guilty of murder.

Not every case of this nature, however, was structured around denial. Honor, albeit understood somewhat differently, was also integral to the defense offered by Moktar, described earlier, during his trial for the murder of one comrade and the attempted murder of another. During the morning of June 18, 1916, Moktar was seen talking to two fellow *tirailleurs*, Ould Ali and Lakdar. In the afternoon Moktar appeared, having shaved off his mustache, brandishing a loaded rifle. On seeing him, Ould Ali immediately sought to hide behind a nearby shack as a bullet, fired by Moktar, "whistled past his ear." Two soldiers tried to disarm Moktar, but he escaped and took off after a *tirailleur* he believed to be Lakdar. Firing again, Moktar mortally wounded the *tirailleur*, who, it turned out, was not Lakdar but a soldier named Babaï.

Asked during his trial why he had tried to kill Ould Ali and Lakdar, Moktar said that he had received a bonus that Ould Ali had persuaded him to take for safekeeping until his next rest period, telling Moktar that he always spent his money too quickly. Subsequently, Moktar saw Ould Ali being kissed by Lakdar. "Jealous," in his own words, and unable to bear the idea that his friend would let himself be kissed "in front of everyone," Moktar asked Ould Ali for his money back. This was the morning of June 18. Ould Ai replied, "Go shave your mustache" (*Va te faire raser la moustache*), which, as the president of the tribunal had clarified, signified that Moktar should "go get dressed up as a 'whore.'" Ould Ali added that he would then give Moktar ten sous for every "favor" until all the money had been returned. At this point Lakdar interjected to say that Ould Ali had given him Moktar's money and that he would pay two sous each time. Insulted and humiliated by this exchange, Moktar confessed that he lost his head, saying to himself, "I can only kill him."[87] However, Moktar did not act

86. SHD, GR 11 J 1319, Boughazi, "Procès-verbal d'information: Kaddour, Eddin," Apr. 15, 1915.

87. The *conseil de guerre* repeatedly asked witnesses if Moktar was drunk at the time of the incident so as to determine how in control he was of his actions. While the witnesses gave a variety of responses, Moktar himself stated that he was not drunk but "mad with anger." SHD, GR 11 J 1323, Moktar, "Notes d'audience. Interroge de Moktar," July 3, 1916. Moktar had given a virtually identical account during prior questioning. See "Procès-verbal: Moktar, Salem ben Tidjani ben," June 27, 1916.

immediately on his emotions, waiting until midafternoon, shaving off his mustache in anger in the meantime. This delay led the tribunal to class his actions as premeditated, qualifying Moktar for the harshest possible sentence: the death penalty.[88] In place of the one-dimensional assessment provided by his commanding officer, who, as we saw earlier, dismissed Moktar as an "impure individual," testimonies collected via the *conseil de guerre* point to a more complex situation involving a broad spectrum of emotions: humiliation and hurt, jealousy and anger, and regret at having killed his comrade Babaï, whom Moktar thought of "like a brother."

Other cases where jealousy seems to have played a role equally gesture to a complicated and constantly evolving set of relationships between men that defy easy characterization. Returning drunk one evening to quarters, Lahoussine saw two other *tirailleurs*, Idir and Sider, chatting. Calling out to Sider that he had already told him that he did not want to see him talking to Idir, Lahoussine proceeded to attack Sider with a razor, prompting the latter to defend himself with a mess tin. As the *conseil de guerre* sought to get to the bottom of the dispute, the evidence it collected suggested that Lahoussine and Idir had been close until Idir suddenly stopped speaking to and associating with his comrade. Lahoussine believed that this was because Idir was now the "friend" of a sergeant and that Sider had been the "matchmaker" in this scenario (both words used by Lahoussine in his deposition), hence his rancor toward Sider.[89] Across the paperwork the term *friend* seems to be used in different ways. Indeed, the relationships in question remain ambiguous. For example, in the immediate aftermath of Lahoussine's stating that Idir no longer spoke to him because "he is the friend of the sergeant now," he was asked, "And you've never been the friend of Idir?" Lahoussine replied, "No." Irrespective of what *friend* actually meant in this context, the altercation between Lahoussine and Sider demonstrates the importance of connections forged between men and the hurt caused when those relationships ended.

This is also apparent in the case of the *tirailleur* Benchelighem, who shot his friend Cheniki and one Corporal Chalal as they lay in their beds. The sergeant who first questioned Benchelighem about his motives swore that Benchelighem stated: "Cheniki was my wife [*ma femme*] for a long time; the corporal

---

88. In his version of events, Ould Ali denied that any money had changed hands and claimed that the two men had been "perfect friends" until Moktar started to pursue him sexually, prompting Ould Ali to ask to transfer to a different company. When Moktar was transferred instead, he made it clear to Ould Ali that "he wanted me dead." SHD, GR 11 J 1323, Moktar, "Notes d'audience. Témoins: Ould Ali," July 3, 1916.

89. SHD, GH 11 J 1324, CG, Lahoussine, Sadik ben Ali (3e RMTA, 37e DI), "Procès-verbal des déclarations reçues par l'officier judiciare: Lahoussine, Sadik ben Ali," Aug. 22, 1916.

wanted to separate me from him. I killed them both."[90] The idea of soldiers taking a "wife" had strong colonial connotations, being particularly associated with behavior in the Armée d'Afrique's disciplinary battalions and *bagnes*.[91] Although Benchelighem subsequently denied saying this and having had any sexual relationship with Cheniki, he was open about the fact that the two men had been close and that he resented Corporal Chalal for coming between them. "Cheniki and me we loved each other like brothers," he stated during an interview on October 27, 1916. "We arrived together [at the front] coming as reinforcements [from Algeria]. Corporal Chalal was opposed to us continuing our companionship [*notre commerce d'amitié*]."[92] Two days later, during his tribunal hearing, Benchelighem explained that he was "angry" (*fâché*) to learn that Cheniki and Chalal were in a relationship—not because of the relations themselves, which he claimed to be indifferent to, but because the corporal had broken up his friendship with Cheniki to commit "unnatural acts" against his friend. It was this, in combination with alcohol, which he normally did not drink, that led him to seek vengeance in the most dramatic terms.[93]

That soldiers experienced deep friendship, jealousy, hurt, and betrayal and that these were all amplified by the wartime context is, on the one hand, a banal observation. Yet it is some of the only evidence we possess that speaks to their inner emotional worlds, certainly when it comes to colonized combatants. Nor are such things always readily attested to in the more voluminous diaries, letters, and memoirs penned by white French soldiers. Even if the sentiments that emerge do not starkly distinguish colonized combatants from their metropolitan French comrades in arms, the ability to draw such distinctions is significant in and of itself, especially since the starting point in the French empire and the military was usually to assume difference and thus to think of and to treat colonial subjects as a category apart.[94] In seeking to justify the continued subjugation of colonized peoples, imperial ideologies repeatedly insisted that these populations did not experience emotions or pain, or experienced them differently from their European counterparts. Therefore much can be gained from reading existing sources in new ways to explore and take seriously traces of the internal lives of

---

90. SHD, GR 11 J 1326, Benchelighem, "Procès-verbal d'information: Djouadi, Mohamed ben Tahar," Oct. 24, 1916; "Rapport sur l'affaire," Oct. 29, 1916.

91. See, e.g., the medical reports cited in Aldrich, *Colonialism and Homosexuality*, 60–61; or Dominique Kalifa's claims about incarcerated men taking a "woman" in order not to become one themselves in *Biribi*, 280.

92. SHD, GR 11 J 1326, Benchelighem, "Interview: Benchelighem," Oct. 27, 1916.

93. SHD, GR 11 J 1326, Benchelighem, "Rapport sur l'affaire," Oct. 29, 1916.

94. My thinking on this point was usefully informed by Michael Roper's caution to historians that "in emphasising only difference, we risk de-humanising those who left less elaborate psychological records" and thus inadvertently reproducing the dominant discourses and stereotypes of others (*Secret Battle*, 32).

colonized combatants and the affective and social context to which they speak. The complicated emotional landscapes that are revealed stand in contrast to the one-dimensional assessments of violence between soldiers that were often applied by military officials and the judicial process that reduced individuals to their perceived innate flaws—"incorrigible drunk," "inveterate pederast," "brutal by temperament and taste"—and divorced their actions from the context of the war. Even if still partial, the resultant information challenges, and shows the men themselves challenging, the reductive explanations and labels attached to them and their behavior by military justice, replacing these with more complex and multifaceted portraits.

Conclusion

During the First World War the trenches served as spaces of support, mutual aid, and comradeship, all of which were invaluable to soldiers on a daily basis. However, they could equally be experienced as "a world of insults, threats and intimidation."[95] Focusing on this latter dimension through the prism of altercations between soldiers on the same side demonstrates the complex interplay between violence and camaraderie. At the same time, using military justice records pertaining to the multiethnic Armée d'Afrique brings an underused set of sources and a new range of voices to the discussion. Although Emmanuel Saint-Fuscien regards *conseil de guerre* files as providing "less information about what men endured or refused than on what justice itself accepted or refused from men at war," this article has argued that it does not need to be an either/or situation.[96] Tribunal records do indeed provide valuable evidence of what behaviors were considered acceptable, tolerable, and unacceptable to those in command, and under what circumstances. Exploring the subjective nature and variable application of military justice with respect to prosecutions for violent acts reveals how colonial mentalities and contemporary notions of race, among other factors, inflected judicial processes and outcomes. It is particularly striking, for example, that all but two cases in this sample of prosecutions for violent acts where same-sex sexual relations were a cited factor pertain to colonized subjects, even though we know that such relationships were not confined to this group of combatants. Military justice thus provides insight into the assumptions certain groups of soldiers faced that were embedded in the minds of those assessing them, reminding us of what they were up against in their daily environment.

95. Cazals and Loez, *Dans les tranchées*, 228.
96. Saint-Fuscien, "Juger et être jugé," 273.

In juxtaposing the military authorities' understanding and assessment of violence with the perspectives of the soldiers themselves, the second half of the article has sought to demonstrate that, to return to Saint-Fuscien's formulation, we can also access "what men endured or refused." By criminalizing or, more specifically, choosing to prosecute certain acts, military justice casts light onto other, often hidden subjects and practices. An examination of violence between comrades via military justice sources thus opens a window onto a far broader range of interlinked topics, such as alcohol and its potential abuse, mental health, and interpersonal and sexual relations. Testimonies provided by those involved illustrate the different ways individuals reacted to the pressures they were placed under between 1914 and 1918, how they related to the men around them in this highly fraught context, and how they framed and justified their choices when called on to explain themselves and their behaviors. Read as situational responses to an unimaginably challenging and violent daily environment, this material offers new insights into questions of soldierly endurance and its limits, as well as where we might usefully look for different kinds of evidence that speaks to these issues.

CLAIRE ELDRIDGE is professor of the history of the Francophone world at the University of Leeds. She is author of "Conflict and Community in the Trenches: Military Justice Archives and Interactions between Soldiers in France's Armée d'Afrique, 1914–1918" in *History Workshop Journal* (2022) and "Migrations of Decolonization, Welfare, and the Unevenness of Citizenship in the UK, France, and Portugal," with Christoph Kalter and Becky Taylor, in *Past and Present* (2023).

Acknowledgments

The author would like to thank Julie M. Powell for proposing that they co-organize the "War Makes Monsters" workshop, for making that such an enjoyable experience, and for being such a great collaborator on this special issue. The author also thanks all the "War Makes Monsters" participants for their invaluable feedback and the *FHS* reviewers for their thoughtful comments. She is equally grateful to Jennifer Sessions and Becky Taylor for their suggestions and support. Research for this article was facilitated by the generous financial support of the Gerda Henkel Stiftung (grant AZ 27/F/19).

References

Aldrich, Robert. *Colonialism and Homosexuality*. London, 2002.

Aldrich, Robert. "Colonial Man." In *French Masculinities: History, Culture, and Politics*, edited by Christopher E. Forth and Bertrand Taithe, 123–40. Basingstoke, 2007.

Andrews, C. M., and A. S. Kanya-Forstner. "France, Africa, and the First World War." *Journal of African History* 19, no. 1 (1978): 11–23.

Attal, Robert, and Denis Rolland. "La justice militaire en 1914–1915: Le cas de la 6e Armée." *Mémoires—Fédération des sociétés d'histoire et d'archéologie de l'Aisne* 41 (1996): 133–58.

Audoin-Rouzeau, Stéphane. *L'enfant de l'ennemi: Viol, avortement, infanticide pendant la Grande Guerre*. Paris, 1995.

Audoin-Rouzeau, Stéphane, and Annette Becker. "Violence et consentement: La 'culture de guerre' du premier conflit mondial." In *Pour une histoire culturelle*, edited by Jean-Pierre Rioux and Jean-François Sirinelli, 251–71. Paris, 1997.

Bach, André. *Fusillés pour l'exemple, 1914–1915*. Paris, 2003.

Bach, André. *Justice militaire, 1915–1916*. Paris, 2013.

Becker, Annette, and Henry Rousso. "D'un guerre l'autre." In *La violence de guerre, 1914–1945: Approches comparées des deux conflits mondiaux*, edited by Stéphane Audoin-Rouzeau, Annette Becker, Christian Ingrao, and Henry Rousso, 11–26. Brussels, 2002.

Blanchard, Emmanuel, and Sylvie Thénault. "Quel 'monde du contact'? Pour une histoire sociale de l'Algérie pendant la période colonial." *Le mouvement social*, no. 236 (2011): 3–7.

Bourke, Joanna. *An Intimate History of Killing: Face to Face Killing in Twentieth Century Warfare*. London, 2000.

Brousseau, Albert. "Essai sur la peur aux armées, 1914–1918." Thèse pour le doctorat en médecine, Faculté de Médecine de Paris, 1920.

Bullard, Alice. "Truth in Madness: Colonial Doctors and Insane Women in French North Africa." *South Atlantic Review* 66, no. 2 (2001): 114–32.

Burton, Antoinette, and Tony Ballantyne. "Introduction: Bodies, Empires, and World Histories." In *Bodies in Contact: Rethinking Colonial Encounters in World History*, edited by Antoinette Burton and Tony Ballantyne, 1–15. Durham, NC, 2005.

Cazals, Rémy, and André Loez. *Dans les tranchées de 1914–1918*. Pau, 2008.

Clark, Anna. *Desire: A History of European Sexuality*. New York, 2008.

Cochet, François. "1914–1918: L'alcool aux armées; Représentations et essai de typologie." *Guerres mondiales et conflits contemporains*, no. 222 (2006): 19–32.

Cochet, François. *Survivre au front, 1914–1918: Les poilus entre contrainte et consentement*. Saint-Cloud, 2005.

Connolly, James E. *The Experience of Occupation in the Nord, 1914–18: Living with the Enemy in First World War France*. Manchester, 2018.

Cronier, Emmanuelle. *Permissionnaires dans la Grande Guerre*. 2nd ed. Paris, 2017.

Crouthamel, Jason. *An Intimate History of the Front: Masculinity, Sexuality, and German Soldiers in the First World War*. Basingstoke, 2014.

Das, Santanu, Anna Maguire, and Daniel Steinbach, eds. *Colonial Encounters in a Time of Global Conflict, 1914–1918*. London, 2022.

Dean, William T. "The French Colonial Army and the Great War." *Historian* 76, no. 3 (2014): 479–517.

Delaporte, Sophie. "Mutilation and Disfiguration (France)." *1914–1918 Online: International Encyclopedia of the First World War*. https://encyclopedia.1914-1918-online.net/article/mutilation_and_disfiguration_france (accessed July 28, 2023).

Duménil, Anne. "En marge du combat? Le crime et la lâcheté devant la justice militaire allemande." *14–18 Aujourd'hui-Today-Heute* 4 (2001): 89–108.

Duménil, Anne. "Soldiers' Suffering and Military Justice in the German Army of the Great War." In *Uncovered Fields: Perspectives in First World War Studies*, edited by Jenny MacLeod and Pierre Purseigle, 43–60. Leiden, 2003.

Echenberg, Myron. *Colonial Conscripts: The Tirailleurs Sénégalais in French West Africa, 1857–1960*. Portsmouth, NH, 1991.

Edele, Mark, and Robert Gerwarth. "The Limits of Demobilization: Global Perspectives on the Aftermath of the Great War." *Journal of Contemporary History* 50, no. 1 (2015): 3–14.

Edington, Claire E. *Beyond the Asylum: Mental Illness in French Colonial Vietnam.* Ithaca, NY, 2019.

Eldridge, Claire. "Absence, Agency, and Empire: Desertion from the French Army during the First World War." *War in History* 30, no. 3 (2023): 277–99.

Eldridge, Claire. "Conflict and Community in the Trenches: Military Justice Archives and Interactions between Soldiers in France's Armée d'Afrique, 1914–1918." *History Workshop Journal* 93, no. 1 (2022): 23–46.

Eldridge, Claire. "'The Forgotten of This Tribute': Settler Soldiers, Colonial Categories, and the Centenary of the First World War." *History and Memory* 31, no. 2 (2019): 3–44.

Englander, David. "The French Soldier, 1914–1918." *French History* 1, no. 1 (1987): 49–67.

Fillaut, Thierry. "Lutte contre l'alcoolisme dans l'armée pendant la Grande Guerre: Principes, méthodes et résultats." In *Expériences de la folie: Criminels, soldats, patients en psychiatrie (XIXe–XXe siècles)*, edited by Laurence Guignard, Hervé Guillemain, and Stéphane Tison, 141–52. Rennes, 2013.

Fogarty, Richard S. *Race and War in France: Colonial Subjects in the French Army, 1914–1918.* Baltimore, 2008.

Foucault, Michel. *La volonté de savoir.* Vol. 1 of *Histoire de la sexualité.* Paris, 1976.

Frémeaux, Jacques. *Les colonies dans la Grande Guerre: Combats et épreuves des peuples d'outre-mer.* Saint-Cloud, 2006.

Geyer, Michael. "Violence et expérience de la violence au XXe siècle—la Première Guerre mondiale." In vol. 1 of *1914–1945 L'ère de la guerre: Violence, mobilisations, deuil*, edited by Anne Duménil, Nicolas Beaupré, and Christian Ingrao, 37–71. Paris, 2004.

Hamilton, Tom. "Sodomy and Criminal Justice in the Parlement of Paris, ca. 1540–ca. 1700." *Journal of the History of Sexuality* 29, no. 3 (2020): 303–34.

Harris, Ruth. "'Child of the Barbarian': Rape, Race, and Nationalism in France during the First World War." *Past and Present*, no. 141 (1993): 170–206.

Hassett, Dónal. *Mobilising Memory: The Great War and the Language of Politics in Colonial Algeria, 1918–1939.* Oxford, 2019.

Hassett, Dónal, and Michelle Moyd. "Introduction: Writing the History of Colonial Veterans of the Great War." *First World War Studies* 10 (2019): 1–11.

Herzog, Dagmar. "War and Sexuality in Europe's Twentieth Century." In *Brutality and Desire: War and Sexuality in Europe's Twentieth Century*, edited by Dagmar Herzog, 1–15. New York, 2009.

Jackson, Paul. *One of the Boys: Homosexuality in the Military during World War II.* Montreal, 2004.

Jahr, Christoph. "Désertion et déserteurs dans la Grand Guerre: Phénomènes et groupe marginaux?" *14–18 Aujourd'hui-Today-Heute* 4 (2001): 111–24.

Jahr, Christoph. "War, Discipline, and Politics: Desertion and Military Justice in the German and British Armies, 1914–1918." In *Justice militaires et guerres mondiales (Europe, 1914–1950) / Military Justices and World Wars (Europe, 1914–1950)*, edited by Jean-Marc Berlière, Jonas Campion, Luigi Lacchè, and Xavier Rousseaux, 73–105. Louvain, 2013.

Joly, Vincent. "Sexe, guerres et désir colonial." In *Amours, guerres et sexualité, 1914–1945*, edited by François Rouquet, Fabrice Virgill, and Danièle Voldman, 62–69. Paris, 2007.

Kalifa, Dominique. *Biribi: Les bagnes coloniaux de l'armée française.* 2nd ed. Paris, 2016.

Keller, Richard. *Colonial Madness: Psychiatry in French North Africa.* Chicago, 2007.

Lafon, Alexandre. *La camaraderie au front, 1914–1918.* Paris, 2014.

Le Naour, Jean-Yves. *Fusillés: Enquête sur les crimes de la justice militaire.* Paris, 2010.

Loez, André. *14–18, les refus de la guerre: Une histoire des mutins.* Paris, 2010.

Lucand, Christophe. *Le pinard des poilus: Une histoire du vin en France durant la Grande Guerre (1914–1918).* Dijon, 2015.

Lunn, Joe. *Memoirs of the Maelstrom: A Senegalese Oral History of the First World War.* Portsmouth, NH, 1999.

Maguire, Anna. *Contact Zones of the First World War: Cultural Encounters across the British Empire.* Cambridge, 2021.

Mangin, Charles. *La force noire.* Paris, 1910.

Mann, Gregory. *Native Sons: West African Veterans and France in the Twentieth Century.* Durham, NC, 2006.

Mann, Michelle. "Not Quite Citizens: Assimilation, World War One, and the Question *Indigène* in Colonial Algeria, 1870–1920." PhD diss., Brandeis University, 2017.

Mariot, Nicolas. "Social Encounters in the French Trenches." *French Politics, Culture, and Society* 36, no. 2 (2018): 1–27.

Mariot, Nicolas. *Tous unis dans la tranchée? 1914–1918, les intellectuels rencontrent le peuple.* Paris, 2013.

Maurin, Jules. *Armée, guerre, société: Soldats languedociens, 1889–1919.* Paris, 1982.

Meyer, Jacques. *La vie quotidienne des soldats pendant la Grande Guerre.* Paris, 1966.

Meynier, Gilbert. *L'Algérie révélée: La guerre de 1914–1918 et le premier quart du XXe siècle.* Geneva, 1981.

Michel, Marc. *L'appel à l'Afrique: Contributions et réactions à l'effort de guerre en A.O.F., 1914–1919.* Paris, 1982.

Michel, Marc. *Les Africains et la Grande Guerre: L'appel à l'Afrique, 1914–1918.* Paris, 2003.

Mosse, George L. *Fallen Soldiers: Reshaping the Memory of the World Wars.* Oxford, 1994.

Moyd, Michelle. "Color Lines, Front Lines: The First World War from the South." *Radical History Review,* no. 131 (2018): 13–35.

Moyd, Michelle. *Violent Intermediaries: African Soldiers, Conquest, and Everyday Colonialism in German East Africa.* Athens, OH, 2014.

Nourisson, Didier. *Le buveur du XIXe siècle.* Paris, 1990.

Offenstadt, Nicolas. *Les fusillés de la Grande Guerre et la mémoire collective.* Paris, 1999.

Pedroncini, Guy. *Les mutineries de 1917.* Paris, 1967.

Pinaud, Pierre. *L'alcoolisme chez les Arabes en Algérie.* Bordeaux, 1933.

Porot, Antoine, and Angelo Hesnard. *L'expertise mentale militaire.* Paris, 1918.

Prost, Antoine. *In the Wake of War: "Les Anciens Combattants" and French Society, 1914–1939.* Oxford, 1992.

Prost, Antoine. "Les limites de la brutalisation: Tuer sur le front occidental, 1914–1918." *Vingtième siècle,* no. 81 (2004): 5–20.

Recham, Belkacem. *Les Musulmans algériens dans l'armée française (1919–1945).* Paris, 1996.

Revenin, Régis. *Homosexualité et prostitution masculines à Paris, 1870–1918.* Paris, 2005.

Ridel, Charles. *L'ivresse du soldat.* Paris, 2016.

Rolland, Denis. *La grève des tranchées: Les mutineries de 1917.* Paris, 2005.

Roper, Michael. *The Secret Battle: Emotional Survival in the Great War.* Manchester, 2009.

Ross, Andrew Israel. "Sex in the Archives: Homosexuality, Prostitution, and the Archives de la Préfecture de Police de Paris." *French Historical Studies* 42, no. 2 (2017): 267–90.

Roux, François. *La Grande Guerre inconnue: Les poilus contre l'armée française.* Paris, 2006.

Roux, Pierre. "Les mutilations volontaires par coup de feu." Thèse pour le doctorat en médecine, Faculté de Médecine et de Pharmacie de Lyon, 1918.

Roynette, Odile. *Bons pour le service: L'éxpérience de la caserne en France à la fin du XIXe siècle.* Paris, 2000.

Saint-Fuscien, Emmanuel. *A vos ordres? La relation d'autorité dans l'armée française de la Grande Guerre.* Paris, 2011.

Saint-Fuscien, Emmanuel. "The End of the Great Military Leader? 'Good' and 'Bad' French Army Officers in the First World War." *First World War Studies* 11 (2020): 61–73.

Saint-Fuscien, Emmanuel. "Juger et être jugé: Prévenus, crimes et délits au sein des armées de la Grande Guerre." In *Dans la guerre, 1914–1918: Accepter, endurer, refuser,* edited by Nicolas Beaupré, Heather Jones, and Anne Rasmussen, 251–73. Paris, 2015.

Saint-Fuscien, Emmanuel. "La justice militaire française au cours de la Première Guerre mondiale: Apports et limites d'une approche quantitative." In *Justice militaires et guerres mondiales (Europe, 1914–1950) / Military Justices and World Wars (Europe, 1914–1950),* edited by Jean-Marc Berlière, Jonas Campion, Luigi Lacchè, and Xavier Rousseaux, 107–23. Louvain, 2013.

Saint-Fuscien, Emmanuel. "Pourquoi obéit-on? Discipline et liens hiérarchiques dans l'armée française de la Première Guerre mondiale." *Genèses* 75, no. 2 (2009): 4–23.

Sheikh, Mustapha, and Tajul Islam. "Islam, Alcohol, and Identity: Towards a Critical Muslim Studies Approach." *ReOrient* 3, no. 2 (2018): 185–211.

Sivan, Emmanuel. "Colonialism and Popular Culture in Algeria." *Journal of Contemporary History* 14, no. 1 (1979): 21–53.

Smith, Leonard V. *Between Mutiny and Obedience: The Case of the French Fifth Infantry Division during World War I.* Princeton, NJ, 1994.

Steinbach, Daniel. "Between Intimacy and Violence: Imperial Encounters in East Africa during the First World War." In Das, Maguire, and Steinbach, *Colonial Encounters,* 98–122.

Stovall, Tyler. "The Color Line behind the Lines: Racial Violence in France during the Great War." *American Historical Review* 103, no. 3 (1998): 737–69.

Suard, Vincent. "La justice militaire française et la peine de mort au début de la Première Guerre mondiale." *Revue d'histoire moderne et contemporaine* 41, no. 1 (1994): 136–53.

Tamagne, Florence. "Guerre et homosexualité." In *Amours, guerres et sexualité, 1914–1945,* edited by François Rouquet, Fabrice Virgill, and Danièle Voldman, 124–31. Paris, 2007.

Tamagne, Florence. *Histoire de l'homosexualité en Europe.* Paris, 2000.

White, Owen. *Blood of the Colony: Wine and the Rise and Fall of French Algeria.* Boston, 2021.

Yedes, Ali. "Social Dynamics in Colonial Algeria: The Question of *Pieds-Noirs* Identity." In *French Civilization and Its Discontents: Nationalism, Colonialism, Race,* edited by Tyler Stovall and Georges Van Den Abbeele, 235–49. Lanham, MD, 2003.

Zack, Lizabeth. "French and Algerian Identities in Formation." *French Colonial History* 2 (2002): 115–43.

Ziemann, Benjamin. *Violence and the German Soldier in the Great War: Killing, Dying, Surviving.* Translated by Andrew Evans. London, 2017.

Zientek, Adam Derek. "Wine and Blood: Alcohol, Morale, and Discipline in the French Army on the Western Front, 1914–1918." PhD diss., Stanford University, 2012.

Znaien, Nessim. "Les territoires de l'alcool à Tunis et à Casablanca sous la période des Protectorats (1912–1956): Des destins parallèles?" *Année du Maghreb* 12 (2015): 197–210.

The Algerian Enemy Within
Policing the Black Market in Marseille and Algiers, 1939–1950

DANIELLE BEAUJON

ABSTRACT   During World War II police officers in Marseille and Algiers relentlessly hunted Algerian black market operatives. Hundreds of reports from these two cities detail the actions taken to prevent individuals from selling contraband goods, exceeding fixed market prices, or ignoring rationing protocols. Long-standing colonial stereotypes had labeled Algerians as prone to theft and violence, but the economic restrictions of war created a new category of the imagined Algerian criminal: the black market trafficker. In police reports the figure of the Algerian profiteer is omnipresent, but internal communications acknowledged that Europeans profited from the black market, too. Why, then, the fixation on Algerians? This article argues that police developed a narrative of Algerians as "internal enemies" of France. Their underlying suspicion of Algerians endured throughout World War II even as governments rose and fell in France and loyalties of the entire nation shifted. In treating Algerians as threats to national security, the police justified a system of control that homogenized the Algerian community along racial lines. The racialized policing of "anti-French" Algerian traffickers built not just on visual codes of race but also on how police practice mapped ideas of race onto the space of the city.

KEYWORDS   Marseille, Algiers, police, World War II, black market

W hen I first opened the manila folder in the archives, I was unsure of the story the pieces of paper told. Dozens of sheets listed the biographic information of Algerian men arrested in the city of Algiers in 1944.[1] Like so many police documents I encountered in my research, the files were both telling and riddled with silences. According to the files, many of the men had been born in

---

1. Archives Nationales d'Outre-Mer (hereafter ANOM), 1F 439, dossier "Dépôts des travailleurs à Kouba." The ANOM holds the key records on French colonialism in Algeria, including police records. I also conducted several months of research in Algiers for this project, gaining access to records including municipal council debates, files on the *ravitaillement* service, and local press collections. I use the term *Algerian* to refer to what French administrators at the time would have called *indigènes*. Although *Algerian* flattens linguistic, citizenship, and class divisions, I use it to distinguish indigenous Algerians from French and European settlers, whom I refer to as *European*.

French Historical Studies • Vol. 47, No. 2 (May 2024) • DOI 10.1215/00161071-11025071
Copyright 2024 by Society for French Historical Studies

rural regions of Algeria before coming to the capital. Only a few had an address to list in Algiers. For the rest, some nameless police officer or secretary had simply typed "homeless" (*sans domicile fixe*) in the space for home address. The police listed a range of professions for these men, mostly day laborers, farmers, and porters. Most of the accused were noted as illiterate. On the otherwise typed form, a handwritten row recorded the men's criminal record. The stack included a few individuals listed as dangerous ex-convicts, but most had no prior encounters with the law. The men fell between the ages of eighteen and thirty-four, most in their mid-twenties. The files all shared two things: these were Algerian men, and they had been arrested for black-market trafficking.

For all the details carefully recorded on the files, I also faced archival gaps. What brought these men to Algiers from the rural districts listed as their birthplace? Perhaps, like so many others, they came to escape the poverty and famine of the Algerian countryside during World War II. But I cannot know for sure. A litany of other questions ran through my mind as I read the stack. What were the circumstances of their arrest? Where had these arrests taken place? What was the fate of these men? Why did not a single European appear in this dossier of accused black-market traffickers? Documents in the same archival box revealed that the men had been arrested as part of a special initiative to remove black-market traffickers from Algiers and send them to agricultural labor camps. What had led to this extreme policing of the black market, rounding up men to ship off to camps?

The dossier of accused traffickers was an anomaly in the archive, an unusually severe example of the French state's carceral response to the black market. But in other ways, these files represent a pervasive trope of the French police archives from World War II. In the French Mediterranean, police officers in both metropole and colony came to identify the black market as the special purview of North Africans.[2] Having labeled North Africans as traffickers, the police used racialized ideas of urban space to battle the black market, focusing on areas of the city that they identified as North African. The violent consequences of these police efforts fell disproportionately on North Africans, despite the largely European clientele buying restricted goods *à la sauvette*.[3] In this article I examine the policing of the black market in two key French port cities—Marseille and Algiers. Through these dual case studies, I argue that officers specifically targeted the spaces they saw as "North African" when trying to stamp out black-market trading, inscribing

2. I use *Algerian* and *North African* roughly interchangeably. This reflects my sources, as French officials often conflated the two, but it also includes the Moroccan and Tunisian populations of Marseille. In both cities the vast majority of North Africans were Algerian. *French Mediterranean* is my own analytic term, not an actor category.

3. Literally translated as "on the sly," the phrase denotes something sold illegally on the streets.

these areas as zones of disloyalty and reinforcing an imaginary of North Africans as enemies of the ongoing French war effort. On both sides of the Mediterranean, officers used control of racialized space as a strategy and stand-in for racial discrimination.

This distinct treatment of North Africans was rooted in colonial discourses of racial difference, narratives that highlighted the supposedly inherent criminality of "Arabs." Local police documents, official government reports, academic studies, and daily newspaper articles in both Marseille and Algiers routinely described North Africans as jealous, proud, fanatically religious, violent, lazy, and innately prone to deceit and theft. These narratives of "colonial suspects" allowed police in both cities to justify a broad mandate of control over North Africans that would have been unthinkable for French or European immigrant populations.[4] Stereotypes of criminality had tangible impacts on how police interacted with North Africans. Scholars have shown, for example, how fears of North African "criminals" prompted the creation of specialized police brigades and aid bureaus in Paris in the 1920s.[5] The targeted policing of North Africans continued during World War II, with Vichy appropriating earlier republican institutions of colonial control to monitor North Africans.[6]

This targeted surveillance was not just a feature of Paris, however. By putting metropole and colony in direct conversation, this article shows how practices of colonial policing circulated within imperial networks. As the architectural historian Sheila Crane writes, "France today was made (and doubtless still is being remade) in Algeria, with and against Algeria."[7] Nowhere is this continual process of making and remaking more evident than in Marseille and Algiers. As key ports, these cities were connected by a constant flow of goods and people. Centering them, then, allows us to see both the shared imperatives of port cities and the legal and administrative distinctions between metropole and colony. As the political loyalties of Marseille and Algiers shifted during the war, police officers in both cities nonetheless remained convinced that North Africans posed a specific, and inherent, threat to France.

4. I take the idea of "colonial suspect" from Kathleen Keller, who traces the fluidity of the meaning of *suspect* in Afrique-Occidentale Française (*Colonial Suspects*).

5. On these Parisian services, see Beaujon, "Policing Colonial Migrants"; Blanchard, *La police parisienne et les Algériens*; Blanchard, "Des Kabyles 'perdus' en région parisienne"; Prakash, "Colonial Techniques in the Imperial Capital"; Prakash, *Empire on the Seine*; and Rosenberg, *Policing Paris*.

6. Aliénor Cadiot's exhaustive dissertation documents the complex history of Vichy administration of North Africans, analyzing Vichy anxieties over North African loyalty and attempts to control North African labor. Cadiot's project focuses, however, on the specialized bureaus rather than on the police and does not discuss North African "black marketeers." On the Marseille North African services, see Cadiot, "Vichy et les Algériens," chap. 4. On Vichy and the French empire, see Cantier and Jennings, *L'empire colonial sous Vichy*; and Cantier, *L'Algérie sous le régime de Vichy*.

7. Here Crane is referencing French architects' comparison of Marseille and Algiers ("On the Edge," 941).

The racialized policing of the North African black market relied, I argue, on police mapping ideas of criminality and race onto urban space. Marseille and Algiers existed within a connected Mediterranean world where visual codes of race were difficult to pin down, due to centuries of migration and shifting imperial boundaries.[8] Instead, police there coded racial identities through language, dress, religious practice, and most notably, space.[9] As Henri Lefebvre has demonstrated, space must be understood as socially constructed, "a set of relations and forms."[10] The police in Marseille and Algiers often discussed black-market crimes in spatial terms. Scholars, too, have analyzed the spatial politics of French policing. Yet these studies, and the police, frame space as a racially neutral category, a unit of policy, or at most, defined by class or crime rates.[11] Yet as Lefebvre points out, space is not neutral. Police and North Africans understood space through a series of social relationships, relations determined by colonial discourses (and realities) of inequality and criminality. Societies produce space and imbue it with meaning. In Marseille and Algiers the actions of local police helped produce the ideas of criminality that haunted North African neighborhoods.[12]

Police decisions about where to operate raids, where to set up networks of surveillance, and how to divide up the city for patrols reflected their "common-sense" understandings of where the black market was located.[13] Although both Marseille and Algiers had distinct "North African" neighborhoods, neither had a regime of formal racial segregation. Unlike other colonial cities that used public health codes, pass systems, or zoning laws to divide the city, segregation in Algiers developed from more de facto practices of expropriation and everyday racism.[14] In Marseille the concentration of North Africans in specific streets resulted

8. The policing of race has been rigorously explored in the US context, but the literature largely focuses on the paradigm of anti-Blackness. See Alexander, *New Jim Crow*; Hattery and Smith, *Policing Black Bodies*; and Muhammad, *Condemnation of Blackness*.

9. Literature on the French empire has looked at other processes of race making in Algeria, including the racialization of religion and economic personhood. See Davidson, *Only Muslim*; and Davis, *Markets of Civilization*.

10. Lefebvre, *Production of Space*, 116.

11. See, e.g., Dikeç, *Badlands of the Republic*; Le Gaoziou and Mucchielli, *Quand les banlieues brûlent*; and Roché, *Le frisson de l'émeute*. One exception to this colorblind view of space is Amit Prakash's discussion of the police "mapping" of the North African community in Paris's Goutte d'Or neighborhood (*Empire on the Seine*). On race and space in US policing, see Balto, *Occupied Territory*; and Shabazz, *Spatializing Blackness*.

12. On the social production of space, see McKittrick, *Demonic Grounds*, xi.

13. In her study of Dakar, Keller also discusses the spatial realities of colonial urban policing but argues that in Dakar police were *less* focused on the Medina because of the limits of colonial authority (*Colonial Suspects*, 71).

14. See Nightingale, *Segregation*. On urban planning in Dakar, see Bigon, *French Colonial Dakar*. On colonial segregation and public health, see Curtin, "Medical Knowledge and Urban Planning"; Echenberg, *Black Death, White Medicine*; Murunga, "'Inherently Unhygienic Races'"; and Swanson, "Sanitation Syndrome."

from a mix of proximity to employment, networks of resource sharing among migrants, and discriminatory rental practices. In targeting North African neighborhoods in their repression of the black market, the police coded these areas as spaces of disloyalty and North Africans themselves as dangerous internal enemies.[15] If the urban segregation of North Africans enabled discriminatory police practices, it could also create moments of resistance and solidarity. North Africans, bound by both discrimination and choice in specific neighborhoods, could resist police interventions in "their" space.

World War II provides a particularly interesting moment to study policing racialized space. The chaos of war exacerbated social tensions, and constantly shifting political alliances pushed French authorities to anxiously debate colonial loyalties. Policing the black market could operate as a proxy for policing the wartime fidelity of North Africans, painted by police as inherently threatening to internal stability. But the police pursuit of North African black-market traffickers also reveals broader patterns in the policing of North Africans, illustrating a system of racial control and collective resistance embedded in the geography of urban life.

War and Rationing in the French Mediterranean

Marseille and Algiers share a history of trade and migration dating back at least to the two cities' Phoenician origins. In the nineteenth century France's violent conquest of Algeria reinforced their ancient connections, linking Marseille and Algiers in a colonial network. As France expanded its Mediterranean empire, the movement of people, goods, and ideas between metropole and colony flowed through the ports of Marseille and Algiers. During World War I France recruited thousands of Algerians as soldiers and workers to serve in the metropole. After the war a steady stream of Algerian workers traveled by boat from Algiers to Marseille in search of higher metropolitan wages. Algerian immigration in this period was typically circular, a seasonal and repeated cycle of exile and return that almost inevitably passed through Marseille and Algiers.[16] This enduring pattern of immigration connected the two cities in a mutual history of movement and surveillance. The stream of goods and people within Marseille and Algiers also made them centers of black-market trading and policing. Police officials feared the transience of life in these bustling ports, imagining webs of untraceable profiteers.

15. I take this idea of how "bodies code/decode space and space codes/decodes bodies" from Rios, *Black Lives and Spatial Matters*, 2.

16. See Blanchard, *Histoire de l'immigration algérienne en France*.

Although linked, Marseille and Algiers also present distinct case studies of North African life during World War II. Marseille was a cosmopolitan port town known for its diverse population. Algerians in Marseille lived alongside neighbors from Dakar, Bastia, Madrid, Saigon, and Naples. In this Mediterranean melting pot, North Africans never formed more than a small minority. French officials suggested that about five thousand North Africans lived in Marseille in 1941, although this number likely does not account for conscripted soldiers or workers.[17] Beginning in the interwar period, the North African community of Marseille had congregated "behind the Bourse," a neighborhood of narrow streets wedged between the Vieux Port and St. Charles train station. The heart of the district was Rue des Chapeliers, a street packed with North African cafés, specialty stores, and rundown hotels where North Africans lived in shared quarters.

Algiers offered a different geography of Algerian life. After their initial conquest of Algiers in 1830, the French carved up the city according to military priorities. Scholars argue that this urban revision was not simply a matter of housing troops but also a symbolic demonstration of France's dominance.[18] As the colonial government rebuilt Algiers, Algerians were increasingly restricted to the neighborhood of the Casbah.[19] French observers indelibly associated the Casbah, named for the walled fortress that once encircled the area, with Algerian social and political life. Algiers had roughly 260,000 residents in 1936; according to some sources, however, the population skyrocketed to over 600,000 during World War II due to rural migrants, international refugees, and French and foreign troops.[20] Many Algerian rural migrants, fleeing scarcity and famine, headed for the Casbah, worsening the already dire overpopulation of the neighborhood. Unable to squeeze into the Casbah, others settled in the shantytowns (*bidonvilles*) that began to dot the city.[21] Although the number of Algerians in Algiers

17. The report noted that it was notoriously difficult to establish the number of North Africans but estimated that there were forty thousand in France in 1941. Archives Départementales des Bouches-du-Rhône (hereafter ADBR), 76 W 205, Oct. 13, 1941. According to census data from the Institut National de la Statistique et des Etudes Economiques, the population of Marseille fell from over 914,000 in 1936 to about 630,000 in 1946, but it fluctuated during the war.

18. Çelik, "Historic Intersections."

19. On the urban history of Algiers, see Benatia, *Alger*; Çelik, *Urban Forms and Colonial Confrontations*; Icheboudene, *Alger*; Kaddache, "La Casbah"; and Lespès, *Alger*. While all these scholars acknowledge segregation as a fact of life in Algiers, none propose an idea of racialized space in the Casbah, nor do they discuss the police.

20. One historian cites a population growth of nearly two hundred thousand between 1940 and 1943, based on American military sources (Salinas, *Les Américains en Algérie*, 189). Mahfoud Kaddache cites the 1936 census data and contends that statistics from during the war are notoriously unreliable ("La Casbah," 26, 35–36).

21. The policing and destruction of the shantytowns animated debates in the postwar, but during World War II police tracking of the black market focused primarily on the Casbah. On the bidonvilles, see Crane, "Housing as Battleground"; and House, "Intervening on 'Problem' Areas and Their Inhabitants."

grew during the war, Europeans continued to form an overall majority of Algiers's urban population. In this colonial city, French law stratified citizenship. Nineteenth-century decrees incorporated native Algerian Jews as French citizens and later extended citizenship to the multinational European population. Most Muslim Algerians, in contrast, were subjects, ruled by the *indigénat* code that supposedly respected Islamic customs but also wrote colonial ideas of racial difference into law.[22]

Despite legal differences, the police, as an organization, looked similar in Marseille and Algiers. In both cities, three branches operated in tandem: the Police d'Etat, the Gendarmerie, and the Sûreté.[23] Each had distinct responsibilities, but all three participated in the policing of North Africans and the repression of the black market, depending on the circumstances. In Marseille the surveillance of North Africans also interested the administrative services designed to control North Africans in the metropole. This bureau had existed in Marseille since 1928, an offshoot of programs launched in Paris.[24] It collaborated closely with police, sending reports on North African "troublemakers" and coordinating on investigations. When Vichy came to power, the new regime reorganized the existing Marseille bureau into two services: the military-led Service des Affaires Algériens (SAA) and the civilian Bureau des Affaires Musulmanes Nord-Africaines.[25] In Algiers the Service de Liaison Nord-Africain, a bureau designed to gather and distribute information on Algerians, also worked closely with police. "The police," then, were not just beat cops but overlapping brigades operating in tandem and office bureaucrats who took on surveillance roles.

After French defeat by the German army in 1940, the collaborationist Vichy regime governed both Marseille and Algiers. Vichy undertook a sweeping reform of the French police system, including creating the infamous units that terrorized French Jews, communists, and members of the Resistance during the war.[26] The Vichy government also streamlined economic control services, creating a national Contrôle Economique charged with enforcing wartime

22. Vichy revoked the citizenship of Algerian Jews, although it was restored with Allied conquest in 1942. On the *indigénat* code, see Thénault, *Violence ordinaire dans l'Algérie coloniale*; Saada, "La loi, le droit et l'indigène"; and Surkis, *Sex, Law, and Sovereignty in French Algeria.*

23. On the structure and function of French policing, see Berlière, *Le monde des polices en France*; and Milliot et al., *Histoire des polices en France.*

24. Similar services also existed in Lyon and Saint-Etienne, although their almost complete lack of funding made them one-man operations. On Lyon, see Begag, *Place du Pont*; and Massard-Guilbaud, *Des Algériens à Lyon.* On the much larger Parisian services, see Beaujon, "Policing Colonial Migrants"; Blanchard, *La police parisienne et les Algériens*; Blanchard, "Des Kabyles 'perdus' en région parisienne"; Prakash, "Colonial Techniques in the Imperial Capital"; Prakash, *Empire on the Seine*; and Rosenberg, *Policing Paris.*

25. On these services in a national context, see Cadiot, "Vichy et les Algériens."

26. On these changes, see Kitson, *Police and Politics in Marseille*; and Berlière and Chabrun, *Les policiers français sous l'Occupation.*

price regulations.[27] During World War II decrees restricted the quantities and standard prices for food staples like flour, sugar, oil, vegetables, and milk, as well as essentials like soap, gasoline, cloth, and rubber and luxuries like chocolate and alcohol.[28] Restaurants could serve only certain types of meals and only during specific hours. Almost immediately a black market sprang up, offering access to forbidden goods for those who could afford to pay the inflated prices. In both Marseille and Algiers, Economic Brigades—special police units focused on economic crimes—monitored marketplaces and tracked food prices throughout the city, although they were perennially understaffed.[29] Local police from other brigades, too, chased after black-market fraud, investigating anonymous denunciations or attempting to catch traffickers red-handed during daily rounds. The vague and expansive definition of illicit activity allowed the police to broadly interpret all informal commerce as illegal. Selling almost anything outside the narrow confines of restricted markets could thus constitute "black-market activity."

The black market was an omnipresent feature of life in France and its empire during World War II, and conflicts over scarce resources deepened existing social divisions.[30] French citizens mobilized categories of the "undesirable" in battles over food and housing, stigmatizing refugees, foreigners, and French Jews in an effort to guard resources.[31] French women, in particular, took to the streets to demand that the government provide food for their families.[32] At first Vichy authorities described black-market traffickers as enemies of the state, greedy individuals stealing food from the starving populace. The historian Fabrice Grenard argues, however, that as the war dragged on, Vichy grudgingly accepted the black market as a practical necessity. Within French Resistance circles, the black market was even celebrated as an act of rebellion against the German occupier.[33] On a more interpersonal scale, exchanges that violated regulations could also serve the needs of families and communities, reinforcing the

27. Economic Brigades collaborated with local municipal police but nationally fell under the jurisdiction of the general secretary for police and the minister of the interior. Grenard, *La France du marché noir*, 75; Grenard, "L'administration du contrôle économique en France," 142; Mouré, *Marché Noir*, chap. 3. On rationing law under Vichy, see Grenard, Le Bot, and Perrin, *Histoire économique de Vichy*; and Mouré, *Marché Noir*, chap. 2.

28. On the history of the Contrôle Économique, see Grenard, "L'administration du contrôle économique en France."

29. For example, in 1947 just ten Economic Brigade agents patrolled all of Algiers. ANOM, 1F 435, Jan. 1947.

30. On the black market, see Grenard, *La France du marché noir*; Grenard, *Les scandales du ravitaillement*; Mouré, *Marché Noir*; Mouré, "*La Capitale de la Faim*"; Mouré, "Black Market Fictions"; Grenard and Mouré, "Traitors, *Trafiquants*, and the Confiscation of 'Illicit Profits'"; and Sanders, *Histoire du marché noir*.

31. Fogg, *Politics of Everyday Life*. On Jews and the black market, see Grenard, *La France du marché noir*, 54.

32. On the policing of women's activism, see Schwartz, *Today Sardines Are Not for Sale*.

33. Grenard, *La France du marché noir*, 98, 185; Grenard, "L'administration du contrôle économique en France," 143.

popular disapproval of strict enforcement.[34] Acknowledging the unpopularity of policing the black market, official policy pivoted in 1942 toward tracking down large-scale operators rather than punishing occasional, nonprofessional traffickers.[35]

This tacit acceptance and focus on kingpins, however, was not true in the North African case.[36] Police officers in Marseille and Algiers knew that demand from French and European customers drove the black market. Government officials acknowledged that the "kings of the black market" running large operations made the bulk of the profits.[37] In most areas of metropolitan France, police focused their efforts on butchers, shopkeepers, and agricultural producers, professions closely connected to the production and sale of rationed food. Yet police reports in Marseille and Algiers obsessed over the idea of a shadowy network of North African black marketers. Police repression of North African participation in the black market focused not on stores or farmers but on small-scale, one-off trades that typically happened on the street. This strategy targeted North Africans not because they made the most money from the black market but because they were the most visible and vulnerable to police surveillance. As the policing of the black market became more unpopular among French citizens, police could point to their pursuit of North African traffickers as an uncontroversial battle against internal enemies.[38] For North Africans selling odds and ends on the streets, they were simply operating as they always had, but the context of war and police discretion now rendered their actions illegal. In their hunt for North African black marketers, the police treated North Africans not as individual criminals but as a racialized block of potential profiteers. In doing so, the police made North Africans' alleged participation in the black market a proxy for their inherent disloyalty, despite a more fluid idea of what participation in the black market meant for other, noncolonial populations.

In the first years of the war, Vichy controlled both Marseille and Algiers. Then, in 1942, Allied forces invaded Algiers, and the Free French Resistance, led by Charles de Gaulle, established a new republican government in the city.

34. See Mouré, *Marché Noir*, chap. 1; and Mouré, "'Economic Tyranny.'"

35. Grenard bases this argument on a quantitative analysis of Paris records, as well as files from other departments (*La France du marché noir*, chap. 6).

36. The black-market literature centers on Paris and German occupation. Little attention has been paid to the south of France, and there is no examination of the empire or of North African participation in the black market.

37. Grenard, *La France du marché noir*, 178; Grenard, "L'administration du contrôle économique en France," 152.

38. Kenneth Mouré points out that the Contrôle Economique measured its efficacy through the number of fines issued. Fining vulnerable North Africans may have been one way to increase numbers without incurring public backlash from the French population. Mouré, *Marché Noir*, chap. 3; Mouré, "Economic Tyranny," 4.

From 1942 to 1944 Marseille and Algiers stood on opposite sides of the ongoing war effort. For years historians and politicians treated Vichy as a radical shift, a tragic ellipsis in France's otherwise republican trajectory.[39] The policing of other marginalized groups, particularly Jews, certainly changed under Vichy, with horrific consequences. But for North Africans, this "break" proved almost imperceptible on the ground, as evidenced by the continuity in the racially targeted policing of the black market. Despite clear political differences and opposing wartime alliances, the police of liberated Algiers and Vichy Marseille proved consistent in their wary treatment of Algerians. In both cities police regarded North Africans accused of black-market sales as internal enemies, ready to sabotage a vulnerable French nation.[40]

Policing the Black Market in Marseille

As the war ramped up and food became scarce, the police and the North African aid services of Marseille scrutinized the local North African community for fraudulent behavior. In a routine surveillance note on Algerian life in Marseille in February 1942, the SAA noted a flux of unemployed North Africans in the city. The head of the SAA, Commandant Wender, suggested that these arrivals could be responsible for the "numerous thefts, illicit trafficking, and diverse infractions" happening in the city.[41] Wender's note included a list of fifty-nine North African men charged with black-market crimes, such as trafficking in forbidden or restricted products, overcharging for price-controlled foods, or fencing stolen goods. Records from the local police stations of Marseille similarly displayed an inordinate number of North Africans accused of black-market crimes.[42] The Marseille police never claimed that North Africans dominated the black market in their city. As they did elsewhere in France, police in Marseille targeted fraud in bars, restaurants, grocery stores, and butcher shops. The "intense" black market in the Phoenician city also included a vibrant trade in illicit pastis, controlled by veritable mob bosses.[43] With North Africans, however, police surveillance moved beyond a focus on "professional" profiteers. If North Africans represented only

39. Robert Paxton, for example, ignited debates when he exposed how Vichy policies continued in the Fourth Republic, framing the legacy of Vichy as one of continuity rather than rupture (*Vichy France*). See also Noiriel, *Les origines républicaines de Vichy*.

40. The idea of an "internal enemy" has been theorized by Mathieu Rigouste, who describes the treatment of postcolonial immigrants as "internal enemies" as an extension of Cold War attitudes about communism and decolonization ("L'ennemi intérieur"). My research demonstrates that this process was already underway during World War II.

41. ADBR, 76 W 205, Feb. 13, 1942. On the complex career of Wender, see Cadiot, "Agir seul ou en réseau?"

42. ADBR, 76 W 144.

43. Grenard, for example, says that police found stashes of black-market goods and even a cow hidden in a cave after the German bombing of Le Panier, a working-class neighborhood associated with Italian and Corsican immigrants (*La France du marché noir*, 161).

a small portion of the overall black market, the police repeatedly insisted that a disproportionate number of North Africans profited off illegal trading.

Administrative bureaus and police officers in Marseille operated under the assumption that North Africans could not be trusted with scarce resources. In 1943, for example, Wender procured rations for North Africans to celebrate Eid al-Fitr.[44] He called for a general distribution of tea and couscous but cautioned that special provisions would be required for rare goods like meat and sugar. Wender suggested that the meat be distributed through controlled halal butchers or European-run aid organizations, warning that passing out meat ad hoc risked seeing the precious commodity immediately sold on the black market. Even when meant to help North Africans, Wender's mission of aid was colored by his conviction that North Africans would succumb to the temptation of trafficking.

Surveillance services highlighted Algerian mobility as a primary reason for suspicion. In 1941 Wender requested a police investigation of an Algerian man named Boulou. Wender accused Boulou, who had recently been released from prison, of selling fake bread-ration tickets.[45] The police tracked down Boulou, an illiterate day laborer who worked on the docks and had a side gig as an amateur boxer. Boulou had arrived in Marseille in 1924 and worked as the manager of a bar owned by his European girlfriend, Georgette. By all accounts, Boulou had a long history with the police. His rap sheet listed charges of fraud, violence, theft, and pimping in Marseille, and he had been accused of falsifying passports in Algiers. However, there was little evidence of Boulou's supposed black-market dealings. The allegation of selling fake bread rations was based entirely on the testimony of a competing restaurant owner. Despite the lack of evidence, the police deemed Boulou a suspect figure because of his frequent movements in and from Marseille since his release from prison.[46] The mobility of Algerians within Marseille, between cities, and across the Mediterranean worried police. The transient nature of Algerian life made them less legible in the eyes of the French state and also provided the opportunity, the police believed, for them to tap into black-market networks.[47]

Fearing Algerian mobility, the police turned their attention to a hub of North African life in Marseille: the port. Officers associated the port with North Africans not only because of circular patterns of North African immigration but

44. ADBR, 76 W 209, Chef du SAINA à M. le Préfet, Oct. 4, 1943.

45. The police and the SAA both misspelled Boulou's name "Bollon," a recurrent issue in police attempts to spell Arabic names. ADBR, 76 W 205, Commissaire Divisionnaire Seignard à M. le Intendant Régional de Police, Dec. 17, 1941.

46. ADBR, 76 W 205.

47. On state efforts to render populations legible, see Scott, *Seeing like a State*. On "undesirable" mobility, see Boittin, *Undesirable*.

also because of the many North Africans employed there as dockers, porters, and sailors. Police suspected that North Africans' connection to the port created opportunity for furtive mobility. For example, a letter from the Prefecture of Constantine alerted the North African services of Marseille that an Algerian who had recently returned to Constantine claimed that his "*coreligionnaires*" had given up regular work altogether in favor of profits from the black market.[48] The source cited a friend who "shuttled" between Paris and Marseille with contraband cigarettes, pulling in a staggering profit of 25,000 to 30,000 francs per trip.[49] Fretting over these rumors, police interpreted Algerians' trans-Mediterranean connections and their mobility between Marseille and other metropolitan cities as evidence of trafficking.

The policing of the black market in Marseille homed in on other spaces long associated with North Africans, such as Rue des Chapeliers. Wender wrote a sprawling report in November 1942 about the dangers of trafficking on this street. Recently, he noted, Rue des Chapeliers had become encumbered with "unsavory *indigènes* . . . the various traffickers who come to sell their products."[50] To curtail the black market, police officers periodically blocked off Rue des Chapeliers and searched those caught between the barricades. Descending on the trapped crowd, the police would verify IDs and confiscate suspect goods. These recurring raids upset the shopkeepers on Rue des Chapeliers. Beyond the disturbance to their businesses, they complained that shady characters would break windows and overturn merchandise in their haste to escape the police cordon. Wender suggested that the police should station a permanent detail on Rue des Chapeliers until the "undesirables" stopped their practice of trafficking on the street.[51] In the chaos and short staffing of the war, however, the Marseille police lacked the resources to carry out Wender's plan. Instead, officers continued their periodic raids, lumping all North Africans on the street into the same category of potential black-market trafficker.

This focus on Rue des Chapeliers continued through the end of the war and the downfall of the Vichy regime. In a report from 1945, the regional general secretary for the police highlighted incidents of violence on Rue des Chapeliers. Although the report focused primarily on bloody fights between North African civilians and West African soldiers, the general secretary also had some choice

48. Officials used *correligionnaire* almost interchangeably with *indigène* to discuss Algerians in Marseille and Algiers. This operated as a racial or colonial category more than as a religious one.
49. ADBR, 76 W 206, Mar. 14, 1942.
50. French actors used the word *indigène* to describe the population I refer to as Algerian. I conserve this word in French because the offensive slur has no clear English equivalent. ADBR, 76 W 205, Nov. 3, 1942.
51. ADBR, 76 W 205, Nov. 3, 1942.

words about the street itself: "It must be noted that it is in this street, where the majority of buildings are occupied by North Africans, that all the traffickers of the black market go, as well as the criminal underworld [pègre]."[52] This letter linked North Africans and Rue des Chapeliers explicitly to the black market, portraying them as the center of this lawless world. More generally, the letter's language marked Rue des Chapeliers as a space of crime and danger, associating everyone who lived there with a criminal netherworld. Rue des Chapeliers was the heart of the North African community in Marseille, home to law-abiding workers, families, and businesses. In police accounts, however, Rue des Chapeliers featured primarily as a space of illicit activity.

Jean Bourgeois, the head of Marseille's Bureau des Affaires Musulmanes Nord-Africaines, echoed the same sentiments in a 1945 note. Bourgeois claimed that Marseille was "overflowing" with unemployed Muslims who "quickly instructed by their *coreligionnaires*, join the Marseille underground" and reap profits from the black market. Bourgeois ominously warned that the growth of black-market trading "can only lead to a new evolution among all the Muslims, who pick up the habit of not working anymore, an evolution whose effects will become clear on their return to North Africa and that will inevitably bring some disastrous disruptions in our colonies."[53] In a tangled and interminable sentence, Bourgeois combined old colonial discourses of North African criminality with new wartime preoccupations. He implied that North Africans had become a threat to public safety because of their participation in illegal trafficking. Evoking a stereotype of North African laziness, Bourgeois further cautioned that the black market was "teaching" North Africans to avoid honest work, creating a long-term labor problem for the French Empire.

Fears of the black market resonated with anxieties about North African collaboration with the Germans, erstwhile allies of the Vichy regime but also a colonial rival. French officials insisted that North Africans' anti-Semitism and naivete made them fall for German propaganda, but Germany also made a concerted effort to win over North African populations.[54] In 1941 the SAA carefully recorded a conversation between one of their informants and an Algerian butcher who had recently left Paris. This anonymous butcher accused a man named Louaid S. of being a German spy.[55] The note further asserted that Louaid made his living from black-market profits, procuring merchandise during frequent trips to Marseille and through connections in Algiers. The report conflated black-market activity with other behaviors seen as being against the interest of the

52. ADBR, 149 W 171, Secrétaire Général pour la Police à M. le Commissaire de la République, June 4, 1945.

53. ADBR, 5 W 374, July 6, 1945.

54. See Herf, *Nazi Propaganda for the Arab World*; and Cadiot, "Vichy et les Algériens," 119.

55. ADBR, 76 W 205, May 10, 1941.

French state, in this case working for the German occupiers. Louaid represented an amalgam of fears that French police and officials harbored about North African profiteers. Not only did these sinister figures accumulate profits by depriving French citizens of food, but they also aligned themselves with Germany, threatening French rule in Algeria.

No one in Marseille thought that only North Africans participated in the black market. Other populations, too, had connections to international ports and global supply chains. Marseille was a notorious center of gang violence, corruption, and criminal networks linked to Corsica and Italy, also associated with the black market.[56] Yet if French officials saw the black market as a general problem, they maintained that North Africans played a particular role. At the port the police highlighted the transient nature of Algerian life as evidence of their participation in the black market. Further inland, police and aid bureau reports portrayed Rue des Chapeliers as a hotbed of criminal activity and treated anyone on the street as a potential trafficker. Officials' fixation on North African participation in the black market reinforced an idea of their questionable loyalty, framing North Africans as a population that required close observation.

"Hunting" the Black Market in Algiers

The black market also plagued wartime Algiers, and police were certain who was to blame. A police report in 1942 noted that while goods like thread could not be found in any store, they were sold on the sidewalk by Algerians "without any authorization and at prohibitive prices."[57] Another police report from 1943 was even more explicit, noting that trafficking was "still and overwhelmingly practiced by the *indigène* element."[58] Unlike in Marseille, the police in Algiers identified Algerians as the core operators of the black market, crediting them for the entirety of illegal commerce in the city. As in Marseille, however, the police of Algiers associated the Algerian black market with particular spaces. The report on thread, for example, highlighted the location of these illicit sales on Rue de la Lyre, a main commercial thoroughfare at the bottom of the Casbah. Many police reports repeated this same association between the Casbah and the black market, a narrative that wove together race and space in the pursuit of illegal commerce.

Officers described Algerian traffickers as rapacious profiteers who gained wealth at the expense of Algiers's European population. What the reports on black-market activity do not acknowledge, however, is the inequality built into

---

56. On "bandes organisées" in Marseille, see Regnard-Drouot, *Marseille la violente*. On the black market in Marseille, see Grenard, *La France du marché noir*, 161.

57. ANOM, 1 F 119, Nov. 3, 1942.

58. ANOM, 1 F 120, Feb. 28, 1943.

rationing. North Africans complained about the discriminatory rationing system.[59] Certain luxuries, like chocolate and alcohol, were accessible only to Europeans, and Algerian and European populations were issued different ration cards. The French state justified this inequality by citing the supposedly simple needs of Algerians. One intercepted telegram from an anonymous European resident of Algiers complained that the ration policy was *too* generous toward Algerians. The government gave unnecessary rations to Algerian families, this telegram proclaimed, since "everyone knows the extreme sobriety of these people." The surplus, it alleged, promptly landed on the black market.[60] This stereotyped understanding of the needs of "primitive" peoples, however, barely disguised a regime intended to prioritize Algeria's European population. Rationing made clear the fallacy at the heart of French colonial rule in Algeria. France had declared Algeria an integral part of France and Algerians French nationals (although not citizens). Algerians were French enough to be drafted as soldiers but not French enough to merit equal access to food. By insisting that Algerians had fewer needs, French authorities and local residents twisted the desperation of Algerians to provide for their families in unequal conditions into a crime against France.

The targeted policing of Algerians could result in moments of tension between Algerians and police officers. In September 1944 police officers attempted to arrest an Algerian merchant for overcharging for his goods. An Algerian soldier, enlisted in the French army, interrupted the police, yelling, "Don't give them your ID card—Don't just go along with it. Surround them."[61] Nor, the central police commissioner of Algiers reported, was this an isolated event. That same day two Economic Brigade agents had been surrounded by an angry Algerian crowd at Rue Randon market on the edge of the Casbah. The report alleged that the two agents were saved from a "bad ending" only because one of them took out his gun and shot at a wall, forcing the crowd to retreat. The police attempted to target fraud in Randon market, an Algerian space. But Algerians challenged the colonial power structure, using their strength of numbers in the Casbah to force the police to back down, at least temporarily.

Eight months later two Economic Brigade agents seized several kilograms of potatoes from a vegetable seller. The officers explained that they confiscated the goods because the vendor, Amrouni A., had been unable to clarify how he procured the starchy roots and had been selling them at an illegally high price. As the two officers took the potatoes, Amrouni called out to his fellow Algerians

---

59. E.g., ADBR, 76 W 206, Jan. 13, 1942.
60. ANOM, GGA 7CAB 12, X à M. Paul Lombard, June 4, 1942.
61. ANOM, 4I 32, Sept. 14, 1944.

in the market: "What are you waiting for, why don't you beat these guys up [*casser la geule à ces gens-là*]? They only go after us—we can't let them get away with it."[62] The agents promptly scattered but later filed a complaint against Amrouni for "threats and provocations to disorder." In his call for solidarity, Amrouni made plain a fact clearly visible in police records: the Economic Brigade did not police the black market evenly in Algiers. Rather, as Amrouni said, the police only went after "us"—Algerians.

Police, however, could trump resistance with violence. In December 1944, for example, the Algerian newspaper *La liberté* reported that the police had raided the shop of Meki Moktar, accused of selling cloth on the black market. When they found nothing in his store, officers brought him to the station. A graphic, haunting passage in the article detailed how officers beat, stripped, and sexually assaulted Moktar, trying to get him to "confess."[63] Following this torture, the article says, Moktar admitted to trafficking despite his innocence. The newspaper, published years after the Allied takeover of Algiers, described the police torture as "Hitlerian," associating this brutality with fascism. Although Moktar's case is rare in the archival record, more mundane incidents of police violence almost certainly characterized the policing of the black market in Algiers. North Africans selling produce, sugary beignets, or bits of cloth from carts or in market squares would have regularly encountered shouts, shoves, and threats to haul them off to the station.

As in Marseille, the police of Algiers saw the black market as connected to Algerians' questionable loyalty to France, although the fear focused on a different international interloper. In 1942 the Allied troops invaded Algiers and set up the colonial capital as the headquarters of their campaign to retake Europe. Although the new French republican leaders of Algiers supposedly saw the Americans as allies, they still feared the influence of American troops on Algerians.[64] In a note from 1943 the prefect of Algiers informed the central police commissioner that "a group of almost exclusively *indigènes* youths" earned money by selling alcohol to Allied soldiers.[65] Catering to the soldiers, the youngsters could avoid wage labor by charging "exorbitant" prices like 150 francs for a bottle of muscatel.[66] The prefect warned that these young men dressed in rags to "elicit pity

62. ANOM, 1 K 212, May 28, 1945.
63. *La liberté* was a republican newspaper published in French in Algiers, with some Algerian contributors. Bibliothèque Nationale de l'Algérie. See "Un commerçant musulman faussement accusé de vente illicite est honteusement torturé dans un commissariat de police," *La liberté*, Dec. 7, 1944.
64. The regime change had little impact on racist police views of Algerians, as these stereotypes were rooted in long-standing colonial tropes rather than in German racial ideologies.
65. ANOM, 1 F 435, Aug. 2, 1943.
66. For reference, the daily wage for dockworkers in Marseille at the time was around 100 francs. ADBR, 4 M 2361, Commissaire Divisionnaire de la Police Spéciale à M. le Préfet, Mar. 27, 1940.

from a police more and more absent yet still to be feared" but appeared much better dressed "outside the theater of their operations."[67] The prefect called on the police to pursue the young tricksters, but it was more than just the black market he seemed to fear. The opportunity for profit and for political influence created by the presence of American soldiers upped the stakes of this black-market trading.

As the war drew to a close, the intense focus on Algerian black-market sellers continued. In 1945 Georges Lafond, the principal police commissioner of Algiers, sent a report to the mayor about the city's black-market problem. Lafond claimed that rural Algerians had flooded into Algiers during the war looking for employment with the Allied troops. These migrants had now become "idlers" and "specialists of the black market," posing a serious public danger.[68] Despite police officers' "daily and unpitying hunt," they seemed incapable of stamping out the Algerian black market. Lafond had long held a grudge against Algerian traffickers. A year earlier he had referred to them as "parasites" and said that these Algerian men "increased the already too numerous idlers who wander the streets, ready to be led astray by any Muslim troublemaker, to the profit of Muslim anti-French movements."[69] Lafond emphasized not just the criminal but the political stakes of the black market, connecting the criminal underworld he described to "anti-French" political movements. Algerians, Lafond argued, were untrustworthy not only because of their illicit trades but also because of their questionable loyalty.

Though they had identified Algerians as the center of the black market, the police of Algiers despaired of methods to suppress the trade. The police complained that those who participated in the black market were impossible to track, referencing long-standing discourses of the dangerous anonymity of Algerians. As a report from the Economic Brigade explained, "Because of the difficulty in carrying out pursuits against 'black-market' traffickers (most of them homeless), the necessity of proceeding to the seizure of goods detained by these individuals and its sale at the tax price has imposed itself."[70] With a homeless, mobile population of traffickers, fines proved moot, as the police could not find the traffickers and force them to pay. Instead, agents would confiscate goods and sell them to cover the cost of fines or donate them to charities for redistribution.[71] Police complained that the profits of the black market far outweighed the paltry fines or occasional confiscation. The law, however, blocked more extreme measures of repression.

67. ADBR, 4 M 2361.
68. ANOM, 1 F 124, June 29, 1945.
69. ANOM, 1F 439, Commissaire Principal Lafond à M. Le Commissaire Central, Sept. 13, 1944.
70. ANOM, 1 K 631, Dec. 5, 1942.
71. ANOM, 1 F 124, Aug. 20, 1945.

In 1944 the prefect of Algiers, Louis Perillier, therefore laid out a new plan. Perillier had ordered regular raids to suppress the black market that he believed festered in the Casbah. As a result of these spatially targeted raids, the police captured many "delinquents" but could not jail them. Perillier claimed that this led to the police arresting and releasing the same men, a discouraging situation. Instead, Perillier suggested a new approach. The Algerian government had recently started requisitioning agricultural laborers. Any individual who did not respond to a requisition order could be arrested and sent to a depot before being assigned to a worksite. Perillier requested that this measure be adapted as a tool for punishing the black market. He proposed that all "black market fraudsters" between the ages of fifteen and fifty, caught trafficking and unable to prove "regular" employment, be sent to agricultural labor camps. Perillier highlighted that this measure was "effective as well as legal" and asked for 100,000 francs to support the initiative.[72]

The prefect framed his plans as responding to the frustrations of the police and the overwhelming size of the black market in Algiers, but he also seemed to be answering the demands of *colons* in the Algerian countryside. The misery of the war had pushed rural Algerians toward the city. This influx, however, left European farmers without a supply of cheap, itinerant labor. European farmers also blamed the temptations of the black market for the emigration of Algerian laborers. The *colons* had lobbied in March 1943 to requisition agricultural laborers, saying that doing so would prevent the city from seeing "so many idlers in the *cafés maures*."[73] Prefect Perillier understood his solution as serving two goals. In his letter outlining the plan, he highlighted that seizing profiteers in the Casbah would reduce the black market while also providing a captive labor force for the European farmers in the countryside left shorthanded by the war.[74]

By September 1944 the plan had been implemented. The thick dossier of accused traffickers I found was the first group of men arrested under the aegis of this new operation. In a letter to the governor-general of Algeria, the prefect noted that fifty men had been arrested in police raids and would be requisitioned for agricultural labor or sent off to public-works projects.[75] The men in the files represent the most precarious segment of Algerian society. Recently arrived rural migrants without industrial or technical job experience, they were vulnerable to wartime scarcity. Without deep ties to the urban center, they had no address to list in Algiers, no friends to put down as employers, no way to avoid being caught in the net of targeted police surveillance.

72. ANOM, 1 F 439, Préfet d'Alger à M. le Gouverneur Générale d'Algérie, Oct. 20, 1944.
73. ANOM, 1 K 130, Mar. 4, 1943.
74. ANOM, 1 F 439, Préfet d'Alger à M. le Gouverneur Générale d'Algérie, Oct. 20, 1944.
75. ANOM, 1 F 439.

No law or decree formally legalized this plan. Rather, the context of the war gave the police the ability to operate purely by internal policy.[76] Defenders of the police claim that officers are neutral representatives of the law, yet as this example shows, the "law" can be nothing more than a series of internal notes. The war gave the prefect the authority to unilaterally enact his plan, and the police had full discretion to decide what counted as black-market activity or "regular" employment. Although all the men in the folder were accused of "black-market" activity, none were tried in a court of law. In metropolitan France, courts occasionally sentenced traffickers with internment, but the Vichy government reserved this harshest punishment for defendants accused of particularly large-scale fraud, the worst of the *rois du marché noir*.[77] This was self-evidently not the case with these Algerian men. Given the vague parameters and wide police discretion, it seems likely that many of these men were arrested while simply wandering the streets of Algiers, selling a spare piece of clothing, some fruit, or a contraband pack of cigarettes, when the police happened on them. Arrested for a crime that legally could not be punished with jail time, they lost their freedom of mobility and of choice.

Perillier's plan quickly ran afoul of reality. On September 29 the director of the depot in Kouba, a suburb of Algiers, shot off a harried letter that, he irritably noted, followed up on telephone calls on the 26th, 27th, and 28th of the same month. The first group of twenty-two arrested Algerian traffickers arrived at the camp in Kouba on September 21. The caravan of men had been given 10 kilos of sugar, 3 kilos of coffee, 5 bars of soap, and 101 liters of gas, but no bread or vegetables. The exasperated director marked this obvious oversight with a series of angry question marks in his letter.[78]

The difficulties only continued from there. The director had been collaborating with local farmers who needed laborers, but when handed the contracts, the potential employers refused to sign. They had hoped that the government would provide room and board for the requisitioned workers, an expense the camp was not equipped to undertake. To make matters worse, the Algerians themselves refused to work. Several of the men in the camp had had been classified in their police files as "dangerous" ex-convicts, and four men had already escaped. Having been kept in the camp for seven days without work, the detained men

76. Scholars have shown that bureaucrats often unofficially governed by internal logics, giving wide discretion to street-level employees. See Lewis, *Boundaries of the Republic*; and Spire, *Etrangers à la carte*.

77. Grenard argues that internment was "systematically" reserved for traffickers of great notoriety (*La France du marché noir*, 88).

78. On the 23rd a contingent of twenty-one more "traffickers" arrived. The letter suggests there were a total of seventy-five men in the camp. ANOM, 1 F 439, Directeur de l'Office Régional du Travail à M. Le Préfet, Sept. 29, 1944.

became restless. To prevent "numerous evasions or even more serious incidents," the camp director placed all the accused traffickers in their rooms under guard. As the director pointed out in his exasperated report, all of this was illegal. The camp at Kouba had been intended to house "agricultural workers" who had refused to answer a requisition order.[79] These accused traffickers could not legally be detained in Kouba. The archives are unclear about the official destiny of the Kouba program, but the example reveals an expansion in the scope of police power.

The men arrested in the Casbah and sent off to Kouba exemplify central tenets of policing the black market in Algiers. Police officers explicitly stated their belief that Algerians were the primary black-market operatives. In their relentless "hunt" for traffickers, the police focused their energy on spaces of Algerian daily life, principally the Casbah. The police found the men sent to Kouba because of how officers mapped ideas of the black market onto neighborhoods they already understood as Algerian. In doing so, police agents criminalized unemployment, scouring the Casbah with a predetermined idea of Algerian culpability. The targeting of black-market repression in "Algerian" spaces mirrors methods of repression in Marseille, showing a circulation of ideas of Algerian criminality and tactics of police discrimination. The difference here, however, was in how far police officers could expand their authority. If Economic Brigade agents throughout France often served as judge and jury, in Algiers the burden of proof was lower and the consequences—forced labor and detention—higher.[80]

Smoking Out the Postwar Black Market

With the end of World War II in 1945, France began to reconstruct a republican ideal from the ashes of the fascist Vichy regime. The new government explicitly rejected all discourse of race in the new constitution, espousing full equality among Frenchmen. Postwar reforms also granted Algerian men citizenship, albeit in a two-tiered system that gutted true political representation. Nonetheless, France had declared Algerians French and thus equal under the law. Despite the national rhetoric of change, however, policing Algerians seemed to undergo little reform. As the commercial traffic of goods across the Mediterranean started to regain its normal cadence, once restricted products became available. However, scarcity remained a recurrent issue and rationing continued for goods like

79. The quoted phrase is underlined in the original document. ANOM, 1 F 439.
80. Grenard, for example, describes a shift to "administrative" justice, with agents of the Contrôle Economique able to hand out fines without court oversight ("L'administration du contrôle économique en France").

cloth, chocolate, and cigarettes, still sold in a vibrant black market.[81] In both Marseille and Algiers repressing the black market after the war reveals continuity in racialized policing despite legal changes.

In Algiers the police held Algerians responsible for trafficking everything from wine to meat, onions to carrots, flour to cigarettes. In the extensive paperwork written by the police of Algiers on the black market, European criminals barely make an appearance, although Europeans made up a majority of the population of Algiers. The files in the Wilaya d'Alger archives demonstrate the rarity of police pursuit of European black marketeers. To give just one example, in November 1944 the Algiers police received a letter about a European butcher allegedly selling meat on the black market. Rather than prosecuting him, however, the police suggested that "public rumors have a tendency to exaggerate the facts." The note concluded by saying that the butcher had simply deployed the "liberty of commerce" allowed to everyone.[82]

In contrast, the correlation between the black market and Algerians continued in the postwar period, evidenced even in articles in local newspapers and letters from concerned citizens. In 1945 the Committee for the Defense of the Interests of the Neighborhood of Babel Oued North complained that "we have observed that outside the market, little *indigènes,* in particular, sell garlic, lemons, lettuce, carrots, peppers, etc. etc. on the black market . . . while housewives can't find [these foods] in the market."[83] Similar grievances about Algerians lurking on the edges of the markets peppered both police reports and citizen complaint letters in the years after the war, demonstrating the longevity of the black-market "problem."

On January 24, 1947, the local newspaper *L'écho d'Alger* ran an exposé lamenting the spread of the black market in Algiers.[84] This article prompted an official investigation, carried out by Inspector Godard, who affirmed the truth of the article, listing the black-market goods sold near the Babel Oued market. He explained that "a multitude of young *indigènes,* veritable thugs who insult and steal from the housewives," sold soap, coffee, milk, rare vegetables like artichokes, and bread.[85] But things were in fact worse than the original article had claimed. Godard said that the black market in Algiers was not just continuing; it was growing. What had once been contained to the Casbah was now spilling out

---

81. The Contrôle Économique existed until 1949. Grenard, "L'administration du contrôle économique en France," 156. Resistance to market controls, however, was rampant from 1945 to 1947 and likely helped bring about the end of official rationing. See Mouré, "Economic Tyranny."

82. Archives de la Wilaya d'Alger, 4 H 89, Nov. 6, 1944.

83. ANOM, 1 F 435, Comité de Défense des Intérêts du Quartier du Bab El Oued Nord à M. Garcia, Adjoint au Président de la Délégation, June 5, 1945.

84. ANOM, 1 F 435, Directeur du Contrôle Économique d'Alger à M. le Préfet, Jan. 28, 1947.

85. ANOM, 1 F 435, Inspecteur Godard à M. le Directeur Départemental, Jan. 25, 1947.

into other areas. Godard's framing, however, remained consistent in its portrayal of Algerians as the ones to blame for this epidemic of trafficking.

Many of the postwar daily police reports in Algiers focused on Algerians selling black-market cigarettes. Report after report from 1945 to 1947 listed almost daily cases of Algerian men arrested for trafficking foreign cigarettes, recognized as such because the products lacked the official "band" printed on rationed cigarettes.[86] In one case, the police even caught an Algerian employee of the mayor of Algiers selling American cigarettes on the sidewalk at a markup.[87] Algerians could also be fined for the sale of cigarettes in a "forbidden zone" of the city, an issue not just of product but of space.[88] The gendered nature of these arrests was no accident. Cigarette sellers were almost invariably male, both because of the mobility needed to sell and the association of cigarettes with women of ill repute.

Protocol instructed police officers to turn over confiscated foodstuffs or luxury products to approved merchants, for resale, or to charitable organizations. In several cases, however, disgruntled locals observed police officers skimming profit off their black-market interventions. In July 1946 Georges Donat, a retired European functionary living in Algiers, wrote to inform the prefect that he had seen an officer, Guyard, who "performs raids . . . and seizes packets of cigarettes . . . and then leaves the *yaouled* along the way. Useless to tell you that three-quarters of the cigarettes . . . go into his pockets." Donat called these actions "an abuse and a theft."[89] This accusation carried enough weight that the police proceeded with an investigation of Guyard, who acknowledged that he had confiscated cigarettes from young Algerian traffickers but protested that he always turned the merchandise over to the Red Cross. Police complicity in the black market, or at least civilian suspicion of such activity, reflected the lingering mistrust of police services after the war.

Conflicts between police and Algerians over black-market accusations could also become moments of resistance, as they had during the war. In August 1946 a Monsieur Saada informed two European police officers near the Randon market, at the base of the Casbah, that a stall owned by Youcef L. was selling beans at an elevated price. After the police officer forced the stall to correct its pricing, Youcef came after them, calling their actions "vindictive" and telling the police officers they had acted "with an excess of zeal."[90] A group of nearly a hundred

86. For example, ANOM, 1 K 631, Dec. 27, 1947.
87. ANOM, 1 K 631, Jan. 1, 1946.
88. ANOM, 1 K 631, May 1947.
89. *Yaouled* is derived from Arabic and used in colonial discourse to denote delinquent Algerian youth. ANOM, 1 F 390, Georges Donat à M. le Préfet, July 18, 1946.
90. Notably, these two officers are *not* Economic Brigade agents. ANOM, 1 F 435, Gardiens de la Paix Ferrer et Pecheur à M. Le Chef de la 3eme Compagnie, Aug. 30, 1946.

people gathered to watch as Youcef lambasted the officers. When the policemen tried to arrest Youcef, he threatened to organize a protest of all the vegetable sellers in front of the police station. The officers retreated but planned to pursue charges against Youcef. The retreating officers had reason to fear: throughout metropolitan France in the previous summer, price control officers had been pelted with vegetables, mobbed by angry crowds, or otherwise assaulted.[91] In this case, the threat of collective action, not outright violence, proved powerful enough to force the officers to retreat. Still, the structures of colonialism meant this was only a temporary reprieve for Youcef, who surely faced the wrath of the two officers later if they pursued legal charges.

Across the Mediterranean in Marseille, police continued to locate the center of the "North African" black market on Rue des Chapeliers. Reports noted that rarely a week passed without special police raids of this area frequented by "*indigènes* traffickers."[92] The police referred to Rue des Chapeliers as the primary gathering spot of "all the black-market traffickers" and insisted that the population of Marseille viewed the street as a "veritable gangrene."[93] Despite police operations, the regional general secretary for the police worried about an untenable situation on Rue des Chapeliers, clogged with bodies to the point where it became "impossible to move" and rife with black-market sales of military goods and rationed food. Describing the chaos on Rue des Chapeliers, the secretary continued, "These very irascible *indigènes*, under the influence of drink, vociferate for hours on end, looking for a fight, insulting and sometimes attempting to assault the guardians of the peace."[94] The police linked the black-market trades on Rue des Chapeliers with a broader vision of North African criminality and violence, including violence directed against the police.

As in Algiers, the police highlighted what they saw as a worrisome trend of solidarity. When officers tried to arrest a North African trafficker, the crowds on Rue des Chapeliers resisted. As the regional general secretary for the police explained, "A hostile and menacing group flocks, cries are proclaimed against the police, and finally, to avoid more serious incidents that could lead even to spilling blood, the officers are obliged to withdraw."[95] Rue des Chapeliers had become a "no-go zone" for the police, who feared arresting supposed traffickers because of the anticipated reaction. When faced with a crowd of North Africans in this North African space, the police retreated, a moment of power for a marginalized community.

91. Mouré, "Economic Tyranny," 7–8. These attacks on Contrôle Economique agents, Mouré explains, reignited in 1947.

92. ADBR, 149 W 171, Secrétaire Général pour la Police à M. le Commissaire, Mar. 30, 1945.

93. ADBR, 149 W 171, Secrétaire Général pour la Police à M. le Commissaire, June 14, 1945.

94. ADBR, 149 W 171, Secrétaire Général pour la Police à M. le General, Mar. 23, 1945.

95. ADBR, 149 W 171, Secrétaire Général pour la Police à M. le General, Mar. 23, 1945.

In 1947 the commissioner of the Public Safety unit (*brigade de la voie publique*) wrote a long letter to the central police commissioner about the tobacco black market, highlighting the assumptions underlying police pursuit of North African cigarette sellers. He emphasized that the traffic in American cigarettes centered on the areas behind the Bourse and along Cours Belsunce, streets strongly coded in police practice as North African. The chief noted that his brigade conducted almost daily raids but remained unable to rid the area of cigarette sellers because of insufficient deterrents. The grumbling about a lack of enforcement tools echoed wartime complaints. The law, he protested, left the police "disarmed." Although the chief remained mum on the ethnoracial identity of the cigarette sellers, he provided a list of those fined for cigarette sales between March and June 1947, a list that disproportionately featured North African names.[96]

Day after day the police carried out "operations" on Cours Belsunce and Rue des Chapeliers. In a typical raid, the police arrived with thirty officers to scour Rue des Chapeliers, searching a hundred people, "mostly North Africans." Of these, the police sent nearly half to the station but managed to discover just eleven North Africans trafficking cigarettes.[97] A similar "vast operation" occurred in 1949 behind the Bourse, an area described as "frequented in particular by North African immigrants, idlers, and traffickers."[98] The language of this report made clear the police's target. Though Europeans might have sold cigarettes, the police associated illicit cigarette sales with North Africans and sought out North African neighborhoods for missions of repression.

This same link was echoed in citizen letters. The owner of a hotel on Rue Poids de la Farine, Monsieur Fossaret, wrote to the police to notify them that his hotel was frequented by "a gang of parasites and North Africans who traffic American cigarettes."[99] This letter, which arrived in the fall of 1951, demonstrates the longevity of black-market stereotypes. The police responded by saying that they had stepped up surveillance on "hot" streets in the center of Marseille, to "prevent nocturnal aggressions."[100] Here the police easily shifted from cigarettes to violence and from a particular street to a network of crime and insecurity. The endless raids behind the Bourse and on Rue des Chapeliers rarely resulted in more than a handful of fines. Yet the association of North Africans with black-market cigarettes translated to a larger vision of criminality. Black-market tobacco became a stand-in for the unwelcome presence of North African immigrants in Marseille.

96. ADBR, 150 W 161, Commissaire de Police à M. le Commissaire Central, June 19, 1947.
97. ADBR, 150 W 160, Commissaire de Police à M. le Commissaire Divisionnaire, June 5, 1947.
98. ADBR, 148 W 271, Commissaire de Police à M. le Commissaire Central, May 5, 1949.
99. ADBR, 148 W 221, Directeur Départemental des Services de Police à M le Préfet, Nov. 14, 1951.
100. ADBR, 148 W 221.

Sales of illegal tobacco calmed as cigarettes became once again readily available. The chase after contraband cigarette sellers, however, reveals a continuity in police visions of North African criminality. In Algiers the police targeted Algerians for all black-market crimes, carrying over the wartime stereotype of "anti-French" Algerian profiteers. In Marseille police pursuit of North African cigarette sellers evolved within a broader mandate to control public space. Fines for selling cigarettes provided a tangible success to point to when the prefect or the public raised fears of violence and crime in North African neighborhoods. French officials became wary of racial language in the wake of Vichy, but the tentative shift in rhetoric did not end the preexisting categories of race that functioned in police practice. Police conceptions of North African criminality determined the types of crime that officers expected to find in North African communities. This discourse of criminality mapped onto North African urban spaces, marking these neighborhoods as inherently dangerous and justifying police surveillance. In both Marseille and Algiers fines for small black-market crimes could be dutifully logged, offered as evidence of success in the police fight to control an amorphous vision of North African criminality.

In police framing, the Casbah and Rue des Chapeliers seethed with crime, but in fact these neighborhoods formed the space of ordinary North African sociability, too. Police raids outed a few traffickers, but they also made the police a constant feature in the lives of all North Africans. Police emphasis on these neighborhoods reflected an understanding of where black-market sales took place. The overt targeting of North African traffickers, however, developed within a set of police assumptions. Responding to newspaper stories, official correspondence, and citizen complaints that portrayed North Africans at the center of illicit trading, the police imbibed an idea of whom they would find profiting off the black market. Attempts to control contraband American cigarettes and stamp out the lingering black-market trade illustrate police strategies that collapsed race and space, with officers seeking out traffickers in areas they identified as North African.

Conclusion

Police reports in Marseille and Algiers consistently focused on North Africans' role in the black market, but this was not the full story. An internal report to the governor-general of Algeria in 1942 admitted that Europeans were overwhelmingly the ones buying black-market goods in Algiers and that the black market could be eliminated if these buyers disappeared.[101] This statement could only

---

101. ANOM, 7 CAB 12, "Quel revenu mensuel un indigène peut-il tirer du trafic de ses tickets d'alimentation?," May 20, 1942.

have been more true in Marseille. The black market fundamentally required a complicit general population. Families, and perhaps more specifically wives and mothers, readily turned to the black market in times of scarcity. The police knew this. At times citizens even accused police officers of abusing their power by taking part in the black market themselves. Yet police officials and individual officers continued to target North African sellers. In doing so, the police criminalized North Africans while treating their European clients as victims of wartime circumstances. Black-market links to North Africans in the popular and police culture of Marseille had tangible ramifications. Weekly, at times daily, raids of the restaurants and stores on Rue des Chapeliers placed North Africans in direct proximity with the police, guilty until proven innocent. In Algiers the policing of the black market implicated almost exclusively Algerians. Identifying Algerians as *the* black-market profiteers, the police portrayed them as the internal enemy France needed to guard against.

Policing the black market in Marseille and Algiers looked different on the ground. In Marseille the police fixated on North African traffickers but never pretended that solely Algerians were to blame. In Algiers, in contrast, the police insisted that *only* Algerian participation in the black market could explain its florescence. Portraying Algerians as the quintessential black-market criminal in Algiers solidified ideas of Algerians as a dangerous other for colonial administrators and French citizens alike. The sheer size of the Algerian population in Algiers also meant that the targeting of Algerian traders looked different in the colonial capital. The cordoned raids on Rue des Chapeliers, for example, would have been difficult to replicate in Algiers.

But when these two cities are put in conversation, something becomes clear: in both Marseille and Algiers the police used practices that wove together imaginaries of race and urban space to police black-market trading. Local officers saw the black market as a particularly North African problem. To control it, they went to the areas of the city already ingrained in police practice as "North African" spaces. By dedicating time and manpower to patrol areas understood as the center of North African life, the police of Marseille and Algiers produced the North African criminals they expected to find. This identification served an administrative purpose for the French state. By categorizing dangerous areas and suspect populations, the police could contain them, offering an illusion of control and a way to maintain colonial hierarchies in the chaos of war.

Even after the "egalitarian" reforms of the postwar, the racialized repression of the black market continued much as before. In their raids and roundups, the police relied on a map of the city that overlaid stereotypes of Algerian criminality onto specific urban sites. By targeting Rue des Chapeliers in Marseille and the Casbah in Algiers, the police treated North Africans as a homogenized block of potential traffickers. Despite some important differences between the two cities, they shared a police vision of North Africans as enemies of France. Police officials consistently saw North Africans as a danger to the French nation, despite the ongoing conflicts between Vichy and the Resistance over who represented the "true" French nation. Police anxiety about North African black marketeers reflected a broader anxiety about how the shifting loyalties and alliances of war opened opportunities for Algerian resistance. Police officers understood North Africans as "anti-French," and hunting down the North African black market became, in turn, a way to monitor this internal enemy. The process of identifying anti-French Algerians would intensify in the postwar, as the growing popularity of Algerian nationalism threw French sovereignty in Algeria into doubt. Having come to understand Algerians, and Algerian spaces, as hubs of "anti-French" clandestine commerce, police now began to construct these same people and spaces as nationalist threats.

DANIELLE BEAUJON is assistant professor of history and of criminology, law, and justice at the University of Illinois Chicago.

Acknowledgments

The author is grateful to the "War Makes Monsters" colloquium, the MacDougal St. History Workshop, Kenneth Mouré, and the anonymous reviewers of *French Historical Studies* for their valuable feedback. Research for this article was sponsored by the American Institute for Maghrib Studies and the Robert Holmes Award for African Scholarship.

References

Alexander, Michelle. *The New Jim Crow: Mass Incarceration in the Age of Colorblindness.* New York, 2010.

Balto, Simon. *Occupied Territory: Policing Black Chicago from the Red Summer to Black Power.* Chapel Hill, NC, 2019.

Beaujon, Danielle. "Policing Colonial Migrants: The Brigade Nord-Africaine in Paris, 1923–1944." *French Historical Studies* 42, no. 4 (2019): 655–80.

Begag, Azouz. *Place du Pont, ou La Médina de Lyon.* Paris, 1997.

Benatia, Farouk. *Alger: Agrégat ou cité; L'intégration citadine de 1919 à 1979.* Algiers, 1980.

Berlière, Jean-Marc. *Le monde des polices en France, XIXe–XXe siècles.* Paris, 1996.

Berlière, Jean-Marc, and Laurent Chabrun. *Les policiers français sous l'Occupation: D'après les archives inédites de l'épuration.* Paris, 2001.

Bigon, Liora. *French Colonial Dakar: The Morphogenesis of an African Regional Capital.* Manchester, 2016.

Blanchard, Emmanuel. "Des Kabyles 'perdus' en région parisienne: Les 'recherches dans l'intérêt des familles' du Service des affaires indigènes nord-africaines (années 1930)." *Revue du monde musulmane et de la Méditerrané,* no. 144 (2018): 29–44.

Blanchard, Emmanuel. *Histoire de l'immigration algérienne en France.* Paris, 2018.

Blanchard, Emmanuel. *La police parisienne et les Algériens, 1944–1962*. Paris, 2011.

Boittin, Jennifer Anne. *Undesirable: Passionate Mobility and Women's Defiance of French Colonial Policing, 1919–1952*. Chicago, 2022.

Cadiot, Aliénor. "Agir seul ou en réseau? La 'résistance' du commandant Robert Wender et le Service des affaires algériennes (1941–1943)." Presentation, French Colonial Historical Society, Martinique, 2023.

Cadiot, Aliénor. "Vichy et les Algériens: Indigènes civils musulmans algériens en France métropolitaine (1939–1944)." PhD diss., Ecole des Hautes Etudes en Sciences Sociales, 2020.

Cantier, Jacques. *L'Algérie sous le régime de Vichy*. Paris, 2002.

Cantier, Jacques, and Eric Jennings. *L'empire colonial sous Vichy*. Paris, 2004.

Çelik, Zeynep. "Historic Intersections: The Center of Algiers." In *Walls of Algiers: Narratives of the City through Text and Image*, edited by Julia Clancy-Smith and Frances Terpak, 198–226. Los Angeles, 2009.

Çelik, Zeynep. *Urban Forms and Colonial Confrontations: Algiers under French Rule*. Berkeley, CA, 1997.

Crane, Sheila. "Housing as Battleground: Targeting the City in the Battles of Algiers." *City and Society* 29, no. 1 (2017): 187–212.

Crane, Sheila. "On the Edge: The Internal Frontiers of Architecture in Algiers/Marseille." *Journal of Architecture* 16, no. 6 (2011): 941–73.

Curtin, Philip. "Medical Knowledge and Urban Planning in Tropical Africa." *American Historical Review* 90, no. 3 (1985): 594–613.

Davidson, Naomi. *Only Muslim: Embodying Islam in Twentieth-Century France*. Ithaca, NY, 2012.

Davis, Muriam Haleh. *Markets of Civilization: Islam and Racial Capitalism in Algeria*. Durham, NC, 2022.

Dikeç, Mustafa. *Badlands of the Republic: Space, Politics, and Urban Policy*. Oxford, 2007.

Echenberg, Myron J. *Black Death, White Medicine: Bubonic Plague and the Politics of Public Health in Colonial Senegal, 1914–1945*. Portsmouth, NH, 2002.

Fogg, Shannon L. *The Politics of Everyday Life in Vichy France: Foreigners, Undesirables, and Strangers*. Cambridge, 2009.

Grenard, Fabrice. "L'administration du contrôle économique en France, 1940–1950." *Revue d'histoire moderne et contemporaine* 57, no. 2 (2010): 132–58.

Grenard, Fabrice. *La France du marché noir (1940–1949)*. Paris, 2008.

Grenard, Fabrice. *Les scandales du ravitaillement: Détournements, corruption, affaires étouffées en France, de l'Occupation à la guerre froide*. Paris, 2012.

Grenard, Fabrice, Florent Le Bot, and Cédric Perrin. *Histoire économique de Vichy: L'Etat, les hommes, les entreprises*. Paris, 2017.

Grenard, Fabrice, and Kenneth Mouré. "Traitors, *Trafiquants*, and the Confiscation of 'Illicit Profits' in France, 1944–1950." *Historical Journal* 51, no. 4 (2008): 969–90.

Hattery, Angela, and Earl Smith. *Policing Black Bodies: How Black Lives Are Surveilled and How to Work for Change*. Lanham, MD, 2017.

Herf, Jeffery. *Nazi Propaganda for the Arab World*. New Haven, CT, 2009.

House, Jim. "Intervening on 'Problem' Areas and Their Inhabitants: The Sociopolitical and Security Logics behind Censuses in the Algiers Shantytowns, 1941–1962." *Histoire et mesure* 34, no. 1 (2019): 121–50.

Icheboudene, Larbi. *Alger: Histoire et capitale de destin national*. Algiers, 1997.

Kaddache, Mahfoud. "La Casbah." Unpublished manuscript, 1950. https://www.glycines.org/la-biblioth%C3%A8que/.

Keller, Kathleen. *Colonial Suspects: Suspicion, Imperial Rule, and Colonial Society in Interwar French West Africa*. Lincoln, NE, 2018.

Kitson, Simon. *Police and Politics in Marseille, 1936–1945*. Leiden, 2014.

Lefebvre, Henri. *The Production of Space*. Translated by Donald Nicholson-Smith. Cambridge, 1991.

Le Gaoziou, Véronique, and Laurent Mucchielli. *Quand les banlieues brûlent: Retour sur les émeutes de novembre 2005*. Paris, 2006.

Lespès, René. *Alger: Etude de géographie et d'histoire urbaines*. Paris, 1930.

Lewis, Mary Dewhurst. *The Boundaries of the Republic: Migrant Rights and the Limits of Universalism in France, 1918–1940*. Stanford, CA, 2007.

Massard-Guilbaud, Geneviève. *Des Algériens à Lyon: De la Grande Guerre au Front populaire*. Paris, 1995.

McKittrick, Katherine. *Demonic Grounds: Black Women and Cartographies of Struggle*. Minneapolis, 2006.

Milliot, Vincent, Emmanuel Blanchard, Vincent Denis, and Arnaud-Dominique Houte. *Histoire des polices en France: Des guerres de Religion à nos jours*. Paris, 2020.

Mouré, Kenneth. "Black Market Fictions: *Au Bon Beurre*, *La Traversée de Paris*, and the Black Market in France." *French Politics, Culture and Society* 32, no. 1 (2014): 47–67.

Mouré, Kenneth. "'Economic Tyranny' and Public Anger in France, 1945–1947." *Contemporary European History* (2022): 1–14. https://www-cambridge-org.proxy.cc.uic.edu/core/journals /contemporary-european-history/article/economic-tyranny-and-public-anger-in-france.

Mouré, Kenneth. "*La Capitale de la Faim*: Black Market Restaurants in Paris, 1940–1944." *French Historical Studies* 38, no. 2 (2015): 311–41.

Mouré, Kenneth. *Marché Noir: The Economy of Survival in Second World War France*. Cambridge, 2023.

Muhammad, Khalil. *The Condemnation of Blackness: Race, Crime, and the Making of Modern Urban America*. Cambridge, MA, 2010.

Murunga, Godwin R. "'Inherently Unhygienic Races': Plague and the Origins of Settler Dominance in Nairobi, 1899–1907." In *African Urban Spaces in Historical Perspective*, edited by Steven J. Salm and Toyin Falola, 98–130. Rochester, NY, 2005.

Nightingale, Carl. *Segregation: A Global History of Divided Cities*. Chicago, 2012.

Noiriel, Gérard. *Les origines républicaines de Vichy*. Paris, 1999.

Paxton, Robert. *Vichy France: Old Guard and New Order, 1940–1944*. New York, 1972.

Prakash, Amit. "Colonial Techniques in the Imperial Capital: The Prefecture of Police and the Surveillance of North Africans in Paris, 1925–circa 1970." *French Historical Studies* 36, no. 3 (2013): 479–510.

Prakash, Amit. *Empire on the Seine: The Policing of North Africans in Paris, 1925–1975*. Oxford, 2022.

Regnard-Drouot, Céline. *Marseille la violente: Criminalité, industrialisation et société (1851–1914)*. Rennes, 2019.

Rigouste, Mathieu. "L'ennemi intérieur: De la guerre coloniale au contrôle sécuritaire." *Cultures et conflits*, no. 67 (2007): 157–74.

Rios, Jodi. *Black Lives and Spatial Matters: Policing Blackness and Practicing Freedom in Suburban St. Louis*. Ithaca, NY, 2020.

Roché, Sebastian. *Le frisson de l'émeute: Violences urbaines et banlieues*. Paris, 2006.

Rosenberg, Clifford. *Policing Paris: The Origins of Modern Immigration Control between the Wars*. Ithaca, NY, 2018.

Saada, Emmanuelle. "La loi, le droit et l'indigène." *Droits: Revue française de théorie juridique, de philosophie et de culture juridiques*, no. 43 (2006): 165–90.

Salinas, Alfred. *Les Américains en Algérie, 1942–1945*. Paris, 2013.

Sanders, Paul. *Histoire du marché noir*. Paris, 2001.

Schwartz, Paula. *Today Sardines Are Not for Sale: A Street Protest in Occupied Paris*. Oxford, 2020.

Scott, James C. *Seeing like a State: How Certain Schemes to Improve the Human Condition Have Failed*. New Haven, CT, 1998.

Shabazz, Rashad. *Spatializing Blackness: Architectures of Confinement and Black Masculinity in Chicago*. Champaign, IL, 2015.

Spire, Alexis. *Etrangers à la carte: L'administration de l'immigration en France, 1945–1975*. Paris, 2005.

Surkis, Judith. *Sex, Law, and Sovereignty in French Algeria, 1830–1930*. Ithaca, NY, 2019.

Swanson, Maynard W. "The Sanitation Syndrome: Bubonic Plague and Urban Native Policy in the Cape Colony, 1900–1909." *Journal of African History* 18, no. 3 (1977): 387–410.

Thénault, Sylvie. *Violence ordinaire dans l'Algérie coloniale: Camps, internements, assignations à résidence*. Paris, 2012.

Dead but Not Buried
Serial Murderer Henri Désiré Landru and a Century of War Critique

JULIE M. POWELL

ABSTRACT   On April 12, 1919, Paris police arrested Henri Désiré Landru, a man who had spent the last four years of war luring women into engagements and confiscating their assets. Many of them were never seen again. Landru, charged with their murders, became an international media sensation—the inspiration for popular crime stories, including books, articles, films, television and radio programs, and theatrical performances, from his execution in 1922 to 2020. This article examines these stories for the revealing ways they bring together conceptions of war and violent crime. It considers a 1926 nonfiction account of Landru by the South African journalist and military veteran William Bolitho, the film *Monsieur Verdoux* (1947) written by Charlie Chaplin, Claude Chabrol's film *Landru* (1963), and a 2006 graphic novel by Christophe Chabouté. These narratives suggest, and this article argues, that stories about Landru—and the multiple murders he committed for profit—have served, at various times and in various places, as vehicles for critiquing warfare and the societies that embrace it.

KEYWORDS   violence, serial murder, war, literature, film

On April 12, 1919, as international statesmen swarmed the Quai D'Orsay to hammer out the details of the Treaty of Versailles and formally end World War I, Inspector Jean Belin of the Sûreté Générale entered the apartment of a bearded man in his fifties, wresting him from the arms of his mistress and taking him into custody.[1] The suspect had been identified the previous day by Mlle. Marie Lacoste as the man to whom her sister, Célestine Buisson, had been engaged and from whose care she had subsequently disappeared. Lacoste knew him as Henri Fremyet and, having visited the couple once in Gambais, recognized him immediately as he stood casually in Au Lion de Faïence on Rue de Rivoli, purchasing a tea set. Lacoste had not heard from her sister since August 1917, and in 1918

---

1. Founded in 1853, under the Second Empire, the Direction de la Sûreté Générale began as a political security force. With a December 30, 1907, decree from Georges Clemenceau, the organization evolved into judicial police with twelve mobile brigades operating across the Hexagon. In 1934 it became the Direction Générale de la Sûreté Nationale.

French Historical Studies • Vol. 47, No. 2 (May 2024) • DOI 10.1215/00161071-11025087
Copyright 2024 by Society for French Historical Studies

she had written to the mayor of Gambais, who knew no one by the name of Frem-yet but notified the correspondent that a Madame Pellat had written a similar letter in October 1917 regarding the disappearance of *her* sister, Anna Collomb. Anna had become engaged to a man named Henri Cuchet and subsequently failed to join her family for New Year's Eve in 1916, as planned. Lacoste reached out to the Pellats, and in February 1919 they lodged a complaint with the prose-cutor's office in the Département de la Seine, launching an investigation.

Though he introduced himself as Lucien Guillet, the man whom Inspector Belin escorted from 76 Rue Rochechouart was quickly identified as Henri Désiré Landru, a husband and father of four who had been sentenced to imprisonment for fraud in 1902, 1904, 1906, 1910, and 1914. He had failed to report for the final sentence, a four-year stint in prison that, if served, would have put an end to *l'affaire Landru* before it even began. Instead, the petty criminal chose to profit from the chaos of an unprecedented global conflict. He spent the war luring middle-aged bourgeoises into engagements, confiscating their assets, and accord-ing to the verdict of his trial, handed down on November 30, 1921, at the assizes of Seine-et-Oise in Versailles, murdering ten of them.[2] No bodies were ever recov-ered, and the prevailing theory, never proved, was that Landru had disposed of the remains by cutting them to pieces and burning them in his kitchen stove. Buisson had not been the first or last woman to disappear, information that was slowly revealed as Brigadier Louis Riboulet decoded Landru's confiscated notebooks, wherein the suspect minutely recorded his expenditures. The most damaging was the repeated purchase of train tickets to Houdan, the nearest station to Gambais: a roundtrip ticket for himself and a one-way ticket for his companion.

The press was ravenous for such details, and Landru became an interna-tional media sensation. Indeed, the French opposition press declared the whole affair a hoax, manufactured by Prime Minister Clemenceau and Minister of the Interior Georges Mandel to draw attention away from what many saw as the disastrous peace negotiations. The timing was fortuitous for the pair, but Landru and his crimes, according to Belin's 1950 autobiography, were very real.[3] The "Bluebeard of Gambais" became—and remains—the inspiration for all manner of popular crime writing, including fiction and nonfiction books, articles, films, television and radio programs, and theatrical performances spanning a century. Remarkable in both depth and breadth, this literature brings narratives about war and violent crime together in revealing ways. This article is not about

2. Landru was also convicted of the murder of one adolescent, André Cuchet, the son of Jeanne Cuchet, to whom he was known as Raymond Diard. For more on Landru, see Béraud, Bourcier, and Salmon, *L'affaire Landru*; Jaeger, *Landru*; Masson, *Number One*; and Darmon, *Landru*.
3. Belin, *Trente ans de Sûreté nationale*.

Landru the man, therefore, but about Landru the story, the variations that it has inspired, and the critical ends that it has served. Writing in 1926, William Bolitho characterized Landru as "a living allegory of large and obvious content." "A whole city, a whole time," he wrote, "thus seems after a ghastly and mocking manner to be summed up in this individual, or at any rate to have distorted reflection in him."[4] The Landru tale, told many times over, remains a vehicle for conveying the anxieties, communicating the failings, and critiquing the excesses of modern society—war chief among them.[5] At the center of all such critiques is the unavoidable comparison between "the individual, artisanal murder" committed by Landru and the "millions of dead . . . killed, massacred, exterminated with all impunity" in an industrial war that provided him cover.[6]

The four Landru stories that I have elected to examine here were produced in four decades and three countries. They each go beyond body count comparisons, offering unique but overlapping critiques to demonstrate the richness and malleability of the Landru story, as well as its reach and longevity. Produced in the wake of World War I and World War II, respectively, Bolitho's *Murder for Profit* (1926) and Charlie Chaplin's *Monsieur Verdoux* (1947) present Landru as a totem for the dangers of unrestrained and belligerent capitalism, a devaluing of human life that terminates inevitably in the mass death of war and serial murder. Filmed in the final year of the Algerian War of Independence, *Landru* (1963), directed by Claude Chabrol and written by Françoise Sagan, activates multidirectional memory—the cross-referencing and borrowing that allows consciousness of one event to be used as a platform to discuss another—to criticize middle-class ambivalence to, and disconnection from, more recent conflicts.[7] *Henri Désiré Landru* (2006) by Christophe Chabouté offers readers perverse versions of the "heroic" *poilu* and of French justice. The integrity of the former is preserved at the expense of the latter in this fact-based reimagining of the Landru narrative that harks back to the Dreyfus affair in its indictment of a militarist society that seems never to have changed its stripes. Historicizing such stories likewise provides a window into how well they have functioned as a means of war critique.

Comparisons pose provocative questions. Are war and serial murder one and the same? Are the perpetrators indistinguishable, or is there an unbridgeable distance between the two? Disparities in public reception of *Monsieur Verdoux* and *Landru*, in particular, suggest that the answers to these questions are historically contingent and that receptiveness to the critique depends both on a

4. Bolitho, *Murder for Profit*, 163–64. An American edition of the book was released in 1926. British editions were released in 1953 and 1962.

5. In the more than fifty iterations of the Landru story that I have examined, critiques of gender and the nature of man are also prevalent.

6. Gonzalez, *Crime Story*, 17.

7. Rothberg, *Multidirectional Memory*, 3.

society's contemporary relationship to war and on the directness with which the critique is deployed.

Murder for Profit and Monsieur Verdoux

The first to record the story of Landru were contemporaries who viewed him as a man not of *a* time but of *their* time—a product and representation of a specific period and place. Bolitho was one such contemporary, and he brought his own experience to bear on the Landru narrative in *Murder for Profit*. Bolitho was born in Cape Town in 1890 into a family struggling to make ends meet. Despite his later success at university, Bolitho's writing—evocative though convoluted—remained inflected by his "poverty-stricken youth."[8] Desiring to fight in World War I, he enlisted in the British Army, nearly losing his life at the Somme when a German shell exploded, burying Bolitho and fifteen other men. Suffering a broken neck, he was the only one to survive. During recovery in hospital, he connected with Eric Maclagen, an intelligence officer and press liaison, who recommended Bolitho to the *Manchester Guardian*. He was hired as the newspaper's Paris correspondent and later, in 1923, became the European correspondent for the *New York World*. According to the 1964 editor's preface of *Murder for Profit*, "Bolitho wrote incisively and with detachment about society and its ways of taking lives, and the reason may be that he had once nearly lost his own life at the hands of society and had had plenty of time to think about it."[9]

As the title, *Murder for Profit*, suggests, Bolitho took particular umbrage at the sacrifice of lives for financial gain, at the valuation of humanity only in terms of its exchange value. The book, originally penned in 1926, examined the motives of serial murderers, practitioners of the "trade of murder."[10] Bolitho contends that Landru was an inevitability and exemplar of a brutally capitalist society. Far from "mark[ing them] a species of men apart," the characteristics of mass murderers like Landru likewise "fit the judge who trie[d] him, and the police-sergeant who arrest[ed] him." "In reality," Bolitho argues,

> such a breed is an inevitable, if unintentional, byproduct of the modern industrial society. Their manufacture may be explained almost mechanically. . . .
>
> The industrial system . . . consists in a possessing-class, and a reservoir of labour. . . . It is the interest of all except those forming it that this basic reservoir, the working proletariat, should be as large and as stable as possible. . . . [Yet] every year unnumbered men escape from the receptacle, against the will and interest of society, some physically and mentally weak falling in spite of the

8. According to Alexander Woollcott, quoted in Sloan et al., *Great Reporters*, 148.
9. Bolitho, *Murder for Profit*, xii.
10. Bolitho, *Murder for Profit*, 157.

meshes of repressive law and philanthropy from a mode of life too hard for
them to the sediment that is called the criminal class. Others squeeze upwards
to an easier life than their education or endowments entitle them to. It is these
latter runaways, who have . . . forced themselves into the more leisured regions
of trade above, that form that large class of unspecialised, sharp individuals to
which, along with a tremendous majority of persons inoffensive to the life of
their fellow-creatures, our mass-murderers clearly belong. . . . Their only ideal is
to follow remorselessly the bright vague light far above them that shines down
from the heaven of possession.[11]

According to Bolitho, the mass murderer and the intelligent trader were similarly
flawed, like the societies and "civilised nations" to which they belonged.[12] "Who
indeed," he asked, "is subtle enough to distinguish between the egotism of an
individual and the patriotism of a nation? Or between private and national
pride?" Finally, "what [can] our mass-murderers have done, that the State cannot outmatch?" Of capital punishment, he argued that "any first-class State in
the world could show (a score or two) killings every year . . . for its cold and cal-
culated self-interest." But for Bolitho, it was in the act of war that the hypocrisy
of society, opposed only inconsistently and with prejudice to the notion of murder for profit, was most clearly illuminated. He writes sarcastically of the apos-
trophized "institution of war,"

> in which the best and noblest sentiments of nations are admittedly manifested.
> Where could a nation so miserable be found that it would not gladly use a thou-
> sand lives for a handkerchief of territory, or so poor-spirited as to see its com-
> merce disappear without a fight for it? In this indeed, its supreme action, the
> State brushes aside all wounding comparisons; in the neighbourhood of a war,
> such as that last in which 12,000,000 perished, the mass-murderer loses all his
> claim to the wholesale, and becomes an infinitesimal wretch, engaged in minute
> wickedness unworthy of attention.[13]

Punishing Landru, who spent the years 1914–18 "conducting a private war of his
own, earnestly mimicking [the Great War], even to the casualties," was a means
by which society could expiate its sins without ever acknowledging them.[14] Killing
"a mere thirteen," Landru was "of the class of mere distractions" for the "assembly of a modern people which had just sacrificed 1,500,000 of its young men to
preserve its institutions and its culture."[15]

In the end, Bolitho affirmed,

11. Bolitho, *Murder for Profit*, 212, 215–19.
12. Bolitho, *Murder for Profit*, 212.
13. Bolitho, *Murder for Profit*, 213–14.
14. Bolitho, *Murder for Profit*, 164–65.
15. Bolitho, *Murder for Profit*, 214, 205. Bolitho incorrectly cites the number of victims attributed to
Landru.

no one can nowadays dare to reproach such men [as Landru], after a collective killing of such magnitude as we have all committed, of an exclusive mark of blood stain. All our foreheads are smeared. Those who innocently persist in imagining that mass-murderers are different from themselves simply in that they had the awful courage to kill and repeat their act, a faculty in which they are to have some gloomy monopoly among the sons of men, I refer to the printed achievements of the heroes of the war; or if they are unwilling to read them again, I call the witness of all ex-combatants that at the Front it was never found difficult to induce even the mildest recruit to kill.[16]

It was the threat of this repetition that most concerned Bolitho, for mass murderers were simply mimics of their states, profiting from death on a smaller scale. "There may be lurking for every murderer for profit in his first crime the deadly enticement to do another," he wrote, "and to so continue until the end of the tether, drawn on by an awakened devil for all time. Not to lose our heads, a perfect analogy for the militarism of nations in the lonely struggles of such individuals."[17] A victim of appendicitis, Bolitho died in Avignon in 1930, unaware that the wars of 1936, 1939, and beyond would, once again, prove societies as guilty as the "monsters" that they sent to the guillotine. Bolitho's book, though, was a success on both sides of the Atlantic. A 1962 edition by Paul Elek Publishers, London, billed it as part of their "Bestseller Library." At least seven editions were printed between 1926 and 1964.[18] Nevertheless, in the 1964 introduction of *Murder for Profit*, the psychiatrist Fredric Wertham lamented that interwar readers had failed to heed the warning that, in the wake of World War II, had become all the more urgent. "A mass murderer used to be a man who killed maybe four or five, or even 10 or 20 people," he wrote. "Mass killing now is more likely to involve millions."[19] What Bolitho had attempted in print—in vain, it seemed—was tried again two decades later in celluloid. Bolitho's complicated prose had perhaps buried the lede. Chaplin's appeal would simultaneously be far more direct in its critique of war and far less well received by the public.

Anticapitalist and antiwar critique came together again in a fictionalized account of Landru's exploits, directed by Charlie Chaplin. The film, *Monsieur Verdoux*, was produced in 1947, just as the Cold War came to replace World War II as the center of global geopolitics. Timing was everything, both for the film's message and for its reception. The star's popular 1940 film, *The Great Dictator*,

16. Bolitho, *Murder for Profit*, 218–19.
17. Bolitho, *Murder for Profit*, 221–22.
18. This includes editions by Jonathan Cape, London (1926); Harper and Brothers, New York (1926); Garden City Publishing, New York (1928); Dennis Dobson, London (1953); Doubleday, New York (1961); Paul Elek, London (1962); and Time, New York (1964).
19. Bolitho, *Murder for Profit*, xvii.

satirized Adolf Hitler, and Chaplin's first postwar project, *Monsieur Verdoux*, was to serve as commentary on the carnage that followed the National Socialist leader's rise to power. Chaplin declared in 1947 that the film was "against war and futile slaughter" and, moreover, that he was "not a Communist . . . [but] a peacemonger."[20] The claim failed to insulate Chaplin against persecution by anticommunists, who branded him a communist sympathizer, questioned his politics and national loyalty, and hounded him about his friendship with the German composer and Jewish refugee Hanns Eisler, a target of the House Un-American Activities Committee. *Monsieur Verdoux* was deemed unacceptable by the Motion Picture Association for rationalizing and minimizing Verdoux's crimes in comparison with the horrors of mass war.[21] Boycotted in several states, it was simultaneously feted by the *Daily Worker* for stirring "the hearts and minds of liberty-loving peoples all over the world."[22]

Chaplin may have been, by his own admission, "not a Communist," but *Monsieur Verdoux* demonstrates a keen recognition on the part of the director that the bloodthirst practiced on the battlefields of Europe and the inhumanity of Wall Street barons shared a common lineage. Chaplin, who takes on the role of the titular Verdoux, keeps the broad strokes of the Landru story intact but brings it forward in time. This "Landru" is no career criminal stalking the Jardin du Luxembourg of World War I Paris but a once "honest bank clerk" who, as Chaplin declares in the voice-over of the film's introductory scene, lost his job during the depression in 1930 and subsequently, "as a strictly business enterprise," "became occupied in liquidating members of the opposite sex" to "support a home and family."[23] Viewers find Chaplin's Verdoux eminently likable; he is not the villain of this story—or at least not the primary one. He is a victim of circumstance, a casualty of market speculation and capitalist greed, but he is also a mirror held up to society. He embodies society's worst excesses, yet he is one man; his crimes pale next to those for which culpability is collective.

Viewers first see Verdoux in the garden of his country home in the south of France. Dressed in a smock and brandishing a pair of shears, Verdoux collects roses as black smoke pours out of an incinerator, venting into the garden and polluting the pastoral scene. A neighbor wonders aloud "how long he's going to keep that incinerator burning," and there is little doubt as to the organic origins of the exhaust. The previous scene establishes that Thelma Varnay, "a woman of fifty flitting off to Paris and marrying a man she's only known two weeks," has withdrawn

20. Cited in Hoberman, "When Chaplin Became the Enemy."

21. Letter from the Motion Picture Association, Feb. 20, 1946, cited in *Chaplin Today: Monsieur Verdoux*, dir. Bernard Eisenschitz with Claude Chabrol, produced for MK2TV (2003).

22. Hoberman, "When Chaplin Became the Enemy."

23. *Monsieur Verdoux*, dir. Charles Chaplin, Mk2 Editions (2003).

all her money and closed her bank account without leaving a forwarding address. Pierre Couvais, Thelma's brother-in-law, chides the distressed family for thinking that "just because she hasn't written, she's either been robbed or murdered." The film insinuates that Thelma has been victimized on both accounts. Smoke rising around him, Verdoux retires indoors where he receives a letter from the Banque du Midi et de Marseille for Madame Thelma Varnay containing sixty thousand francs and confirming the termination of her account. Verdoux tallies the bills with the efficiency of a counting machine and matter-of-factly places them in his pocket. According to Chaplin, Verdoux feels that "murder is the logical extension of business," just as Carl von Clausewitz viewed war as the logical extension of diplomacy.[24] Business and war merge in the scene, which ends with Verdoux returning to Paris, signaled by a close-up shot of train wheels in motion scored with a jarring and unsettling string accompaniment. The smoke, the train, and the incineration of human flesh were unequivocal allusions to the industrialized murder of the Holocaust, a memory fresh in the minds of midcentury audiences. Back in Paris, Verdoux is approached by an old bank colleague who asks after his affairs and, seeing the murderer's wad of cash, casually remarks, "Well, you must've made a killing." Indeed, he had, and not for the last time.

Mass death and business collide once more as a conversation between Verdoux and a houseguest brings together the rationalization of work and chemical homicide, thereby recalling the monstrous Final Solution and Aktion T4, the coordinated euthanasia of physically and mentally disabled adults and children in Nazi Germany. While visiting his wife and son, Verdoux hosts Maurice, a pharmacist who is working on "a humane way to do away with dumb animals." Maurice announces that he has created a chemical compound that leaves no trace and asks, "Can you imagine such a weapon in the hands of an archcriminal?" Verdoux replies coolly that such properties promised a windfall if the poison were put to use in insurance scams. He argues that it could be tested by "pick[ing] a derelict off the street," a trial deemed "diabolical" by his wife. Verdoux concedes that "such experiments we had better leave to the archcriminals," and the scene ends with another close-up shot of the pumping of pistons and the spinning of wheels as a train transports the *père de famille* back to the French capital.

Back in Paris, Verdoux prepares to conduct the "diabolical" trial, which, if successful, could streamline his business in short order. Armed with a chemistry set, he evokes the work of Nazi doctors, proclaiming, "And now for the experiment." He heads out into the rain and encounters a young woman, a Belgian war refugee, whom he escorts back to his apartment. The young woman is the widow of an *invalide de guerre* and is just out of jail, having served three months

24. Quoted in Hoberman, "When Chaplin Became the Enemy."

for pawning a rented typewriter. She is a victim, like Verdoux, but not a helpless one. He sees in her a kindred spirit, spares her, and offers her some money. "This is a ruthless world," he tells her, "and one must be ruthless to cope with it." He encounters her again, as the shadow of war casts itself over Europe once more. Now the partner of a munitions manufacturer and soon-to-be war profiteer by proxy, she laments that her "very kind and generous" *proche* is "in business quite ruthless." Verdoux replies frankly that "business is a ruthless business, my dear." For a munitions manufacturer, and for Chaplin, however, war and business were one and the same: brutal and uncaring, creating what Verdoux called a "world of fear and uncertainty."

Moments before Verdoux's second encounter with the refugee, audiences are bombarded by a chaotic montage of death and destruction, the fallout both of economic and military adventurism and of greed. In rapid succession viewers see the press of frantic crowds at the stock exchange; the November 17, 1932, *L'humanité* headline "BANKS FAIL; RIOTS ENSUE"; the shattering of glass as anxious customers storm the bank; a Wall Street speculator putting a gun to his temple; a businessman defenestrating himself. The frenetic pace of cuts slows as Verdoux puts a call in to his broker, only to realize that he was "wiped out hours ago." A close-up on the wide-eyed Verdoux fades into a printing press, pumping out more bad news. The August 31, 1933, edition of *La gazette* announces, "CRISIS IN EUROPE," and audiences see citizens running through the streets, a large political rally seething, Mussolini orating from a balcony, Hitler gesturing emphatically, and the two dictators conversing first on a veranda, then in military uniform, and lastly with military planners and advisers. We see battalions assembled outside the Colosseum, troops marching, and, finally, a headline from *Le Figaro*: "NAZIS BOMB SPANISH LOYALISTS; THOUSANDS OF CIVILIANS KILLED: War Imminent in Europe." The scene ends when Verdoux, seated in a Parisian café, closes the paper and steps into the street, where he is nearly run over by a car chauffeuring the young Belgian refugee. If the film's previous attempts to bring war to mind were crafted through insinuation and allusion, the time for subtlety has ended.

In short order, Verdoux is recognized by the Couvais family, arrested, and finally brought to trial, a venue that allows Chaplin to make his critique of the business of killing in no uncertain terms. In his closing statements the prosecutor argues that "never, never in the history of jurisprudence have such terrifying deeds been brought to light," a statement that rings false from the start and is made more absurd when he continues: "Gentlemen of the jury, you have before you a cruel and cynical monster. Look at him." Everyone turns to look at Verdoux, who in turn looks behind himself in search of the "cruel and cynical monster" of the prosecutor's description. For a man who "made a business" of robbing and murdering unsuspecting women, "for this mass killer," and for "the protection of society," the prosecutor demands death by guillotine. Duly convicted, Verdoux takes the opportunity to speak to the court, noting that for thirty-five years he used his brains honestly, but after that "nobody wanted them, so [he] was forced to go into business for [him]self." "As for being a mass killer," he argues, "does not the world encourage it? Is it not building weapons of destruction for the sole purpose of mass killing? Has it not blown unsuspecting women and little children to pieces and done it very scientifically? As a mass killer, I'm an amateur by comparison." As a final flourish, he announces that if he is to be condemned for coldly trading French lives for francs, then he will not be alone, for all are implicated. "On leaving this spark of earthly existence," he promises, "I shall see you all very soon . . . very soon."

In the last minutes of what the *nouvelle vague* director Chabrol called "a radical indictment of society through . . . one murderer," Chaplin drives his criticism home.[25] Lying on a cot in his cell, Verdoux awaits his sentence. A reporter enters and sits at the end of the bed like a priest giving last rites. What the journalist craves is reassurance; he wants to know that Verdoux is an aberration, a man apart from society. Verdoux offers no such comfort. The reporter prompts the condemned man: "Crime doesn't pay, does it?" "No sir, not in a small way," Verdoux responds; "to be successful in anything, one must be well organized." "Give me a story with a moral to it," the reporter prods, "you, the tragic example of a life of crime." Verdoux replies, "I don't see how anyone can be an example in these criminal times." "You certainly are," his visitor charges, "robbing and murdering people." Verdoux answers frankly, "That's business." Naively, the reporter retorts, "Well, other people don't do business that way." "That's the history of many a big business," Verdoux continues. "Wars, conflict, it's all business. One murder makes a villain, millions make a hero. Numbers sanctify, my good fellow." Verdoux's crime, his business of "liquidating members of the opposite sex," is no different, Chaplin argues, from the crimes of Western civilization, but the former is paltry in comparison. Chaplin makes this final point not to exonerate Verdoux, who is escorted to the guillotine in the final scene, but to force a reckoning among audiences who have heroized villains—the warmongers whose victories bring death and suffering in their wake, the capitalists whose magnificent empires have been built on misery and exploitation—and to hold them to account for their complicity.

Landru

Fifteen years after the release of *Monsieur Verdoux*, Claude Chabrol set out to do his own film about Landru. Comparisons to Chaplin's work were unavoidable.

---

25. Chabrol, *Chaplin Today*.

The same macabre allusions to the Holocaust pervade the film: the trains, the postmortem theft of goods, the black smoke and stench of cremated bodies, a "routinization of murder as a kind of Fordist assembly line," according to Budd Wilkins, that sees four women in the span of forty-five seconds "embarking one after the other on the train . . . destined for immolation."[26] Nevertheless, Chabrol insisted that the two films were worlds apart, noting that "'Monsieur Verdoux' was not Landru, but the character of Landru adapted to the Chaplinesque spirit. We will be more faithful to the truth."[27] Yet, like their predecessor, Chabrol and screenwriter Françoise Sagan aimed to craft a "sympathetic" Landru, one with whom viewers could identify, a requisite for reflection on society and the self. This Landru is the consummate bourgeois. His crimes seem less in the service of survival than in the maintenance of a certain lifestyle, but in a middle-class world structured around appearance and presentation, the distance between the former and the latter might be considered minute. This Landru regularly attends the theater; he quotes Molière; he lives in a pastel world "bathed in music and flowers" and surrounded by sumptuous fabrics, well-appointed rooms, and a surfeit of accumulated *objets*.[28]

Chabrol and Sagan both made their careers offering midcentury cultural consumers biting critiques of the French middle class, and *Landru* is, in this sense, faithful to their larger oeuvres. According to a 2010 eulogy in the *New Yorker*, Chabrol's "cynical satire was aimed in particular at the pompous bourgeoisie."[29] Known for "anatomis[ing] the middleclass French body politic with a sadistic twist of the scalpel," the director found his match in Sagan, whose books presented "laconic dissection[s] of the lives of the *haute bourgeoisie*."[30] The pair invited audiences to make themselves at home with Landru. The "soft and poetic" colors of *Landru* created "a feeling of euphoria," according to Chabrol.[31] It is no "horror film," argued Sagan, but "a tender film, made a little smoky from time to time by cadaveric emanations." If it is a dream world, however, it is one in which reality inevitably intrudes. "It takes place between 1917 and 1920. The drama," Sagan remembers, "was first on the battlefields, then in the [League of Nations]."[32]

26. Wilkins, "Two by Claude Chabrol on Kino Lorber Bluray"; Claude Veillot, "Chabrol a brûlé ses vedettes," *Candide*, Jan. 1963, in Françoise Sagan, *Landru: Film réalisé par Claude Chabrol; Scenario, adaptation et dialogue de Françoise Sagan*, unpublished scrapbook, 1962, 69–71, 8-SW-1019, Bibliothèque Nationale de France, Richlieu.

27. Press release for Landru, Unifrance film, Oct. 22, 1962, in Sagan, *Landru*, 13.

28. Press release for Landru.

29. Brody, "In Memoriam Claude Chabrol."

30. Bradshaw, "Claude Chabrol Anatomised the French Middle Class"; *Guardian*, "'Lost' Françoise Sagan Novel Causes Stir in France."

31. Press release for Landru.

32. Press release for Landru.

Such "drama," shown in grainy, colorless newsreel footage, repeatedly bursts in on Chabrol and Sagan's rose-colored bourgeois dreamscape. The juxtaposition is jarring for the viewer, who is immediately reminded that, *Oh right, there's a war on.* The first cut between worlds follows the opening scene of the film. Landru, seated with his family in his lush dining room, complains: "Ground beef again! I'm beginning to have my fill of this ground beef." His wife responds coolly, "What do you want, Henri? *C'est la guerre.*" Moments later Mireille, the family maid, enters the room in tears to offer him a second reminder that, less than fifty kilometers away, men are dying. Prompted by Madame Landru, she reveals that her fiancé, Georges, has disappeared at the Marne. What follows is a montage—set to the tense rhythm of military percussion and the haunting wail of horns—of soldiers marching, bombs exploding, the desolation of no-man's-land, and the destruction of the invaded territories surveyed by airplane. Another cut brings the viewer back to a placid lake, surrounded by lush green trees, reflecting a blue sky; a woman's dulcet singing voice soothes the audience as the title cards announce that this is the world of *Landru*. It is calm and beautiful but quietly sinister—the mirrored surface of the pond is broken by a plume of fabric cresting the water and a pair of women's shoes floating casually along.[33]

Cuts between Landru's soft dream world (masking its own horrors) and the harsh, black-and-white reality of war continue throughout the film. The intrusions are for the audience's eyes only; Landru—our emblem of bourgeois self-interest and indifference to suffering—remains unaffected. In the second case, as in the first, the juxtaposition accompanies an attempt to remind Landru both that he is in the midst of war and that it is a tragedy worthy of recognition. Following the murder of Berthe Héon, Landru returns to his family to distribute his "earnings." Madame Landru plucks the newspaper from the crook of her husband's elbow and announces: "What horror! Ten thousand dead!" "So what?" he replies. "Life is blood and terror." The audience is transported to that horror as trumpets sound, bombs explode, and soldiers climb from the trenches and race into no-man's-land, bayonets at the ready. Fire and smoke shroud the desolate field; the screen fades and viewers are returned to the home of Célestine Buisson, where Landru stands among her gilt frames and crystal chandeliers to declare that "everyone dies. And it's nothing."

Indeed, reminders of the war are everywhere; unacknowledged by the disinterested bourgeois, soldiers dot the periphery of Landru's scenes. Early in the film he sits in the Jardin du Luxembourg reading letters, oblivious to the uniformed soldier and his sweetheart kissing on the bench in front of him. Later Landru takes a stroll with Anna Collomb. He is positioned in the foreground of

33. *Landru*, dir. Claude Chabrol, Rome Paris Films (1963).

the final shot, and just behind him is a disabled soldier perched on the edge of a fountain. The *poilu*, his right sleeve pinned up, takes a drag off his cigarette and regards the couple—a gesture that is not returned. When Berthe Héon and Landru await the train to Houdan, they share the frame with a soldier on leave. Seated against the wall of the ticket office under a giant war bonds poster prompting passersby to "Turn over your Gold for France; Gold fights for Victory," he remains out of sight and out of mind.

Landru is concerned only with his own affairs, and as Georges Sadoul noted in a 1963 review of the film, "The portrait of the petty bourgeoisie, through this bearded assassin, is exact."[34] Driving the point home is a flurry of black-and-white clips that directly follow a scene in which Landru visits the bank to close out Buisson's account. Soldiers march through a trench, run across barren terrain with shells bursting around them, and gather with refugees in camps; a newspaper column declares that "our troops at the front are retreating," but the message is dwarfed by the headline "The price of butter will remain the same throughout the summer," suggesting that interest in the war has been minimized in relation to more quotidian concerns and recalling Landru's tone-deaf laments over his dinner menu. "Rudely bourgeois," according to Richard Neupert: "while other men die in the trenches, Landru is unwilling to accept his minor sacrifice of eating ground meat."[35]

The war concerns Landru and, by extension, his ilk only insofar as it impacts him personally. Hardly relevant to World War I, in which nearly every family was touched by death, Chabrol and Sagan's social critique aims at the contemporaries of later wars of the twentieth century—World War II and the Algerian War of Independence—who, like the neighbors in the film who close windows and light candles to cover the stench of cremation coming from Landru's victims, blithely ignored a host of atrocities in a bid to carry on with their lives. Such a critique relies on what Michael Rothberg has termed "multidirectional memory," an exploration of the relationship between different traumatic events. Rothberg argues that memory of one mass-death event "doesn't simply compete with that of other pasts, but provides . . . a greater level of 'comfort' than confrontation with more 'local' problems would allow . . . open[ing] up lines of communication."[36] Put otherwise, multidirectional memory allows Chabrol and Sagan to critique bourgeois indifference not by directly attacking those they wish to indict but by displacing the criticism onto contemporaries of a different conflict entirely and offering parallels that invite reflection.

---

34. Georges Sadoul, "La revanche de Chabrol," *Lettres françaises*, Jan. 24, 1963, in Sagan, *Landru*, 49–52.
    35. Neupert, *History of the French New Wave Cinema*, 155.
    36. Rothberg, *Multidirectional Memory*, 18.

At another level, however, Chabrol and Sagan's social critique moves beyond the charge of indifference and self-interest to unmask the violence, plastered over by niceties and presentation, at the center of bourgeois French society. With plumes of black smoke rising from the chimney of a country villa and billowing fabric in a scenic pond, we are reminded that the ugly truth of things is always just below the surface. In 1963 Jean-Louis Bory remarked of this "ironic satire of society" that "all that, [Landru's] charm, that slightly insipid prettiness, that politeness of tone, that generalized mannerism, all that is a lie: it's a trap. Like the villa of Gambais. Like Landru's 'old France' courtesy, his reassuring respectability. The truth of Landru is the oven. Like the truth of this society . . . is the war. . . . This society of florists and bandstands pillages and murders." Bory notes, moreover, that the film contains "many ellipses." Landru's crimes are not seen but alluded to by black smoke, bags of coal, the appropriation of personal effects, and visits to the bank. "The story must remain 'correct,' better still," he argues, "elegant. Never violence, never a harsh word—violence, murder, that's society's business," as demonstrated by the black-and-white montages that punctuate the film.[37] Nearly sixty years later Wilkins remarked that the film's "interspersed newsreel footage of the war provides a documentary parallel to Landru's more modest efforts at depopulation. . . . Landru isn't a rebel in opposition to the dominant social order, but a logical extension and internalisation of its values."[38]

Henri Désiré Landru

While color, and its absence, was integral to Chabrol and Sagan's *Landru*, the story told by Christophe Chabouté makes its point compellingly, starkly, in black and white. According to Alain Huberty and Marc Breyne, codirectors of Christie's Comic Strips and Illustrations Department, the Alsatian graphic novelist works in black and white "so as to escape aesthetic and narrative constraints," "leaving his readers free to fill in the colours of their choosing." The experts note that Chabouté's "different visual take on the world . . . frees us from our habitual ways of seeing"; indeed, the artist presents Landru in an entirely new light, fashioning a new narrative, a new motive, a new villain.[39] What emerges from this reimagination of the Landru story is an unambiguous critique of militarist society, one that subordinates justice to the preservation of the strength and reputation of its armed forces. In rewriting *l'affaire Landru*, Chabouté recalls *l'affaire Dreyfus*, a cultural flashpoint in the French belle epoque, which saw Captain Alfred Dreyfus convicted of treason for passing secrets to the Germans.

37. Jean-Louis Bory, "Landru: Un régal pour initiés," *Arts*, Jan. 23, 1963, in Sagan, *Landru*, 42–44.
38. Wilkins, "Two by Claude Chabrol on Kino Lorber Bluray."
39. Huberty and Breyne, "Christophe Chabouté."

Railroaded by the French Army, which produced forged documents and pursued the case against him despite the discovery of the real culprit, Dreyfus was, for some, an acceptable sacrifice to conserve the honor and standing of the military. For others, the farce was a symptom of the rot at the center of French society.[40]

Far from reformed or cowed by the military defeats of the mid-twentieth century, the France of the late twentieth and twenty-first centuries has proved unapologetically militarist. Since the Algerian War of Independence, French armed forces have engaged in almost 130 military operations, including 61 in Africa, 30 in the Near and Middle East, 20 in Europe, 6 in Asia and the Pacific, and 9 in the Americas, mostly in the Caribbean.[41] According to a report on military doctrine presented to the National Assembly in 2015, France's military interventions have multiplied since the end of the Cold War, and the growth and maintenance of French power and reputation have been both the stated objectives and the celebrated outcomes of such actions. "France is a great military nation," the report declared. "While our country is at peace and does not experience any direct military threat against its territory, external action and the projection of forces outside the national territory allow the military tool to be fully employed. It has thus forged combat experience in a wide variety of theaters, which is today the admiration of all our partners." The report argued further that France should maintain a military "consistent with its level of ambition" and that there was an "imperative of power" now that France had become "a recognized military power on the international scene" whose advantage must not be allowed to erode.[42]

It is this fervent militarism on which Chabouté throws cold water, and the timing of his critique is opportune. In 2001 France had joined the United States in prosecuting US president George W. Bush's war in Afghanistan and, in the course of thirteen years, deployed some seventy thousand soldiers. Between 2002 and 2006, as part of Opération Pamir, French troops occupied Kabul in an effort to stabilize the Afghani capital and, in the words of Christophe Lafaye, "to make sure France would keep its influence in the world as a member of the United Nations Security Council."[43] Nevertheless, in 2004 French president Jacques Chirac led the opposition against the American president's proposed war on Iraq. As Charles Cogan notes, "The French political class overwhelmingly supported its government's aggressive opposition to the US," with very few "intellectuals and public figures challeng[ing] the [idea] . . . that the Iraq war

---

40. For more on the Dreyfus affair, see Harris, *Dreyfus*.
41. Chauveau and Gaymard, "Rapport d'information," 113–53.
42. Chauveau and Gaymard, "Rapport d'information," 7, 9, 75–77.
43. Lafaye, "France's Lessons," 55.

was ill-advised and morally wrong."[44] In reality, the opposition of French elites was a condemnation less of militarism than of US unilateralism. Nevertheless, the very public, very unified pushback against the US invasion of Iraq opened a space in which to critique war, and it is this space that Chabouté exploited to great effect, both by highlighting the horror and brutality of war and by reimagining the soldier—and, by extension, the military—as a cold, calculating, and self-interested murderer.

The graphic novel begins on November 12, 1921. The first thirteen pages take us to Landru's trial, where a fly perches on the bust of Marianne, the symbol of French values, before migrating to the gavel and finally to the head of one of the elderly trial judges, signifying the decrepitude of all they embody. The judges, the jury, the gendarmes, and all those in the gallery are heavy-lidded, bored by proceedings, which, we know in truth, to have been engaging and dynamic: a circus-like atmosphere prevailed in Versailles in 1921, and Landru was the consummate performer, around whom everything revolved.[45] Such boredom nevertheless recalls Bolitho's 1926 observation that "at the Landru trial, no lawyer dared to say that the prisoner made him shudder, or to lift the trial and condemnation of a man who had killed a mere thirteen out of the class of mere distractions."[46] Chabouté presents a society brutalized by war, unable to muster shock in the face of Landru's crimes.

A turn of the page reveals the real horror of the epoch. Transported back to January 1915, readers see rain-soaked rats feasting on a uniformed corpse. Soldiers in a trench huddle against the inclement weather; the anxiety on their faces is plain. One, Paul, takes the opportunity to write a letter to his sweetheart, Hélène. Over five pages the script of the missive unfolds, laid out between frames of a chaotic and bloody offensive, where shells burst and viscera explode from wounds. "I am going to flee this butchery, Hélène, escape this hell; they will not count me among their corpses," Paul confides. "I will meet you in Paris as soon as possible, the deserters are being hunted down and I will be forced to hide. . . . You absolutely must find us money, my love, a lot of money, quickly and by any means."[47] An explosion just in front of Paul covers his face in darkness and debris; he falls down, and all is dark. When he comes to, it is revealed that he has sustained major injuries to his face. He approaches a body on the ground and trades identification tags with it before stumbling off into the night. Paul's disfiguration associates him with the complex legacy of the *gueules cassées*, those soldiers

44. Cogan, "Iraq Crisis and France," 123.
45. See, e.g., Béraud, Bourcier, and Salmon, *L'affaire Landru.*
46. Bolitho, *Murder for Profit,* 213–14.
47. Chabouté, *Henri Désiré Landru,* 23–24.

whose wounds were the most visible and jarring of the conflict. Accompanying Clemenceau to the signing of the Treaty of Versailles, such veterans became emblems of the horrors of war and of the heroism that it supposedly stimulated.[48] Paul, as readers will discover, is no hero but a brutalized villain.

Back in Paris, the story continues. Hélène is wooed by Landru in the park, an encounter watched closely by a mysterious mustachioed man, identifiable as one of the spectators to Landru's courtroom drama. At the same time, collapsing the space between the front and the home front, between the military and civilian spheres, and implicating both in what ensues, a cadaverous Paul enters the gate of a country estate and falls to the ground. He calls out to the inhabitant, Charles, who drags the unrecognizable defector inside to administer relief. Days later Hélène boards a train to Houdon with Landru. From the departing car she tosses a piece of paper onto the platform. Seized by a trench-coated figure with face and hands swaddled in bandages, it reads: "Gambais, Villa l'Ermitage (near the cemetery)." Roused in the night, Landru descends into the kitchen of the villa, where he finds Hélène with the bandaged Paul. In a turn of events, Paul blackmails Landru and declares that the swindler will henceforth place his aptitude for seduction in the service of the mutilated man, who ostensibly requires money to get himself and Hélène far away from the war and from the French "justice" that would pursue him for desertion.

The plan unfolds over subsequent pages. Landru brings Jeanne Cuchet and her son André to the villa, where they are introduced to Landru's "sister Hélène and her husband Paul."[49] On the first night Jeanne is awakened by Paul, who hands her a pistol and tells her that thieves have broken into the house; she should not hesitate to shoot anything that moves. Making her way downstairs, Jeanne fires the gun into the darkness and, on seeing the shocked faces of Hélène, Paul, and André, realizes that she has shot her own fiancé, who lies bleeding on the floor. The police will certainly arrest her, Paul charges; she and her son should leave the country, board a boat to Argentina. She'll need to get all her money together for the voyage; he'll clean up the mess. Paul drags Landru's body out into the courtyard, where it miraculously reanimates. Landru must return to Paris, Paul says, with Jeanne's keys and the power of attorney that will allow him to empty her bank account. Landru departs, as instructed, and Hélène visits the local café to make a mysterious telephone call. The process repeats: two more women brought to Gambais, gunshots in the night, screams of recognition, and mysterious phone calls.

Autumn comes, and the already tense relationship between Landru and Paul frays. The latter's request for saws sets the former on edge and a follow-up

---

48. For more on the *gueules cassées*, see Powell, "About-Face"; and Delaporte, *Les gueules cassées*.
49. Chabouté, *Henri Désiré Landru*, 53.

inspection of the tools—purportedly for cutting firewood—reveals blood. Between December 18, 1915, and November 26, 1917, five more women are brought to the villa; there are five shots, five cries in the night; the clandestine calls continue. On this last occasion, however, Landru does not depart for Paris as usual. He follows Hélène to the café and watches as thick black smoke pours from the chimney of the Gambais house. After a brief interval in Paris, Landru returns to Gambais, where he empties the ash from the kitchen stove and finds a safety pin among the debris. The discovery prompts him to ask Paul if previous visitors to the villa had made it safely to their destination—arrangements had been left to the blackmailer. Paul assures Landru that he is doing his part, but Landru quips that Paul's wounds, after three years, seem hardly to have gotten any better. Paul responds that Landru had better concern himself with his little old ladies and forget about the injuries.

When the latest visitor to the villa fails to take the customary shot at her fiancé, all is revealed—the women are being murdered. Paul follows the woman and clubs her over the head, calling out to Hélène to take care of the body. A stunned Landru sits in disbelief until Charles arrives. Landru is sent off to Paris with the victim's house keys, instructions to sell all the jewelry and furniture found therein, and an ominous threat against the safety of his family should he feel compelled to tell anyone what he has seen. Landru returns to Paris, watched by the same man who stalked his first meeting with Hélène. The armistice is signed, and in the first weeks of 1919, Landru returns to Gambais with another companion, whom Paul summarily shoots. The charade is well and truly over, the true villain revealed. "What did you think!!" Paul shouts at the astounded Landru. "Did you really think we were busting our asses to make them flee abroad for a few miserable francs?!" "Look at my face, Henri!!" he shouts, unspooling the bandages from his head. "Take a good look!!!" Paul's face is a patchwork of scar tissue, the result of "successive grafts" performed by Charles. "Some skins are more compatible than others," he reveals. "Maybe this charming lady that you've brought me will be the right one!!" Paul sends Landru away with instructions to remain silent unless he is keen to find his own son's skin on the murderer's face.[50] Landru makes for the train station and for Paris, where he pens a letter to the attorney general, alerting him to the violence that he witnessed and confessing his role as a pawn in the bloody misadventure. That innocent lives are claimed by the soldier to literally "save face" is a striking metaphor for the modern French military, whose exploits seem largely in service of maintaining prestige and reputation.

Chabouté's *bande dessinée* exploits the gaps in the Landru case—there were no bodies discovered and no confession offered—and takes as its central

50. Chabouté, *Henri Désiré Landru*, 109–11.

truth the prevailing conspiracy theory of the time, that the Landru trial was a put-on by the government for its own ends. There is an added element, though: the military is to be shielded at all costs. In the final pages Marie Lacoste identifies Landru as the man with whom her sister went missing; he is arrested and questioned. Mandel approaches Clemenceau with Landru's letter, and it is decided that press coverage of the disappearances should be encouraged to divert attention from treaty negotiations. "All that is needed is a few twists and turns, cleverly orchestrated with false leads," Mandel offers. Clemenceau agrees but adds, "Be sure to keep the *gueule cassée* out of this business!! The blood spilled in the trenches is still too fresh!! It would be unpleasant and clumsy to implicate a veteran in the current situation!! So throw this Landru as food for the crowd!!!" Mandel subsequently visits Landru in jail and assures him that if he plays along, he and his family will be well taken care of, treated to a "golden retirement" in the Americas.[51]

Readers are returned to the trial with which the novel began, and Landru, despite proclamations of innocence, is sentenced to death. The blade of the guillotine falls in the prison courtyard, but the condemned is nowhere to be seen. Mandel receives a call to "do what's necessary," and in short order Paul and Hélène are shot dead in their bed, the mysterious accomplice is murdered in the street, and Charles dies quietly by fatal injection. Seemingly in the clear, Landru looks out over the deck of an ocean liner as he is approached by a man seeking a light for his cigarette. The unassuming man launches himself at Landru and tosses him overboard. A splash below signifies that Landru has been swallowed by the dark waters of the Atlantic. To protect itself, and the military that it reveres, the French state perverts justice and betrays Landru not once but twice. Here we find echoes again of the Dreyfus affair. Convicted twice in a bid to safeguard the reputation of the French military and shipped off to the penal colony on Devil's Island, Dreyfus ultimately had his sentence commuted and was pardoned in 1906 by President Emile Loubet. There is no such redemption for Landru, whose unjust punishment is irreversible.

In the end, it is a sign of postwar brutalization that Landru is disposed of so summarily. His executioner, who indifferently lights a cigarette after murdering him, appears as bored as those who attended his trial. The message, as *Landru* producer Georges de Beauregard commented in 1962, appears to be that "death was common in 1914, 15, 16, 17, 18" and marked Landru and men like him.[52] Indeed, Chabouté, whose story is based on rumor and conspiracy, had every opportunity to provide Landru a happy ending. That the author's villainous *gueule cassée* purported to send his "murderesses" to Argentina to escape scrutiny suggests that Chabouté was well aware of the rumor, recurrent in France throughout

---

51. Chabouté, *Henri Désiré Landru*, 119–23.
52. Press release for Landru.

the twentieth century and the subject of a popular 1989 novel, that Landru was secretly released from prison and sent off to Argentina with an annuity from the French government. The book was based on the account—corroborated by the police prefect of Buenos Aires—of the renowned comic Charles-Adrien "Grock" Wettach, who allegedly encountered Landru in Argentina in 1926.[53] This is not the denouement that Chabouté wanted for Landru, and the choice—more unnecessary death—speaks volumes.

Reception: A Tale of Two Wars

In 1919 the Landru story, unfolding in real time, was not a cipher for war but a diversion from it. As accounts of the trials of Alfred Dreyfus, Henriette Caillaux, and Violette Nozière have shown, causes célèbres provide windows into the national temper.[54] L'affaire Landru demonstrated a desire both to move beyond the war and to settle wartime scores. The year of the armistice was marked by ongoing nationalist sentiment, culminating in moments such as the Fête de la Victoire, the "crowning of a war unparalleled in History and the triumph of the victors," but it was likewise, as Mary Louise Roberts writes, an opportunity to "ignore the war . . . and insist on the vitality of the moment."[55] Put otherwise, by the journalist Emmanuel Bourcier, who attended and wrote about the Landru trial: the affaire signaled that "the war [was] definitely over, we [could] talk about something else!"[56] Indeed, the two sentiments were so intertwined that appearances of bearded men among the Fête de la Victoire crowds provoked jovial shouts of "Hey, Landru!" from uniformed soldiers, and attention to the case often rose and fell inversely with popular investment in demobilization, peace negotiations, and postwar political life.[57]

Landru's "dreadful exploits" allowed war-weary France to reimagine death in impersonal and emotionally anodyne ways by providing the populace with "some killings it could bear to discuss."[58] The trial allowed the nation to slay its demons in carnivalesque fashion. It was a spectacle, and Landru, by all contemporary accounts, was its able jester. He represented the shirker and was always bound for the gallows. His route to the scaffold was littered with jokes, both by him and about him, but his victims were pilloried as well. Landru had carried out society's revenge on women who had so flagrantly violated wartime gender

---

53. See Jaeger, *Landru*, 10. This nonfiction account of the Landru affair, published in 2005, would likely have been a starting point for research for Chabouté's novel, published the following year.
54. Harris, *Dreyfus*; Berenson, *Trial of Madame Caillaux*; Maza, *Violette Nozière*.
55. Béraud, Bourcier, and Salmon, *L'affaire Landru*, 145; Roberts, *Civilization without Sexes*, 2.
56. Béraud, Bourcier, and Salmon, *L'affaire Landru*, 26.
57. Béraud, Bourcier, and Salmon, *L'affaire Landru*, 141–53; Bolitho, *Murder for Profit*, 158.
58. Editors' preface in Bolitho, *Murder for Profit*, ix.

norms, and it was this that allowed him to escape public ire. Men had gone to war to protect women, who, in turn, owed their humble support. Yet Landru's fiancées, and women like them, had seemingly violated the arrangement, using the war years to seek only their own pleasure. Roberts notes that debates over female identity were an important cultural site for processing the war and its impacts on French society.[59] It is perhaps no surprise, then, that commentary on the victims took a misogynist turn. An exemplary political cartoon in *Le journal* featured Landru asking his attorney, "A woman's place is in the home [*foyer*], is it not, my dear sir?"[60] The joke, made by the man who had supposedly burned his fiancées' remains in his oven, turned on the word *foyer*, meaning both "home" and "hearth." Landru had unequivocally put women "back in their place." For a France looking to move beyond the war, the punishment of the *embusqué*'s victims was as necessary as his own.

Response to the Landru trial hinged on French society's experience of World War I, and reactions to later retellings of the Landru story must be similarly understood. As a vehicle for war critique, the Landru story is first and foremost a sacrilege. Comparisons with serial murder rob war of the halo of sacrality that surrounds it. They reduce war to bare, self-interested killing. War becomes not glorious but contemptible; its architects become not heroes but perpetrators and villains. This is the intention of those who deploy the Landru story for critical ends, but it likewise means that in periods of intense nationalism, the comparison is rendered unpalatable at best, wholly indigestible at worst. Stateside reception of *Monsieur Verdoux* in the late 1940s makes the point most plainly. The United States was belligerently capitalist, embarking on an extended ideological war against the Soviet Union, and it had beatified those who had fought World War II as the "greatest generation." Americans were simply not having any of what Chaplin was offering.

Neither was the film embraced in France, where critics noted its "unbearable pretentiousness" and considered it "obviously a failed film" both as a comedy and as a *film à thèse*.[61] One French critic wrote dismissively that "Charlot only played Monsieur Verdoux, who is Landru, and Landru only killed his wives to get the better of Truman and Yankee capitalism."[62] To be sure, the film was a departure for Chaplin, who discarded the character of "Charlot" that had endeared him to French audiences. Nevertheless, postwar France was deeply invested in the nationalist Resistance myth, wherein, according to Charles de Gaulle, the French nation had liberated itself and would "continue the struggle today as [it had] not

59. Roberts, *Civilization without Sexes*, 8–9.
60. Guillaume, "Brulates amours."
61. Clément, "Charles Chaplin"; A.B., "Monsieur Verdoux," 297.
62. H.Q., "De Landru au Pakistan," 297–98.

ceased to do since June 1940," likewise painting the period between 1939 and 1944 as part of a "thirty years' war" against Germany in which the French were righteous combatants.[63] French critics largely refused to engage with or even recognize Chaplin's critique of war; moreover, during this period, according to Julian Jackson, "censorship intervened" if cinematic depictions of the war "too dramatically contradicted the official myth."[64] France's complicated relationship with World War II, which replaced the memory of tens of thousands of Jews deported from the Hexagon to Auschwitz-Birkenau with a heroic myth of resistance, left little room for critique.

When *Landru* was released in 1963, reception was favorable despite obvious parallels to *Monsieur Verdoux*. The film was a commercial success for Chabrol amid a string of box office failures, and reviewers readily engaged with the antiwar message of the film.[65] Henry Rabine wrote in *La croix* that "the Landru they present to us today resembles a war machine going to war against war." He continued:

> Chaplin contented himself with having his Monsieur Verdoux say that the eleven crimes of which he was accused were a trifle compared to the great slaughter which had bloodied the world fifteen years before. Claude Chabrol, for his part, insists heavily on the chapter, at regular intervals slipping news shots of the 1914–1918 war into the sequences of the film itself. As a result, this is no longer an unpleasant allusion from Landru but an affirmation, a firm stance, no less unpleasant, from the authors.[66]

Reviewers from *L'humanité* and *Candide* likewise evaluated the film's message in relation to that proffered by Chaplin.[67] Claude Veillot, writing for the latter publication, declared that "when Chabrol's Landru is surprised by the emotion aroused by the disappearance of a few women while millions of young men are dying in the trenches, we still hear Mr. Verdoux: One murder, you are a villain. A million, you are a hero."[68]

The release of the film came a safe distance from World War II and occupied a space, between 1954 and 1971, that Henry Rousso defines as a period when "the subject of Vichy was less controversial, except for occasional eruptions in the period 1958–1962."[69] Indeed, it was in these years that the Algerian War of

---

63. Jackson, *France*, 602. See also Rousso, *Vichy Syndrome*.

64. Jackson, *France*, 604.

65. Colombani, "Le boucher de Claude Chabrol."

66. Henry Rabine, "Landru," *La croix*, Feb. 6, 1963, in Sagan, *Landru*, 78–79.

67. Samuel Lachize, *L'humanité*, Jan. 28, 1963, in Sagan, *Landru*, 66–67, 69–71; Veillot, "Chabrol a brûlé ses vedettes."

68. Veillot, "Chabrol a brûlé ses vedettes."

69. Rousso, *Vichy Syndrome*, 10.

Independence, Rousso notes, revived memories of World War II, which were mobilized to call certain sectors of French society to account for complicity in suffering.[70] Chabrol's *Landru* should be understood as part of this mobilization, an early attempt—preceding the "Broken Mirror" period of 1971–74, when the Gaullist myth was definitively shattered—to reckon, at once, with French involvement in the crimes of both World War II and the Algerian War. Unlike *Monsieur Verdoux*, *Landru*'s message, coated for digestion in soft colors and administered by graceful starlets, was less confrontational. Chaplin's film had been released immediately after World War II, and its director had played with the chronology of the Landru story to directly criticize the recent conflict and the rise of fascism. Chabrol's criticism was oblique, and it was offered at a time when it might be conceded that not all of France had behaved heroically.

Conclusion

In 2005, more than eighty years after Landru's execution, the historian Gérard Jaeger noted that it was the mystery surrounding Landru that allowed the caricature to perpetuate itself and "to be transformed over time according to circumstances and needs, according to the freedoms of interpretation which attach themselves to legends."[71] The story of Landru is indeed malleable, and it has been approached in myriad ways in the last century by a broad range of journalists, scholars, filmmakers, and storytellers. Yet they have one thing in common: they must confront and contend with war. Landru's story is inextricable from the slaughter of the Western Front. The war provides a counterweight to Landru's crimes, and accounts of his crimes, according to a review of Chabrol's film in the magazine *Temoignage chrétien*, inherently revolve around "a comparative value of corpses."[72] The evocations of war that pepper these stories "remind us," in the words of Georges Sadoul, "that, during this period, for one woman killed by Landru, a million dead were immolated on various European fronts."[73] More than inviting a comparison between war and crime, the Landru story demands it.

While the Landru story has been retold and reinvigorated many times over, reception of the war critique has been inconsistent. To be sure, social critique emerges when it is least welcome. In the case of war, criticism often arises when official and popular narratives of the righteousness of conflict are most entrenched. However, it is likewise during these periods, when war is proximate

70. Rousso, *Vichy Syndrome*, 75.
71. Jaeger, *Landru*, 10.
72. "Landru," *Temoignage chrétien*, Mar. 1, 1963, in Sagan, *Landru*, 85.
73. Sadoul, "La revanche de Chabrol."

and nationalist sentiment is high, that comparing war with serial murder is most alienating. The public will not suffer the sacrilege of seeing its heroes turned to monsters. Struck by the obvious similarities between *Monsieur Verdoux* and *Landru*, Veillot wondered if they were best explained as homage, or "should we believe," he asked, "that . . . it is impossible to tell the story of Landru otherwise?"[74] Similarities between the two films, as I have shown, did not extend to the reactions they garnered. Both films indicted audiences through the indictment of Landru, but they were not equally confrontational and, importantly, they were released into very different milieus. In each case, French audiences were called to reflect on their role in World War II. Had France been unambiguously heroic, as the Gaullist myth suggested, or, on the contrary, had it (or a portion of it) played the villain? The question, which had been dismissed in 1948, became permissible just fifteen years later.

JULIE M. POWELL is adjunct research fellow at University College Dublin. She is author of *Bodies of Work: The First World War and the Transnational Making of Rehabilitation* (2023) and "Doctoring the Script: Crime Writing, Order, and Medical Authority in the Oeuvre of Dr Augustin Cabanès, 1894–1928" in *Social History of Medicine* (2022).

Acknowledgments

The author thanks the Irish Research Council for its generous support of this research (grant GOIPD/2023/35).

References

A.B. "Monsieur Verdoux." *Esprit*, new ser., 142, no. 2 (1948): 297.

Belin, Jules. *Trente ans de Sûreté nationale*. Paris, 1950.

Béraud, Henri, Emmanuel Bourcier, and André Salmon. *L'affaire Landru*. Paris, 1924.

Berenson, Edward. *The Trial of Madame Caillaux*. Berkeley, CA, 1992.

Bolitho, William. *Murder for Profit*. New York, 1964.

Bradshaw, Peter. "Claude Chabrol Anatomised the French Middle Class with a Twist of the Scalpel." *Guardian Film Blog*, Sept. 12, 2010. https://www.theguardian.com/film/filmblog/2010/sep/12/claude-chabrol-death-hitchcock.

Brody, Richard. "In Memoriam Claude Chabrol." *New Yorker*, Sept. 12, 2010. https://www.newyorker.com/culture/richard-brody/in-memoriam-claude-chabrol.

Chabouté, Christophe. *Henri Désiré Landru*. Issy-les-Moulineaux, 2006.

Chabrol, Claude, dir. *Chaplin Today: Monsieur Verdoux*. YouTube, posted June 18, 2018, 26:39. https://www.youtube.com/watch?v=GVM1GaMzRMA.

Chauveau, Guy-Michel, and Hervé Gaymard. "Rapport d'information déposé par la Commission des affaires étrangères en conclusion des travaux d'une mission d'information constituée le 14 novembre 2012, sur 'engagement et diplomatie: quelle doctrine pour nos interventions

74. Veillot, "Chabrol a brûlé ses vedettes."

militaires?'" No. 2777, Assemblée nationale constitution du 4 octobre 1958, quatorzième légis-
lature. May 20, 2015. https://www.assemblee-nationale.fr/14/rap-info/i2777.asp.

Clément, Maurice. "Charles Chaplin: Monsieur Verdoux, l'oeuf et moi." *Hommes et mondes* 5, no. 20 (1948): 528–30.

Cogan, Charles. "The Iraq Crisis and France: Heaven-Sent Opportunity or Problem from Hell?" *French Politics, Culture, and Society* 22, no. 3 (2004): 120–34.

Colombani, Florence. "Le boucher de Claude Chabrol: Noirceur et ironie." *Le monde*, Oct. 21, 2004. https://www.lemonde.fr/archives/article/2004/10/31/p-6-le-boucher-de-claude-chabrol-p-p-noirceur-et-ironie-p_4305084_1819218.html.

Darmon, Pierre. *Landru.* Paris, 1994.

Delaporte, Sophie. *Les gueules cassées: Les blessés de la face de la Grande Guerre.* Paris, 1996.

Gonzalez, Christian. *Crime Story: Monsieur Landru.* Paris, 1993.

Guardian. "'Lost' Françoise Sagan Novel Causes Stir in France." Sept. 19, 2019. https://www.theguardian.com/books/2019/sep/19/francoise-sagan-lost-novel-france-four-corners-heart.

Guillaume, Albert. "Brulates amours." *Le journal*, May 23, 1919.

Harris, Ruth. *Dreyfus: Politics, Emotion, and the Scandal of the Century.* New York, 2013.

Hoberman, J. "When Chaplin Became the Enemy." *New York Times*, June 8, 2008. https://www.nytimes.com/2008/06/08/movies/08hobe.html.

H.Q. "De Landru au Pakistan." *Esprit*, new ser., 142, no. 2 (1948): 297–98.

Huberty, Alain, and Marc Breyne. "Christophe Chabouté." Hubert and Breyne. https://hubertybreyne.com/en/artists/presentation/68/christophe-chaboute (accessed Mar. 6, 2024).

Jackson, Julian. *France: The Dark Years, 1940–1944.* Oxford, 2001.

Jaeger, Gérard. *Landru: Bourreau des coeurs.* Paris, 2005.

Lafaye, Christophe. "France's Lessons." *US Army War College Quarterly: Parameters* 49, no. 3 (2019): 55–63.

Masson, René. *Number One: A Story of Landru.* London, 1964.

Maza, Sarah C. *Violette Nozière: A Story of Murder in 1930s Paris.* Berkeley, CA, 2011.

Neupert, Richard. *A History of the French New Wave Cinema.* Madison, WI, 2007.

Powell, Julie M. "About-Face: Gender, Disfigurement, and the Politics of French Reconstruction, 1918–1924." *Gender and History* 28, no. 3 (2016): 604–22.

Roberts, Mary Louise. *Civilization without Sexes: Reconstructing Gender in Postwar France, 1917–1927.* Chicago, 1994.

Rothberg, Michael. *Multidirectional Memory: Remembering the Holocaust in the Age of Decolonization.* Stanford, CA, 2009.

Rousso, Henry. *The Vichy Syndrome: History and Memory in France since 1944.* Cambridge, MA, 1991.

Sloan, William David, Julie K. Hedgepeth, Patricia C. Place, and Kevin Stoker. *The Great Reporters: An Anthology of News Writing at Its Best.* Northport, AL, 1992.

Wilkins, Budd. "Two by Claude Chabrol on Kino Lorber Bluray: *Bluebeard* and *Blue Panther*." *Slant*, Sept. 23, 2021. https://www.slantmagazine.com/dvd/claude-chabrol-bluebeard-blue-panther-blu-ray/.

News

Call for Papers: Special Issue on Incarceration in French and Francophone Histories

The term *incarceration* implies more than the modern prison, but how far does and can it stretch? What are the experiences, ideologies, and power dynamics of nonvoluntary confinement? For this special issue, we invite articles that explore any facet of incarceration within France and its empire in any historical period. Given recent developments in historical and carceral scholarship, we particularly welcome articles that allow us to think through understandings of incarceration broadly and that shed light on the continuities and discontinuities in practices and conceptualizations of confinement in time and space.

Fresh historical research has been complicating foundational assumptions about histories of incarceration. While the work of Michel Foucault continues to shape the terrain, historians have been rethinking chronologies, connections, and spatial considerations. Historians of the early modern period, for instance, have been pushing back against interpretative narratives that emphasize the novelty of the modern period, drawing attention instead to the deep historical roots of conceptions and systems of confinement. This research is also opening debate on the relationships between types of institutions of confinement over time. Historians of empire, meanwhile, have been calling into question long-standing assumptions about the primacy of the modern penitentiary as a technology of power and social control, pointing to the enduring history of the transportation and exile of convicts, enslaved individuals, and "suspect" populations.

Together, these new approaches are destabilizing orthodoxies on the unfolding dynamics of practices, spaces, and uses of incarceration, providing new insights into the experiences of people enclosed in these spaces and new understandings of the connections that existed between them and communities on the outside.

Writing the history of incarceration can encompass more than just a consideration of official and textual expressions of power. What did incarcerated subjects and communities make of confinement? Drawing on the concept of the "anarchive," how might alternative forms of archives supplement and/or complicate the official archives held on prisoners in repositories like the French Ministry of Justice and the Archives Nationales d'Outre-mer? What perspectives are revealed by considering visual materials? How have observers beyond the confines of incarcerated spaces viewed those inside?

French Historical Studies • Vol. 47, No. 2 (May 2024) • DOI 10.1215/00161071-11036263

Possible themes include (but are not limited to)

- cultures and imaginaries of incarceration
- incarceration in and beyond the prison, for instance, asylums, port-city *bagnes*, overseas penal colonies, sites of captivity of enslaved people, juvenile reformatories, military disciplinary camps, camps for prisoners of war and other "suspect" populations, and so on
- politics of space and mobilities (exile, isolation, networks, community)
- reportage, photography, public campaigns on incarceration
- architecture and technologies of control and constraint
- gendered and racialized practices and experiences of incarceration
- incarceration and family life
- forms of self-expression (art, writing, etc.) and resistance
- colonial and postcolonial forms of incarceration
- guards, doctors, lawyers, and other workers in carceral spaces
- legacies, heritage, and material cultures of sites of confinement

We ask for submissions of a maximum of 10,000 words, excluding notes. Submissions can be in either English or French but should be accompanied by a 150-word abstract and up to five keywords; abstract and keywords, as well as the article's title, should be submitted in both languages. Please submit your manuscripts via https://read.dukeupress.edu /french-historical-studies. Please follow the information for authors, and mark your manuscript to be considered for the special issue.

For any questions, please contact the guest editors, Briony Neilson (brionyneilson@ gmail.com) and Sophie Fuggle (sophie.fuggle@ntu.ac.uk).

The deadline for submissions is **August 23, 2024**.

Appel à contributions: Numéro spécial sur l'incarcération dans les histoires françaises et francophones

Pour ce numéro spécial, nous invitons des articles qui abordent la question de l'incarcération dans tous ses aspects et dans des contextes variés en France et à travers l'Empire colonial français. Compte tenu des développements récents dans les travaux des historiens et sociologues, nous cherchons surtout des travaux qui nous permettront de réfléchir à l'incarcération au sens large, et qui mettront en lumière les continuités et ruptures dans les pratiques et les conceptualisations de l'enfermement dans le temps et dans l'espace.

Quelles sont les expériences, les idéologies et les dynamiques de pouvoir de l'incarcération ? Cette question a beaucoup préoccupé les historiens ces derniers temps. Alors que les analyses de Michel Foucault exercent toujours une influence importante sur la recherche, de nouvelles approches reviennent sur l'histoire du confinement, ses chronologies, ses croisements et ses aspects spatiaux. Pour l'époque moderne, par exemple, les historiens ont remis en question l'importance et la nouveauté des idées et pratiques de la période contemporaine, mettant l'accent sur les racines profondes des conceptions et des systèmes de confinement ; des racines qui remontent loin dans l'histoire. Ces recherches provoquent aussi des discussions sur les continuités et les discontinuités entre les différents types d'institutions d'enfermement—entrepôts de personnes esclavisées, hôpitaux, asiles, colonies, camps, et ainsi de suite. Les historiens de l'empire, quant à eux, ont interrogé la primauté du pénitencier moderne en tant que technologie de pouvoir et de contrôle social, en montrant l'histoire longue et continue de la captivité, de la déportation, et de l'exil des condamnés et d'autres populations exploitées ou estimées « suspectes ».

Dans son ensemble, ces nouvelles approches offrent de nouvelles perspectives sur les expériences des personnes enfermées et leurs rapports avec les communautés à l'extérieur.

Ecrire l'histoire de l'incarcération peut englober bien plus que des analyses des expressions officielles et textuelles du pouvoir. Quelles étaient les attitudes des sujets et des communautés incarcérées concernant le confinement ? En s'appuyant sur le concept d'« anarchive », comment est-ce que des formes alternatives d'archives pourraient-elles compléter ou contester les archives officielles sur les prisonniers détenues par l'Etat ? Quelles perspectives sont produites par des études des matériaux visuels et sonores ? Depuis le « tournant visuel » en criminologie, les chercheurs ont montré jusqu'à quel point les « iconographies » de la punition et les diverses formes de « spectateur pénal » déterminent les connaissances et les réponses du public aux pratiques d'incarcération à différents moments dans le temps. Comment les observateurs situés à l'extérieur ont-ils perçu les espaces carcéraux et les personnes qui se trouvaient dedans ?

Voici une liste non exhaustive de sujets possibles :

- cultures et imaginaires de l'incarcération
- incarcération dans les prisons, mais aussi dans les asiles, les bagnes, les maisons de correction pour mineurs, les entrepôts des personnes esclavisées, les camps disciplinaires militaires, les camps de prisonniers de guerre et d'autres populations « suspectes », etc.
- politiques de l'espace et des mobilités (par ex. l'exil, l'isolement, réseaux sociaux à l'intérieur des institutions d'incarcération, rapports entre le dedans et le dehors)
- reportages, photographies, campagnes publiques sur l'incarcération
- architectures et technologies de contrôle et de contrainte
- pratiques et expériences d'incarcération genrées et racialisées
- incarcération et vie de famille
- formes d'expression (art, écriture, etc.) et de résistance
- formes d'incarcération dans les contextes coloniaux et postcoloniaux
- perspectives et cultures de ceux qui travaillent dans les espaces carcéraux (gardiens, médecins, avocats et autres)
- héritages, patrimoines et cultures matérielles des lieux de confinement

Pour soumettre un article, veuillez consulter https://read.dukeupress.edu/french-historical -studies. Suivez les instructions de la section « For Authors ». Les articles peuvent être soumis en anglais ou en français, mais dans les deux cas, ils doivent être conformes au style de *FHS*, et doivent être accompagnés d'un résumé de 150 mots et jusqu'à cinq mots clés, ainsi que le titre de l'article, dans les deux langues. Les manuscrits ne doivent comporter plus de 10 000 mots, plus les notes.

Les questions sont à adresser aux directrices du numéro spécial : Briony Neilson (briony.neilson@sydney.edu.au) et Sophie Fuggle (sophie.fuggle@ntu.ac.uk).

La date limite pour soumettre les articles est fixée au **23 août 2024**.

Recent Books and Dissertations on French History

Compiled by SARAH B. SUSSMAN

This bibliography is designed to introduce readers to recent publications on French history, broadly defined. It is organized according to commonly recognized periods, with works that bridge multiple categories listed under "General and Miscellaneous."

General and Miscellaneous

Aprile, Sylvie, and Hervé Leuwers, eds. *Révolutions et relectures du passé, XVIIIe–XXe siècle.* Villeneuve-d'Ascq: Presses Universitaires du Septentrion, 2023. 352p. €25.00.

Astoul, Guy, Jean Le Pottier, and Jean-Luc Nespoulous. *Migrants et migrations dans le Midi des origines à nos jours: Actes du 1er congrès de la Fédération historique de la région Occitanie, Montauban, 11–13 octobre 2019.* Montauban: SMERP, 2022. 477p. €25.00.

Ayling, Lindsay. "Fractured Nationalism and the Crises of French Identity, 1789–1899." PhD diss., University of North Carolina at Chapel Hill, 2023.

Bard, Christine, Pauline Boivineau, and Marion Charpenel. *Les féministes et leurs archives.* Rennes: Presses Universitaires de Rennes, 2023. 266p. €24.00.

Boisdron, Matthieu. *Joseph Paul-Boncour, 1873–1972.* Paris: Sorbonne Université Presses, 2023. 514p. €28.00.

Cage, E. Claire. *The Science of Proof: Forensic Medicine in Modern France.* Cambridge: Cambridge University Press, 2022. 237p. $110.00.

Chadefaud, Catherine. *Histoire des femmes en France: De la Renaissance à nos jours.* Paris: Ellipses, 2023. 553p. €26.00.

Chanteranne, David. *Chroniques des territoires: Comment les régions ont construit la nation.* Paris: Passés Composés, 2023. 316p. €21.00.

Condette, Jean-François, Arnaud-Dominique Houte, Jean Le Bihan, and Aurélien Lignereux, eds. *Former, encadrer, surveiller: Documents d'histoire sociale de la France contemporaine (XIXe–XXIe siècles).* Rennes: Presses Universitaires de Rennes, 2023. 362p. €25.00.

Demeure, Brigitte. *La figure maternelle dans la vie politique française, 1789–1914.* Avignon: Editions Universitaires d'Avignon, 2023. 426p. €29.00.

Denglos, Guillaume, and Philippe Vial, eds. *Au cœur de l'Etat: Une histoire du Secrétariat général de la défense et de la sécurité nationale (XIXe–XXIe siècles).* Paris: Nouveau Monde, 2023. 754p. €29.00.

French Historical Studies • Vol. 47, No. 2 (May 2024) • DOI 10.1215/00161071-11025103

Depretto, Laure, Christian Renoux, Christophe Speroni, and Gabriele Vickermann, eds. *Cultures du secret à l'époque moderne: Raisons, espaces, paradoxes, fabriques.* Paris: Classiques Garnier, 2023. 370p. €38.00.

Dupuy, Pascal. *De la création à la confrontation: Diffusion et politique des images (1750–1848).* Mont-Saint-Aignan: Presses Universitaires de Rouen et du Havre, 2023. 264p. €28.00.

Duvert, Cyrille. *Le foulard et la balance: Une histoire juridique de l'Islam en France.* Paris: Passés Composés, 2023. 199p. €19.00.

Eymeoud, Juliette, and Claire-Lise Gaillard. *Histoire de célibats: Du Moyen Age au XXe siècle.* Paris: Presses Universitaires de France, 2023. 181p. €18.00.

Fehrenbach, Jérôme. *Les fermiers: La classe sociale oubliée.* Paris: Passés Composés, 2023. 559p. €27.00.

Fournier, Eric, and Arnaud-Dominique Houte, eds. *A bas l'armée! L'antimilitarisme en France du XIXe siècle à nos jours.* Paris: Editions de la Sorbonne, 2023. 310p. €25.00.

Geneix, Gilles. *Antoine-Laurent de Jussieu (1748–1836): Fabrique d'une science botanique.* Paris: Publications Scientifiques du Muséum National d'Histoire Naturelle, 2022. 727p. €45.00.

Gicquel, Jean-François, Catherine Guyon, and Bruno Maes, eds. *Sacres et couronnements en Europe: Rite, politique et société, du Moyen Age à nos jours.* Rennes: Presses Universitaires de Rennes, 2023. 303p. €25.00.

Grévy, Jérôme, and Dino Mengozzi, eds. *Michel Vovelle: Il suo pensiero storiografico in Italia e in Francia.* Milan: FrancoAngeli, 2023. 219p. €30.00.

Histoire(s) de la région Bourgogne-Franche-Comté: Fragments d'un territore. Cinisello Balsamo (Milan): Silvana Editoriale Spa, 2023. 400p. €35.00.

Ingram, Mark, and Kathryn A. Kleppinger, eds. *The Marseille Mosaic: A Mediterranean City at the Crossroads of Cultures.* New York: Berghahn, 2023. 335p. $145.00.

Jacquet, Florence. *Charente, La Rochefoucauld: "L'histoire, la famille, le château, la cité, les alentours et le château de Verteuil."* Paris: Indes Savantes, 2023. 515p. €35.00.

Lalouette, Jacqueline. *L'identité républicaine de la France: Une expression, une mémoire, des principes.* Paris: Fayard, 2023. 351p. €24.00.

Laloux, Ludovic, Romane Monnier, and Raphaël Chauvancy, eds. *Guerre et paix: Enjeux géostratégiques, diplomatie et opérations militaires.* Huningue: Presses Universitaires Rhin et Danube, 2022. 301p. €24.00.

Leopoldie, Nicole. *Transnational Coupling in the Age of Nation Making during the Nineteenth and Twentieth Centuries.* London: Anthem, 2023. 161p. £80.00.

Luis, Jean-Philippe, Karine Rance, and Michel Streith, eds. *Migrations: Le creuset clermontois, XIXe–XXIe siècle.* Clermont-Ferrand: Presses Universitaires Blaise Pascal, 2023. 300p. €20.00.

Miot, Claire, Thomas Vaisset, and Paul Vo-Ha, eds. *Cessez-le-feu, cesser les combats? De l'époque moderne à nos jours.* Villeneuve-d'Ascq: Presses Universitaires du Septentrion, 2022. 308p. €25.00.

Muchembled, Robert. *La séduction: Une passion française.* Paris: Belles Lettres, 2023. 326p. €25.00.

Ohlen, Frédéric. *Le monde flottant: Nathalie Lemel, Bretonne et révolutionnaire.* Pirae: Au Vent des Iles, 2023. 216p. €16.00.

Phipps, Catherine. "Sex, Race, and Power: Colonial and Interracial Sexuality in the French Empire in Morocco, 1912–1956." PhD diss., University of Oxford.

Posener, Salomon. *Essai d'une bibliographie critique des œuvres de l'abbé Grégoire.* Edited by Jean Dubray. Paris: Classiques Garnier, 2023. 213p. €26.00.

Raveux, Olivier, Anne Montenach, and Gilbert Buti, eds. *Chaînes et maillons du commerce, XVIe–XIXe siècles.* Aix-en-Provence: Presses Universitaires de Provence, 2023. 300p. €30.00.

Ross, Andrew Israel, and Nina Kushner, eds. *Histories of French Sexuality: From the Enlightenment to the Present.* Lincoln: University of Nebraska Press, 2023. 360p. €35.00.

Ross, Kristin. *The Politics and Poetics of Everyday Life.* London: Verso, 2023. 309p. $29.95.

Smith, Macs. *Paris and the Parasite: Noise, Health, and Politics in the Media City.* Cambridge, MA: MIT Press, 2021. 296p. $40.00.

Whitehead, Julian. *Calais: A History of England's First Colony.* Barnsley: Pen and Sword History, 2022. 227p. $49.95.

Medieval and Renaissance

Adams, Tracy. *Agnès Sorel and the French Monarchy: History, Gallantry, and National Identity.* Leeds: Arc Humanities, 2022. 164p. $119.00.

Akard, Lucia. "Victims and Survivors of Rape in Late Medieval France and Burgundy." PhD diss., University of Oxford, 2022.

Berkhofer, Robert F. *Forgeries and Historical Writing in England, France, and Flanders, 900–1200.* Woodbridge: Boydell, 2022. 348p. $125.00.

Brouquet, Sophie. *Marguerite de Provence et Eléonore de Provence: Sœurs et reines de France et d'Angleterre.* Paris: Perrin, 2023. 462p. €24.00.

Coulon, Damien. *Un port sans rivage? Grand commerce, réseaux et personnalités marchandes à Perpignan à la fin du Moyen Age.* Madrid: Casa de Velázquez, 2023. 315p. €35.00.

Deyber, Alain. *Vercingétorix, un aristocrate gaulois.* Paris: Ellipses, 2023. 502p. €26.00.

Launay, Vincent. *Le roi en son duché: L'aristocratie de Bretagne et la construction de l'Etat royal (1270–1328).* Rennes: Presses Universitaires de Rennes, 2023. 354p. €26.00.

Minvielle-Larousse, Nicolas. *L'âge de l'argent: Mines, société et pouvoirs en Languedoc médiéval.* Aix-en-Provence: Presses Universitaires de Provence, 2023. 343p. €35.00.

Morand-Métivier, Charles-Louis, and Tracy Adams, eds. *The Waxing of the Middle Ages: Revisiting Late Medieval France.* Newark: University of Delaware Press, 2023. 283p. $120.00.

Périsse, Sébastien. *La Saintonge maritime au sortir de la guerre de Cent Ans.* Paris: Indes Savantes, 2023. 410p. €33.00.

Rivault, Antoine. *Le duc d'Etampes et la Bretagne: Le métier de gouverneur de province à la Renaissance, 1543–1565.* Rennes: Presses Universitaires de Rennes, 2023. 393p. €30.00.

Roch, Jean-Louis. *Vivre la misère au Moyen Age.* Paris: Belles Lettres, 2023. 249p. €25.50.

Sarindar-Fontaine, François. *Charles V le Sage, ou les limites d'un grand règne.* Paris: Harmattan, 2023. 459p. €47.00.

Thiérus, Anaïs, and Damien Millet. *Les Chappuys d'Amboise: Chronique historique d'une famille lettrée de la Renaissance.* Rennes: Presses Universitaires de Rennes, 2023. 596p. €30.00.

Villard de Honnecourt. *The Worlds of Villard de Honnecourt: The Portfolio, Medieval Technology, and Gothic Monuments.* Edited by George Brooks and Maile S. Hutterer. Leiden: Brill, 2023. 588p. $186.00.

Zink, Michel. *Parler aux simples gens: Un art médiéval.* Paris: Cerf, 2023. 225p. €20.00.

Ancien Régime

Alcouffe, Alain. *Seignelay Colbert de Castlehill (1735–1811): Un évêque entre Lumières écossaises et Contre-Révolution*. Toulouse: Presses de l'Université Toulouse 1 Capitole, 2022. 405p. €35.00.

Amis de Talleyrand. *Talleyrand et ses contemporains: Colloque 2022*. Valençay: Association des Amis de Talleyrand, 2023. 151p. N.p.

Bercé, Yves-Marie. *Bons princes et ministres haïssables aux XVIe et XVIIe siècles*. Paris: Cerf, 2023. 248p. €22.00.

Bertière, Simone. *Chroniques de l'Ancien Régime*. Paris: Perrin, 2023. 576p. €22.50.

Bustarret, Claire. *Inventorier les correspondances des Lumières: Analyse matérielle et traitements numériques*. Ferney-Voltaire: Centre International d'Etude du XVIIIe Siècle, 2023. 238p. €60.00.

Crogiez Labarthe, Michèle, ed. *Thémis et Flore: Les savoirs de Malesherbes*. Paris: Classiques Garnier, 2023. 352p. €32.00.

Da Vinha, Mathieu. *Le plaisir de vivre, ou les libertés de la Marquise de Jaucourt*. Paris: Tallandier, 2023. 349p. €24.50.

Debré, Guillaume. *L'affaire XYZ: Un scandale signé Talleyrand*. Paris: Fayard, 2023. 364p. €23.00.

Dejardin, Camille. *Patronnes au XVIIIe siècle*. Paris: Nouveau Monde, 2023. 189p. €20.90.

Desserrières, Laëtitia. *Les guerres de Religion (1559–1610): La haine des clans*. Paris: In Fine, 2023. 332p. €39.00.

Di Gioa, Michele, ed. *99 lettres d'un témoin de la Fronde (1649–1653), ou des lettres de renseignements détaillés sur des événements de France adressées de Paris par M. Camillo Genouini à moi-même Giovanni Battista Ciambotti à Rome*. Paris: Harmattan, 2023. 294p. €31.00.

Dolan, Claire. *Histoire de capitouls: "Gens de peu de naissance" et promotion sociale à Toulouse (XVIIe–XVIIIe siècles)*. Toulouse: Presses Universitaires du Midi, 2023. 430p. €29.00.

El Hage, Fadi. *La guerre de succession de France (1584–1610): Henri IV devait-il être roi?* Paris: Passés Composés, 2023. 378p. €23.50.

Gillain, Christophe. "Cardinal de Retz, French Noble Exile, and Political Mobility in Seventeenth-Century Europe." PhD diss., University of Cambridge, 2022.

Leca-Tsiomis, Marie. *La guerre des dictionnaires: Le Trévoux, aux sources de l'Encyclopédie*. Paris: Centre National de la Recherche Scientifique, 2023. 229p. €24.00.

Le Roux, Nicolas. *Les guerres de Religion: Une histoire de l'Europe au XVIe siècle*. Paris: Passés Composés, 2023. 399p. €24.00.

Leuveren, Bram van. *Early Modern Diplomacy and French Festival Culture in a European Context, 1572–1615*. Boston: Brill, 2023. 330p. $139.00.

Lever, Evelyne. *Les princesses mazarines: La gloire du cardinal*. Paris: Tallandier, 2023. 349p. €23.50.

Lilti, Antoine. *Actualité des Lumières: Une histoire plurielle*. Paris: Collège de France, 2023. 80p. €12.00.

Malcor, Fabrice. *L'ascension du cardinal de Fleury (1653–1726)*. Rennes: Presses Universitaires de Rennes; Versailles: Centre de Recherche du Château de Versailles, 2023. 311p. €26.00.

Marchini, Anna Maria. *Women in the French Enlightenment: From Femme Savante to Mother of the Family*. New York: Routledge, 2023. 154p. $136.00.

Martysheva, Lana. *Henri IV roi: Le pari de l'hérétique*. Ceyzérieu: Champ Vallon, 2023. 335p. €25.00.

McShea, Bronwen. *La Duchesse: The Life of Marie de Vignerot; Cardinal Richelieu's Forgotten Heiress Who Shaped the Fate of France.* New York: Pegasus, 2023. 466p. $28.95.

Neat-Ward, Lucy. "Caring for Animals in Early Modern France, 1550–1750." PhD diss., University of Manchester, 2022.

Pollin, Jean-Paul, Michel Pertué, and Anthony Mergey, eds. *Guillaume-François Le Trosne (1728–1780): Itinéraire d'une figure intellectuelle orléanaise au siècle des Lumières.* Paris: Mare et Martin, 2023. 316p. €33.00.

Rabaud, Jacques, and Jean Cabanes. *Lacaune et le négoce maritime au XVIIIe siècle: Correspondance entre Jacques Rabaud et Jean Cabanes, 4 octobre 1771–18 septembre 1793.* Edited by Gilbert Buti and Jacques de Larambergue. Nages: Centre de Recherches du Patrimoine de Rieumontagné, 2022. 213p. €20.00.

Roche, Daniel. *Les Lumières minuscules d'un vitrier parisien: Souvenirs, chansons et autres textes (1757–1802) de Jacques-Louis Ménétra.* Chêne-Bourg: Georg, 2022. 456p. CHF 30.00.

Roussel, Claude Youenn. *Des capitaines protestants et Louis XIV: Des Antilles au Golfe de Gascogne.* Paris: Harmattan, 2023. 243p. €26.50.

Sarmant, Thierry. *Le Régent: Un prince pour les Lumières.* Paris: Perrin, 2023. 256p. €25.00.

Schambil, Clara. *Ces dames du Parlement: Une histoire des femmes de magistrats à Bordeaux au XVIIe siècle.* Bordeaux: Confluences, 2023. 332p. €23.00.

Statman, Alexander. *A Global Enlightenment: Western Progress and Chinese Science.* Chicago: University of Chicago Press, 2023. 356p. $45.00.

Tabacchi, Stefano. *Richelieu.* Rome: Salerno, 2022. 320p. €27.00.

Vergé-Franceschi, Michel, Marie-Christine Varachaud, and André Zysberg. *Les marins du Roi Soleil.* Paris: Perrin, 2023. 363p. €24.00.

Waresquiel, Emmanuel de. *Jeanne du Barry: Une ambition au féminin.* Paris: Tallandier, 2023. 585p. €27.90.

Winn, Colette H. *Les femmes témoins de la révocation de l'édit de Nantes.* Paris: Classiques Garnier, 2023. 401p. €49.00.

Zeller, Olivier. *La Bresse et le pouvoir: Le papier journal de Jean Corton, syndic du tiers état (1641–1643).* Dijon: Editions Universitaires de Dijon, 2023. 164p. €13.00.

French Revolution and Napoleon

Aristide, Isabelle, Jean-Christian Petitfils, and Emmanuel de Waresquiel, eds. *Louis XVI, Marie-Antoinette et la Révolution: La famille royale aux Tuileries (1789–1792).* Paris: Gallimard, 2023. 189p. €30.00.

Benoit, Michel. *L'affaire de la Compagnie des Indes: Un scandale politico-financier sous la Terreur.* Paris: Ramsay, 2023. 245p. €20.00.

Benzoni, Riccardo. *"Dieu lui accorde un fils": Napoleone, il re di Roma e la legittimazione della dinastia imperiale.* Milan: FrancoAngeli, 2022. 258p. €37.00.

Biard, Michel. *Les derniers jours de la montagne (1794–1795): Vie et mort des premiers irréductibles de gauche.* Paris: Presses Universitaires de France, 2023. 233p. €18.00.

Callaway, H. B. *The House in the Rue Saint-Fiacre: A Social History of Property in Revolutionary Paris.* Cambridge, MA: Harvard University Press, 2023. 297p. $45.00.

Coursin, Régis. *Jacques-Pierre Brissot: Sociologie historique d'une entrée en Révolution.* Rennes: Presses Universitaires de Rennes, 2023. 355p. €28.00.

Du Mesnil Du Buisson, Françoise. *Portraits d'un sans-culotte.* Chamalières: LEMME, 2022. 224p. €19.00.

Ermisse, Gérard. *Marescot, le Vauban de Napoléon*. Paris: Pierre de Taillac, 2023. 209p. €22.90.

Favier, Franck. *Le maréchal Ney*. Paris: Perrin, 2023. 392p. €24.00.

Figeac, Michel. *Helena Potocka: Une princesse européenne au temps des révolutions*. Paris: Vendémiaire, 2023. 326p. €24.00.

Gallinella, Fabien. *La république des Girondins: La pensée constitutionnelle d'une mouvance politique sous la Révolution*. Paris: Dalloz, 2023. 757p. €79.00.

Goupilleau, Jean Victor. *L'aveuglement: Lettres du révolutionnaire vendéen Jean Victor Goupilleau, 1791–1795*. La Roche-sur-Yon: Centre Vendéen de Recherches Historiques, 2023. 512p. €28.00.

Green, Netta. "Revolutionary Succession: Families, Inheritance Law, and the Social Sciences in France, 1789–1815." PhD diss., Princeton University, 2022.

Guicheteau, Gérard. *Les treize journées qui ont fait la Vendée: Récits de contemporains*. Paris: Cerf, 2023. 285p. €22.00.

Ihl, Olivier. *Le vieux de la montagne: Filippo Buonarroti à Grenoble*. Vulaines-sur-Seine: Croquant, 2023. 319p. €20.00.

Klein, Charles-Armand. *Savants et artistes de l'extravagante expédition d'Egypte*. Nice: Campanile, 2023. 248p. €20.00.

Louviot, Isabelle, and Georges Peignard. *Elisée Reclus: Penser l'humain et la terre*. Paris: Tripode, 2022. 161p. €23.00.

Luxardo, Hervé. *La Révolution française et la violence: "Une logique infernale . . ." (1789 à nos jours)*. Antony: Clefs pour l'Histoire de France, 2023. 233p. €16.00.

Ortholan, Henri. *Le général Humbert, 1767–1823: Héros de l'Irlande*. Saint-Barthélemy-d'Anjou: Olizel, 2022. 415p. €27.00.

Pouffary, Marion. *Robespierre, monstre ou héros?* Villeneuve-d'Ascq: Presses Universitaires du Septentrion, 2023. 342p. €25.00.

Riaud, Xavier. *La santé de Napoléon Ier*. Paris: Harmattan, 2023. 150p. €17.00.

Schiappa, Jean-Marc. *Gracchus Babeuf*. Paris: Fayard, 2023. 376p. €23.00.

Tomasso, Jean-Jacques. *Mariages en révolution: Les mariages irréguliers avant la mise en œuvre de l'état civil laïc en 1793, et ceux de Pierre Sylvain Maréchal et de Jacques René Hébert*. Paris: Harmattan, 2023. 167p. €19.00.

Tulard, Jean. *L'empire de l'argent: S'enrichir sous Napoléon*. Paris: Tallandier, 2023. 200p. €19.90.

Valmori, Niccolò. *Banking and Politics in the Age of Democratic Revolution*. Oxford: Voltaire Foundation, 2023. 320p. $99.00.

1815–1870

Dadoune, Jean-Pierre. *François-Vincent Raspail: Apôtre de la République et de la science*. Paris: Harmattan, 2023. 243p. €25.00.

Finkelberg, John Richard. "Becoming a Man in the Age of Fashion: Gender and Menswear in Nineteenth-Century France, 1830–1870." PhD diss., University of Michigan, 2022.

Lequime, Jérôme. *Simon Rouet: Consul de France à Mossoul en 1845, pionnier méconnu de l'archéologie assyrienne; Au cœur des rivalités entre la France et l'Angleterre*. Drémil Lafage: Mergoil, 2022. 195p. €29.00.

Mauduit, Xavier. *Napoléon III*. Paris: Presses Universitaires de France, 2023. 239p. €14.00.

Michelet, Maxime. *Napoléon III, la France et nous*. Paris: Passés Composés, 2023. 199p. €18.00.

Ploux, François. *Bruit public: Rumeurs et charisme napoléonien, 1814–1823*. Ceyzérieu: Champ Vallon, 2023. 264p. €24.00.

Poirot, Léonie, and Sébastien Poirot. *Un cuirassier en Turquie, 1854–1855: Correspondance.* Edited by Delphine Dubois-Milet and Jérémie Benoit. Paris: Harmattan, 2023. 227p. €25.00.

Tomasello, Federico. *The Making of the Citizen-Worker: Labour and the Borders of Politics in Post-revolutionary France.* New York: Routledge, 2023. 162p. $170.00.

Third Republic

Abbal, Odon. *Les prisonniers de guerre français dans "L'illustration" (1914–1919).* Paris: Harmattan, 2023. 244p. €25.50.

Berlière, Jean-Marc. *La police à Paris en 1900.* Paris: Nouveau Monde, 2023. 295p. €19.90.

Boulouque, Sylvain. *Maurice Tréand: L'inquisiteur rouge; La vie trépidante de l'homme des basses besognes du PC.* Neuilly-sur-Seine: Atlande, 2023. 338p. €19.00.

Bourlet, Michaël. *Verdun 1916: La guerre de mouvement dans un mouchoir de poche.* Paris: Perrin/Ministère des Armées, 2023. 381p. €25.00.

Chaluleau, George. *Le camp oublié des Espagnoles: Couiza-Montazels 1939.* Baixas: Balzac-Le Griot, 2023. 183p. €22.00.

Courrière, Henri. *Les Alpes-Maritimes et la République: Histoire politique d'un département modéré (1879–1898).* Rennes: Presses Universitaires de Rennes, 2023. 282p. €25.00.

De Courcy, Anne. *Magnificent Rebel: Nancy Cunard in Jazz Age Paris.* New York: St. Martin's, 2023. 330p. $29.99.

Foley, Susan K. *Republican Passions: Family, Friendship, and Politics in Nineteenth-Century France.* Manchester: Manchester University Press, 2023. 336p. £85.00.

Li, Antoine. *Les vingt-et-un du Porthos (et quelques autres): Histoires d'immigration.* Paris: Atelier des Cahiers, 2023. 299p. €23.00.

Millet, Sylvain. *Lettres de guerre du caporal Silvain Millet, dit Maurice, à son épouse: Fin février 1915 au 15 juillet 1918.* Plessala-le-Mené: Association Bretagne 14–18, 2022. 247p. €15.00.

Orzech, Rachel. *Claiming Wagner for France: Music and Politics in the Parisian Press, 1933–1944.* Rochester, NY: University of Rochester Press, 2022. 250p. $115.00.

Paulin-Booth, Alexandra. *Time and Radical Politics in France: From the Dreyfus Affair to the First World War.* Manchester: Manchester University Press, 2023. 277p. £85.00.

Petit, Dominique. *Fortuné Henry et la colonie libertaire d'Aiglemont: De la propagande pour Ravachol au syndicalisme révolutionnaire.* Paris: Noir et Rouge, 2023. 260p. €22.00.

Poulain, Martine. *Marie Arconati Visconti: Le passion de la République.* Paris: Presses Universitaires de France, 2023. 350p. €25.00.

Pouliquen, Arthur. *Georges Sorel: Le mythe de la révolte.* Paris: Cerf, 2023. 242p. €20.00.

Renard, Jacques-Marcel. *Les prisonniers allemands en mains françaises durant le Premier Conflit mondial, 1914–1920.* Paris: SPM, 2023. 176p. €18.00.

Rose, Thomas. *Les socialistes en France de 1871 à 1914.* Pantin: Bons Caractères, 2023. 112p. €8.20.

Rycx, Julien. *Georges Laguerre, un bel-ami en politique (1858–1912).* Villeneuve-d'Ascq: Presses Universitaires du Septentrion, 2023. 431p. €29.00.

Sachs, Miranda. *An Age to Work: Working-Class Childhood in Third Republic Paris.* New York: Oxford University Press, 2023. 256p. $83.00.

Sancé, Benoît. *Filles soumises et femmes rejetées: Prostitution et prostituées dans les Deux-Sèvres du milieu du XIXe siècle à 1946.* La Crèche: Geste, 2022. 217p. €18.00.

Schildknecht, Clara. *Hardi, compagnons! Masculinités et virilité anarchistes à la Belle Epoque.* Paris: Libertalia, 2023. 252p. €10.00.

Tropeau, Christophe. *Le plaisir du lien: La sociabilité associative rurale en Mayenne des années 1830 aux années 1930.* Rennes: Presses Universitaires de Rennes, 2023. 367p. €25.00.

Wagnon, Sylvain. *Marie Huot, 1846–1930: Libertaire, néomalthusienne, antispéciste, théosophe . . .* Lyon: Atelier de Création Libertaire, 2023. 130p. €12.00.

1940–Present

Amiel, Bastien. *La tentation partisane: Engagements intellectuels au seuil de la guerre froide.* Paris: Centre National de la Recherche Scientifique, 2023. 377p. €26.00.

Andrieu, Claire. *When Men Fell from the Sky: Civilians and Downed Airmen in Second World War Europe.* Cambridge: Cambridge University Press, 2023. 348p. $39.99.

Bollier, Vianney. *André Bollier "Vélin": Artisan héroïque des journaux clandestins (1920–1944).* Paris: Félin, 2023. 216p. €22.00.

Bourcart, Jean. *Le général Delestraint: La Résistance, de l'armée secrète jusqu'à Dachau.* Paris: Perrin, 2023. 364p. €24.00.

Broche, François. *Ils n'avaient pas vingt ans: La révolte des jeunes, 1940–1944.* Paris: Tallandier, 2023. 279p. €20.90.

Busseau, Laurent. *Auxiliaires féminines et prisonniers de guerre allemands fusillés: Poitou, 1944–1945.* Paris: Indes Savantes, 2023. 207p. €25.00.

Cabanel, Patrick. *Mireille Philip: Passeuse de frontières.* Maisons-Laffitte: Ampelos, 2023. 94p. €10.00.

Chauvy, Gérard. *L'Abwehr, 1939–1945: Les services secrets allemands en France.* Paris: Perrin, 2023. 487p. €24.00.

Chevassus-au-Louis, Nicolas. *La guerre des bactéries: L'Institut Pasteur sous l'Occupation.* Paris: Vendémiaire, 2023. 230p. €21.00.

Clift, Aaron. *Anticommunism in French Society and Politics, 1945–1953.* New York: Oxford University Press, 2023. 257p. $110.00.

Colvin, Kelly Ricciardi. *Charm Offensive: Commodifying Femininity in Postwar France.* Toronto: University of Toronto Press, 2023. 230p. $95.00.

Denoël, Yvonnick, and Renaud Meltz, eds. *Mensonges d'Etat: Une autre histoire de la Ve République.* Paris: Nouveau Monde, 2023. 559p. €24.90.

Desprairies, Cécile. *Voyage à travers la France occupée, 1940–1945: 4.000 lieux familiers à redécouvrir.* Paris: Presses Universitaires de France, 2023. 960p. €49.00.

Dodd, Lindsey. *Feeling Memory: Remembering Wartime Childhoods in France.* New York: Columbia University Press, 2023. 375p. $140.00.

Erkenbrecher, Andrea. *Oradour und die Deutschen: Geschichtsrevisionismus, strafrechtliche Verfolgung, Entschädigungszahlungen und Versöhnungsgesten ab 1949.* Berlin: De Gruyter Oldenbourg, 2023. 674p. $93.99.

Fourcade, Olivier. *La France et l'OTAN depuis 1989.* Paris: Sorbonne Université Presses, 2023. 288p. €9.90.

Gatineau, François. *Les trois jours qui ont fait tomber la France: Essai.* Paris: Artilleur, 2023. 313p. €20.00.

Geagea, Mathieu. *Dunkerque, la dernière forteresse nazie (1944–1945).* Paris: Passés Composés, 2023. 330p. €23.00.

Grenard, Fabrice. *Jean Moulin, le héros oublié*. Paris: Plon, 2023. 262p. €15.90.

Hampton, Ellen. *Doctors at War: The Clandestine Battle against the Nazi Occupation of France*. Baton Rouge: Louisiana State University Press, 2023. 173p. $34.95.

Hébert, Lucie. *Les victimes n'étaient pas assez belles: Déportation, mémoire et exclusion*. Caen: Grevis, 2023. 250p. €15.00.

Jackson, Julian. *France on Trial: The Case of Marshal Pétain*. London: Lane, 2023. 444p. $35.00.

Joly, Laurent. *La falsification de l'histoire: Eric Zemmour, l'extrême droite, Vichy et les Juifs*. Paris: Grasset, 2022. 140p. €12.00.

Joly, Laurent, Roger Arditi, Aurélie Audeval, Isabelle Backouche, et al. *La France et la Shoah: Vichy, l'occupant, les victimes, l'opinion (1940–1944)*. Paris: Calmann-Lévy, 2023. 557p. €25.00.

Kedward, H. R. *The French Resistance and Its Legacy*. London: Bloomsbury Academic, 2022. 148p. $24.95.

Lemieux, Emmanuel. *Bloncourt et les siens: Les fantômes du Palais-Bourbon*. Paris: Piranha, 2022. 241p. €18.00.

Lemieux, Emmanuel. *Le réseau: Les derniers secrets de la Résistance*. Paris: Cerf, 2023. 444p. €22.00.

Lesieur, Jennifer. *Rose Valland, l'espionne à l'œuvre; Récit*. Paris: Laffont, 2023. 226p. €19.50.

Lucand, Christophe. *Le vin des nazis: Comment les caves françaises ont été pillées sous l'Occupation*. Paris: Grasset, 2023. 349p. €23.00.

Lugassy, Maurice. *Les Justes en Occitanie: Cette page de lumière dans la nuit de la Shoah*. Toulouse: Privat, 2023. 245p. €19.90.

Manenti, Pierre. *Albin Chalandon: Le dernier baron du gaullisme*. Paris: Perrin, 2023. 432p. €24.00.

Mathieu, Lilian, Vincent Porhel, Jean-Yves Seguy, and Yves Verneuil, eds. *Ecoles en révolte: Le moment 1968 à Lyon, du collège à l'université*. Lyon: Presses Universitaires de Lyon, 2023. 272p. €18.00.

Missika, Dominique. *L'affaire Bernard Natan: Les années sombres du cinéma français*. Paris: Denoël, 2023. 254p. €20.00.

Mouré, Kenneth. *Marché Noir: The Economy of Survival in Second World War France*. Cambridge: Cambridge University Press, 2023. 324p. $110.00.

Ott, Sandra, ed. *Negotiating the Nazi Occupation of France: Gender, Power, and Memory*. Reno, NV: Center for Basque Studies Press, 2021. 197p. $30.00.

Pourcher, Yves. *L'exil des collabos, 1944–1989*. Paris: Cerf, 2023. 329p. €24.00.

Sutcliffe, John William. "L'Armée et l'Atome: The French Fourth Republic and the Armed Forces' Negotiations of a Nuclear Future." PhD diss., University of Leeds, 2022.

France and the World

Baccini, Elisa. *L'impero culturale di Napoleone in Italia: Stampa, teatro, scuola secondo il modello francese*. Rome: Carocci, 2022. 513p. €55.00.

Barnes, Whitney Abernathy. "Remaking Religion: Islam, Empire, Race, and the Secularization of French Christianity, 1830–1920." PhD diss., Boston College, 2023.

Barthélémy, Pascale. *Sororité et colonialisme: Françaises et Africaines au temps de la guerre froide (1944–1962)*. Paris: Editions de la Sorbonne, 2022. 416p. €35.00.

Bélénus, René. *Les abolitions de l'esclavage aux Antilles et en Guyane françaises, 1794–1848: Textes et recueil de documents sur l'émancipation des esclaves.* Fort-de-France: Exbrayat, 2022. 375p. €58.00.

Bellescize, Ramu de. *La déchirure: Sur les derniers instants de l'Algérie française.* Paris: Balland, 2023. 741p. €29.00.

Boukenouche, Saïd. *Guide du Marseille colonial.* Paris: Syllepse, 2022. 227p. €10.00.

Buttoud, Gérard. *Alger sous les bombes de Louis XIV, 1661–1698.* Paris: Harmattan, 2023. 200p. €23.00.

Chamelot, Fabienne. "The Politics of French Colonial Archives: Mainland France, French West Africa, and the Indochinese Union, 1894–1960." PhD diss., University of Portsmouth, 2022.

Clammer, Paul. *Black Crown: Henry Christophe, the Haitian Revolution, and the Caribbean's Forgotten Kingdom.* London: Hurst, 2023. 378p. £25.00.

Cooper, Austin Rory. "Saharan Fallout: French Explosions in Algeria and the Politics of Nuclear Risk during African Decolonization (1960–66)." PhD diss., University of Pennsylvania, 2022.

Cross, Elizabeth. *Company Politics: Commerce, Scandal, and French Visions of Indian Empire in the Revolutionary Era.* New York: Oxford University Press, 2023. 312p. $55.00.

Davis, Jennifer J. *Bad Subjects: Libertine Lives in the French Atlantic, 1619–1814.* Lincoln: University of Nebraska Press, 2023. 370p. $65.00.

Dodman, Thomas, and Aurélien Lignereux, eds. *From the Napoleonic Empire to the Age of Empire: Empire after the Emperor.* Cham: Springer, 2023. 336p. $159.99.

Duluermoz, Quentin, Emmanuel Fureix, and Clément Thibaud, eds. *Les mondes de 1848: Au-delà du printemps des peuples.* Ceyzérieu: Champ Vallon, 2023. 345p. €27.00.

Fabbiano, Giulia, and Abderahmen Moumen, eds. *Algérie coloniale: Traces, mémoires et transmissions.* Paris: Cavalier Bleu, 2022. 376p. €25.00.

Fageol, Pierre-Eric. *Discours colonial et sentiment d'appartenance national à La Réunion: Années 1880–1950.* Paris: Indes Savantes, 2023. 511p. €36.00.

Fournier, Marcel. *Faux-sauniers et contrebandiers: Déportés au Canada au nom du roi.* Paris: Archives et Culture, 2023. 176p. €15.00.

Gérard, Gilles. *Je suis né libre: Portraits de l'esclave Furcy et de la société coloniale de Bourbon au XIXe siècle.* Paris: Harmattan, 2023. 188p. €21.00.

Ghali, Driss. *Une contre-histoire de la colonisation française.* Paris: Godefroy, 2023. 318p. €24.00.

Glaser, Noah. "The Age of Regeneration: Capitalism and the French Intervention in Mexico (1861–1867)." PhD diss., University of Illinois Chicago, 2022.

Gloriant, Frédéric. *Le schisme franco-britannique: De Suez au veto de 1963.* Rennes: Presses Universitaires de Rennes, 2023. 374p. €28.00.

Gojosso, Eric. *Aux origines du Laos.* Poitiers: Presses Universitaires Juridiques de Poitiers, 2023. 340p. €30.00.

Guibert, Jean-Sébastien, and Boris Lesueur, eds. *Entre exclusif et contrebande: Les navigations commerciales aux Antilles (1600–1830).* Paris: Harmattan, 2022. 294p. €32.00.

Guide du Rouen colonial et des communes proches. Paris: Syllepse, 2022. 158p. €10.00.

Henneman, Jennifer R., and Jacob Rama Berman, eds. *Near East to Far East: Fictions of French and American Colonialism.* Denver, CO: Denver Art Museum, 2023. 285p. $65.00.

Jean-Baptiste, Rachel. *Multiracial Identities in Colonial French Africa: Race, Childhood, and Citizenship.* Cambridge: Cambridge University Press, 2023. 309p. $110.00.

Jennings, Jeremy. *Travels with Tocqueville beyond America.* Cambridge, MA: Harvard University Press, 2023. 525p. $39.95.

Kranz, Mendel. "The Postcolonial Jewish Question: Jewish and Arab Entanglements in Postwar France." PhD diss., University of Chicago, 2023.

Little, Will C. "Instruments of Culture: Refashioning the French Empire between the French and Haitian Revolutions." PhD diss., University of Mississippi, 2022.

Marignan, Jean-François de. *En reconnaissance au Maroc: Sur les pas de Charles de Foucauld explorateur.* Paris: Cerf, 2023. 301p. €22.00.

Médard, Frédéric, and Serge Barcellini. *Algérie, 1960–1962: L'armée française dans la tourmente; D'un désengagement douloureux à la confrontation des mémoires.* Paris: SOTECA, 2023. 414p. €23.00.

Morin, Paul Max. *Les jeunes et la guerre d'Algérie: Une nouvelle génération face à son histoire.* Paris: Presses Universitaires de France, 2022. 432p. €22.00.

Ofrath, Avner. *Colonial Algeria and the Politics of Citizenship.* London: Bloomsbury Academic, 2023. 194p. $115.00.

Perego, Elizabeth M. *Humor and Power in Algeria, 1920 to 2021.* Bloomington: Indiana University Press, 2023. 270p. $85.00.

Perlman, Susan McCall. *Contesting France: Intelligence and US Foreign Policy in the Early Cold War.* Cambridge: Cambridge University Press, 2023. 273p. £47.99.

Phipps, Catherine. "Sex, Race, and Power: Colonial and Interracial Sexuality in the French Empire in Morocco, 1912–1956." PhD diss., University of Oxford, 2023.

Piccinato, Joseph. *Les harkis pendant la guerre d'Algérie: Février 1956–septembre 1962.* Paris: Maisonneuve et Larose, 2023. 222p. €20.00.

Prest, Julia. *Public Theatre and the Enslaved People of Colonial Saint-Domingue.* Cham: Palgrave Macmillan, 2023. 278p. $129.99.

Quemeneur, Tramor, Ouanassa Siari Tengour, and Sylvie Thénault, eds. *Dictionnaire de la guerre d'Algérie.* Paris: Bouquins, 2023. 1,424p. €34.00.

Ralantoaritsimba, Nirina. *En Californie, les Français écrivent leur ruée vers l'or (1848–1915).* Paris: Champion, 2023. 240p. €55.00.

Roberts, Richard L. *Conflicts of Colonialism: The Rule of Law, French Soudan, and Faama Mademba Sèye.* Cambridge: Cambridge University Press, 2022. 288p. $39.99.

Rodionoff, Marius Loris. *Désobéir en guerre d'Algérie: La crise de l'autorité dans l'armée française.* Paris: Seuil, 2023. 232p. €21.90.

Rosenstein, Brent Matthew. "The Face of the Nation: Drogmans and the French State, 1669–1880." PhD diss., State University of New York at Buffalo, 2023.

Ruscio, Alain. *Marseille, la Provence et l'Indochine: Une histoire humaine à l'ère coloniale.* Paris: Indes Savantes, 2023. 168p. €24.00.

Sergio, Marialuisa Lucia. *How the Church under Pius XII Addressed Decolonization: The Issue of Algerian Independence.* Milton: Routledge, 2023. 216p. $128.00.

Sergio, Marialuisa Lucia. *Pio XII e l'indipendenza algerina: La Chiesa cattolica nella decolonizzazione dell'Africa francese.* Rome: Studium, 2022. 256p. €25.00.

Shanda Tonme, Jean-Claude. *France-Afrique, l'inéluctable rupture: Convergences, divergences et influences dans les rapports entre les nations.* Paris: Harmattan, 2023. 247p. €26.50.

Smith, Leonard V. *French Colonialism: From the Ancien Régime to the Present.* New York: Cambridge University Press, 2023. 250p. $90.00 cloth, $29.99 paper.

Steinmetz, George. *The Colonial Origins of Modern Social Thought: French Sociology and the Overseas Empire*. Princeton, NJ: Princeton University Press, 2023. 551p. $45.00.

Stice, Elizabeth. *Empire between the Lines: Imperial Culture in British and French Trench Newspapers of the Great War*. Lincoln: University of Nebraska Press, 2023. 219p. $60.00.

Tardieu, Jean-Pierre. *La lutte de Vincent Ogé pour la citoyenneté des gens de couleur de Saint-Domingue: La perspective espagnole, 1790–1791*. Paris: Harmattan, 2023. 279p. €28.00.

Vermeren, Pierre. *L'empire colonial français en Afrique: Métropole et colonies, sociétés coloniales de la conférence de Berlin (1884–1885) à la fin de la guerre d'Algérie (1962)*. Paris: Colin, 2023. 268p. €26.00.

Villette, François. *Liberté! Le rôle décisif de la France dans l'indépendance américaine*. Marseille: Caraktère, 2023. 216p. €27.00.

Translated Abstracts

QUENTIN VERREYCKEN

Miséricorde en guerre : Violence militaire et politiques du pardon royal en France au XVe siècle

Cet article examine la construction de la criminalité militaire et l'octroi de pardon aux soldats dans la France à la fin du Moyen Age. Au début du XVe siècle, les crimes perpétrés par les gens de guerre constituent un problème récurrent d'ordre public pour le pouvoir royal. Les registres criminels ainsi que les sources narratives exploitent une riche terminologie pour qualifier les abus militaires subis par la population, distinguant les soldats criminels des délinquants ordinaires. Bien que ces abus soient fréquemment dénoncés par la littérature politique et qu'ils soient sévèrement punis par la législation, le roi de France accorde régulièrement des lettres de pardon aux soldats, leur permettant d'échapper aux poursuites judiciaires en échange de leur service de guerre. Loin d'être le simple résultat d'une attitude laxiste du roi, ces pardons reflètent le fragile équilibre du pouvoir royal au XVe siècle, qui exige du roi qu'il concilie l'exercice de la justice et la conduite de la guerre. En explorant les politiques de pardon royal à l'égard des soldats criminels et les réactions qu'elles suscitent, cet article montre comment la Couronne française fait face à la criminalité militaire à la fin et au lendemain de la guerre de Cent Ans.

MOTS CLÉS   crime, France, guerre de Cent Ans, lettres de pardon, violence militaire

JOSEPH CLARKE

L'incendie de Bédoin : Crime, complicité et guerre civile dans la France révolutionnaire

Le 28 mai 1794, une enquête criminelle commencée près d'un mois auparavant se conclut sur l'exécution de soixante-trois hommes et femmes, l'emprisonnement de quinze autres et, après quelques jours de retard, la destruction d'un village. Cet article examine l'incendie de Bédoin, le crime qui l'a provoqué et le procès judiciaire qui l'a accompagné, pour explorer la relation entre cause criminelle et effet punitif pendant la Terreur de l'an II. En tant qu'étude de cas dans la justice révolutionnaire, cet épisode semble extrême, mais l'article soutient qu'il permet d'interroger les significations que les révolutionnaires ordinaires attachent à des termes comme *crime* et *complicité* lorsque la survie de l'Etat semble être en jeu. En regardant au-delà de la Terreur jusqu'aux controverses qui ont finalement enveloppé cet acte de destruction exemplaire, cet article examine également les conséquences de l'atrocité pour examiner comment une société peut comprendre le crime lorsque la définition de la criminalité et l'identité du criminel sont en pleine mutation.

MOTS CLÉS   Révolution française, Terreur, justice révolutionnaire, atrocité

CLAIRE ELDRIDGE

« Brutal par tempérament et par goût » : Violence entre camarades dans l'Armée d'Afrique, 1914–1918

Au cœur de l'historiographie de la Première Guerre mondiale, les études sur la violence se sont concentrées sur les formes abstraites et impersonnelles de violence entre forces opposées ou sur les formes plus personnelles de violence entre civils et combattants ennemis. En revanche, cet article utilise les archives de la justice militaire afin d'explorer les cas de violences interpersonnelles graves et de brutalité soutenue entre soldats d'une même unité de combat. Il offre un nouveau point de vue pour explorer l'enchevêtrement complexe de la violence et de la camaraderie et la manière dont ces événements se sont déroulés dans le contexte spécifique de l'Armée d'Afrique, corps militaire multiethnique de la France. L'analyse des accusations, des explications et des justifications qui émergent des sources polyphoniques de la justice militaire illustre ce que signifiait commettre et être criminalisé pour certains actes de violence dans un contexte totalement saturé de violence ; comment et où la ligne était tracée entre une conduite acceptable et inacceptable ; et, plus important encore, ce que la violence révèle sur les expériences de combat individuelles et les relations entre camarades. En donnant accès aux perspectives et aux mondes intérieurs de ce groupe diversifié de soldats, dont nombreux étaient membres de communautés racialement ou autrement marginalisées, la justice militaire met en évidence un ensemble complexe et riche de réponses situationnelles et de relations sociales qui renforcent notre capacité à penser l'impact du conflit sur les hommes qui y sont pris.

MOTS CLÉS   Première Guerre mondiale, Armée d'Afrique, violence, justice militaire, empire

DANIELLE BEAUJON

L'ennemi intérieur algérien : La répression du marché noir à Marseille et Alger, 1939–1950

Pendant la Deuxième Guerre mondiale, les policiers de Marseille et d'Alger se sont lancés dans la poursuite des trafiquants algériens. Des centaines de rapports venant de ces deux villes décrivent les mesures prises pour empêcher la vente de la contrebande, faire respecter les prix fixés, et imposer les règles de rationnement. Si dans les décennies précédentes, les stéréotypes coloniaux avaient déjà identifié les Algériens comme vecteurs de vol et de violence, les restrictions économiques de la guerre ont créé une nouvelle catégorie de criminel algérien imaginé— le trafiquant du marché noir. Dans les rapports de police, la figure de l'Algérien profiteur est omniprésente. Cependant, les communications internes reconnaissent que les Européens profitaient également du marché noir, alors pourquoi cette fixation officielle sur les Algériens ? Cet article vise à démontrer que la police a développé une représentation des Algériens comme des « ennemis intérieurs ». En traitant les Algériens comme une menace à la sécurité intérieure, la police a justifié un système de contrôle qui a homogénéisé la communauté algérienne. Cette répression racialisée des trafiquants algériens, considérés comme « anti-français », s'appuyait non seulement sur des codes visuels de la race, mais aussi sur la manière dont la police a reconfiguré l'espace urbain en y superposant des idées de race.

MOTS CLÉS   Marseille, Alger, Deuxième Guerre mondiale, police, marché noir

JULIE M. POWELL

Mort mais pas enterré : Le tueur en série Henri Désiré Landru et un siècle de critique de la guerre

Le 12 avril 1919, la police de Paris arrête Henri Désiré Landru, un homme qui avait passé les quatre dernières années de guerre à courtiser des femmes et à confisquer leurs biens. Beaucoup d'entre elles n'ont jamais été revues. Landru, accusé de leurs meurtres, devient une sensation médiatique internationale—inspirant des histoires de crime populaires, y compris des livres, des articles, des films, des émissions de télévision et de radio, et des spectacles—de son exécution en 1922 jusqu'en 2020. Cet article examine ces histoires pour déceler la manière révélatrice dont elles rapprochent les conceptions de la guerre et du crime violent. Il considère un récit (1926) par le journaliste sud-africain et ancien combattant William Bolitho, le film *Monsieur Verdoux* (1947) écrit par Charlie Chaplin, le film *Landru* (1963) de Claude Chabrol, et une bande dessinée (2006) de Christophe Chabouté. Ces récits suggèrent que les histoires sur Landru—et les multiples meurtres qu'il a commis à des fins lucratives—ont servi, à divers moments et en divers lieux, comme véhicules pour critiquer la guerre et les sociétés qui l'embrassent.

MOTS CLÉS   violence, meurtre en série, guerre, littérature, film

Eugen Weber Book Prize

The UCLA Department of History is pleased to announce that

Owen White and Marc André

are co-winners of the **2024 Weber Book Award**. A prize for the best book in modern French history (post 1815) over the previous two years, this award is named for the eminent French historian Eugen Weber (1925-2007) and brings a cash award of $15,000.

Owen White, Professor of History at the University of Delaware, *The Blood of the Colony: Wine and the Rise and Fall of French Algeria* (Harvard University Press), a deeply researched and elegantly written history of Algeria told through wine, which was introduced by the French, controlled by the colonists, and then finally largely dismantled by independent Algeria.

Marc André, Professor of History at Rouen University (France), *Une prison pour mémoire: Montluc, de 1944 à nos jours* (ENS Éditions), a remarkable combination of history, memory studies, and museology based on original research in prison documents using interviews with Algerians sentenced to death during the Algerian war, conscientious objectors, and a host of others. Montluc was a notorious Gestapo prison also used to house those who opposed the Algerian War.

For more information, visit http://history.ucla.edu.

 College | Social Sciences
History

Printed and bound by CPI Group (UK) Ltd, Croydon, CR0 4YY

06/05/2024

14498310-0001